DICTIONAR
ECONOMICS

Frank Livesey

30

PITMAN
PUBLISHING

Pitman Publishing
128 Long Acre, London WC2E 9AN

A Division of Longman Group UK Limited

First published in 1993

© Longman Group UK Limited 1993
Reprinted 1994

British Library Cataloguing in Publication Data
A CIP catalogue record for this book can be obtained from the British Library.

ISBN 0 273 60034 6

Printed and bound by Bell and Bain Ltd., Glasgow

PREFACE

In preparing this dictionary I have tried to take account of the current rapid rate of change in economic institutions and ideas. The impact of this change can be seen in substantial entries that would probably not have rated a mention in a dictionary written five years ago, e.g. environmental economics, cohesion, principal-agent relationship. The other side of this coin is the need to omit other entries because of a lack of space. No biographies of economists have been included, because however interesting they may be to read, I do not believe that they contribute a great deal to people's understanding of economics.

I have also had in mind the criticism that has been levelled at economics in recent years by people within and outside the profession; a mild version of this criticism is that the subject is in a muddle. Two reasons for this perception are, first, that competing schools of economists advance theories based on different sets of assumptions, and second, that economists are prone to assert a theory's validity on evidence that other scientists would consider to be rather insubstantial. In those entries concerned with economic theories and models I have drawn attention to weaknesses as well as strengths.

The dictionary should be helpful to two broad groups of readers: the professional economist and student of economics, and the layman who has a more general interest in the subject. Economic affairs receive a substantial amount of media coverage today, but the presenters do not always have the opportunity to explain some of the terms being discussed. This is a gap which I hope the dictionary will fill.

I have tried to make the layout of the dictionary as user-friendly as possible. The meaning of an entry (word or term) is often understood more clearly or more fully if that entry is considered together with another, associated entry (or entries). These instances have been denoted by highlighting in small capitals associated entries which it would be helpful to consult. For example, the entry **necessities** includes a reference to INCOME ELASTICITY OF DEMAND. Where it is felt that it is *essential* to consider two (or more) entries together, the explanation is given under one entry, and the other entry tells the reader to consult that entry. For example: **vertical integration**. *See* GROWTH OF THE FIRM.

The significance of some economic variables can be understood most clearly when they are measured, and a number of tables have been included in the dictionary. Although each table has particular relevance to one entry, it may also be consulted in conjunction with other entries. The entries which include tables are: average propensity to consume, balance of payments, balance sheet, bank, commercial, Bank of England, comparative advantage, consumers' expenditure, cost schedule, discount houses, distribution of income, distribution of wealth, European Currency Unit, fixed capital formation, government expenditure, index number, monetary aggregates, national income accounting, payback, Retail Price Index, retail trade, social security, taxation, and wealth.

There are several possible ways of ordering entries in a dictionary. The one chosen can be illustrated by the following list:

capital.

capital, issued.

capital goods.

capital-output ratio.

capital services.

capitalization.

ABBREVIATIONS

Many terms, and especially the names of institutions, are frequently abbreviated. Abbreviations are used, but never as entry headings. To help readers who know some terms only by their abbreviations, we give a selection of commonly used abbreviations together with the corresponding entries in the dictionary.

ACAS	Advisory, Conciliation and Arbitration Service
BES	Business Expansion Scheme
BIS	Bank for International Settlements
BOTB	British Overseas Trade Board
CAP	Common Agricultural Policy
CBI	Confederation of British Industry
CCC	Competition and Credit Control
cif	cost, insurance, freight
CSO	Central Statistical Office
DCF	discounted cash flow
EC	European Communities
ECGD	Export Credits Guarantee Department
ECSC	European Coal and Steel Community
ECU	European Currency Unit
EDF	European Development Fund
EEC	European Economic Community
EFTA	European Free Trade Association
eftpos	electronic funds transfer at point of sale
EIB	European Investment Bank
EMS	European Monetary System
EMU	European Monetary Union
ERDF	European Regional Development Fund
ERM	Exchange Rate Mechanism
ESF	European Social Fund
FAO	Food and Agriculture Organization
FCI	Finance Corporation for Industry
FED	Federal Reserve System
FIFO	first in first out
FIMBRA	Financial Intermediaries, Managers and Brokers Regulatory Association
fob	free on board
G7	Group of Seven
G10	Group of Ten
GATT	General Agreement on Tariffs and Trade
GDP	gross domestic product
GNP	gross national product
IBRD	International Bank for Reconstruction and Development
ICFC	Industrial and Commercial Finance Corporation
ILO	International Labour Organization

IMF	International Monetary Fund
IMRO	Investment Management Regulatory Organization
LAUTRO	Life Assurance and Unit Trust Regulatory Organization
LDC	less developed country
LDT	licensed deposit-taker
LIBOR	London inter-bank offer rate
LIFO	last in first out
LIFFE	London International Financial Futures and Options Exchange
MLR	minimum lending rate
MNE	multinational enterprise
NIC	newly industrializing country
OECD	Organization for Economic Co-operation and Development
OFFER	Office of Electricity Generation
OFGAS	Office of Gas Supply
OFTEL	Office of Telecommunications
OFWAT	Office of Water Services
ODA	official development assistance
OPEC	Organization of Petroleum Exporting Countries
PAYE	pay-as-you-earn
PEP	personal equity plan
PSBR	public-sector borrowing requirement
R&D	research and development
RPI	Retail Price Index
RPM	resale price maintenance
SAYE	save-as-you-earn
SDRs	special drawing rights
SEAQ	Stock Exchange Automated Quotation
SEC	Securities and Exchange Commission
SIB	Securities and Investment Board
SIC	Standard Industrial Classification
SRO	self-regulatory organization
TEC	Training and Enterprise Council
TESSA	tax exempt special savings account
3i	Investors in Industry
TPI	Tax and Price Index
TUC	Trades Union Congress
UNCTAD	United Nations Conference on Trade and Development
VAT	value-added tax
YTS	Youth Training Scheme

A

ability to pay principle. The principle that people should be taxed in accordance with their income or wealth. The principle is advocated by those who have a concern for VERTICAL EQUITY.

above the line. All items above the line at which a total is made, i.e. items included in that total. For example the line might be drawn at the profits or earnings of a company. It has been an accounting convention that exceptional items that derive from a company's ordinary business are included above the line, whereas extraordinary items which arise from transactions outside the company's ordinary business are included below the line. Since this distinction affects the company's reported profit and earnings per share, it is of considerable significance. For example Rank Hovis McDougall reported 'extraordinary closure costs' of between £12 and £24 millions each year between 1984 and 1991. During that period these costs averaged over 22 per cent of reported net profits. The wide discretion enjoyed by companies in classifying items as extraordinary was ended when the Accounting Standards Board introduced, with effect from Autumn 1992, new procedures for calculating profits.

above-the-line promotion. Advertising through television, radio and the press.

absolute advantage. (1) When two countries are able to produce two (or more) products and the first country could produce each product at a lower resource cost than the second country, the first country is said to have an absolute (cost) advantage. International trade may or may not take place, depending upon whether the countries have a COMPARATIVE ADVANTAGE. (2) One producer is said to have an absolute advantage over another producer when it can supply a product at a lower cost, whatever the amount produced. If the low-cost producer sets a price which would not yield the high-cost producer an adequate profit, the latter will not be able to compete, i.e. the absolute cost advantage acts as a BARRIER TO ENTRY into the market.

absolute prices. *See* NOMINAL PRICES.

absorption costing. A system of management accounting whereby all costs are allocated to (absorbed by) the various products supplied by the firm. The idea behind absorption costing is that if, following FULL-COST PRICING procedures, prices are set that yield a profit for each product, then the firm will earn an adequate profit overall. However, it is often impossible to allocate all costs except on an arbitrary basis, and there is no guarantee that absorption costing will lead to the pattern of prices that would maximize the firm's profits, or even yield an adequate profit.

abstinence theory. *See* INTEREST, THEORIES OF.

accelerated depreciation. *See* DEPRECIATION.

acceleration principle. This refers to the fact that a change in output, sales or, more generally, gross domestic product, in one period, causes a change in INVESTMENT in the following period. Producers know from experience how much capital equipment they require to produce a given output. They often keep some spare capacity to meet sudden increases in demand, but when that capacity has been brought into operation, they install more equipment to restore the CAPITAL-OUTPUT RATIO to the desired level. The principle can be expressed formally as follows:

$$I = a(Y_{t2} - Y_{t1})$$

where I is the net investment,

       $Y_{t2} - Y_{t1}$ is the change in output, sales or GDP,

       a is the accelerator coefficient.

If £4 millions of equipment is required to produce £1 million of output a year, the capital-output ratio is 4. The accelerator coefficient would also be 4 in the absence of other influences. But in practice other influences might exist. For example if producers had capacity in excess of the desired level, they might be able to supply the additional output without installing any new equipment, giving a value for the accelerator coefficient of zero. (Where, for this or any other reason, the value of the coefficient is less than the capital-output ratio, the accelerator is said to be dampened.)

accelerationist view. *See* INFLATION, THEORIES OF.

accelerator coefficient. *See* ACCELERATION PRINCIPLE.

accelerator-multiplier model. A model which helps to explain how BUSINESS CYCLES, fluctuations in the level of economic activity, can result from the interaction of the accelerator and multiplier mechanisms. An increase in the output of consumer goods (increased consumption) leads, via the accelerator, to an increase in the output of investment goods. The increased income corresponding to this increased investment, magnified by the multiplier, gives rise to a further increase in consumption. This in turn leads to more investment, the process continuing until the economy reaches full capacity. The initial stimulus to economic activity might comprise an increase in investment which leads, via the multiplier, to higher consumption and subsequently, via the accelerator, to a further increase in investment. This sequence of events can be described by means of a multiplier-accelerator model. These events occur during an upswing in economic activity. Both models can also be used to show how an initial fall, either in consumption or investment, leads to a bigger fall in economic activity.

accepting houses. MERCHANT BANKS which specialize in accepting BILLS OF EXCHANGE, i.e. they guarantee that the bills will be honoured when they are presented for payment. Any bank of sufficient standing can undertake acceptance business, but membership of the Accepting Houses Committee is confined to those institutions, at present sixteen, a major part of whose business is bill acceptance.

account. (1) An arrangement whereby a purchaser can obtain credit, i.e. obtain goods in advance of payment. (2) A period during which transactions on the STOCK EXCHANGE take place, again in advance of settlement. (3) A record of financial transactions in the form of stocks or flows, e.g. the UNITED KINGDOM NATIONAL ACCOUNTS include a record of the flow of incomes in a given year.

account day. The day on which all transactions made during the previous account at the STOCK EXCHANGE must be settled (hence it is also known as settlement day). It is normally ten days after the final day of dealing of the account.

accounting costs. *See* COSTS.

accounting identity. An equation which will always by definition be found to be true. For example the conventions adopted in the UNITED KINGDOM NATIONAL ACCOUNTS mean that actual saving always equals actual investment. However, this information does not help us to predict the future course of the economy; this requires knowledge of planned saving and planned investment.

accounting period. The period over which a firm prepares its TRADING AND PROFIT AND LOSS ACCOUNT and at the end of which it draws up its BALANCE SHEET. Joint stock companies are required to prepare these accounts at least once a year, but many companies prepare trading accounts far more frequently, perhaps weekly, in order to monitor the progress of their business.

accounting profit. *See* PROFIT.

accrued expenses. Liabilities incurred by the firm in respect of services received but not yet paid for, e.g. wages owed for work already undertaken.

acid-test ratio. *See* CURRENT RATIO.

active balances. Money that is held either for TRANSACTIONS or PRECAUTIONARY MOTIVES or that is invested in financial assets expected to yield a positive return.

activity rate. *See* PARTICIPATION RATE.

ad valorem tax. A tax expressed as a fixed percentage of the selling price of a product, e.g. VALUE-ADDED TAX. With a tax of 17½ per cent, if an article is sold to the final purchaser for £117.50, the tax element of this would be £17.50 (i.e. 17½ per cent of £100).

adaptive expectations. People's behaviour is influenced by their predictions of the future, and these predictions are in turn influenced by their past experience. Assume that prices, including wages, have been rising by 3 per cent a year, but that in a given year higher import prices lead to an overall price rise of 5 per cent. Adaptive (or extrapolative) expectations implies that workers will expect a price rise of 5 per cent next year and so will require a wage increase of 5 per cent. However the combination of higher import prices and higher wages may well lead to a price rise of 7 per cent, higher than workers expected. To generalize, adaptive expectations will always result in the underestimation of any variable which is consistently rising.

adding-up problem. Refers to a series of transactions undertaken by several people. Each transaction may benefit the person undertaking the transaction, but it also leaves the other people worse off; consequently the total benefit from the round of transactions cannot be obtained by adding up the individual benefits from each transaction. For example consider a situation where a group of people are competing for a limited number of jobs. One person investing in education will benefit from improved job opportunities (and all that follows from that), but at the expense of poorer opportunities for the remaining people. The same will apply to the investment in education undertaken by each of the other people.

adjustable peg. If, under a system of FIXED EXCHANGE RATES, the agreed rates or parities can be changed, we have an adjustable peg system. Many countries operated such a system in the 1950s and 1960s.

administered prices. (1) Prices set by the supplier rather than as a result of negotiation between supplier and buyer are said to be administered. However the term has a further connotation – more true of some administered prices than others – that prices are less responsive to changes in the balance between demand and supply than is desirable. In particular it is argued that some prices are maintained at a higher level than is justified. (2) The term is also applied to the prices of products set under COMMODITY AGREEMENTS, and to the price of a currency set by the government under a FIXED EXCHANGE RATE system.

advanced corporation tax. *See* CORPORATION TAX.

advances. *See* BANK ADVANCES.

adverse selection. This can arise when the information available to the buyers of a product differs from that available to sellers (information is asymmetric). For example, since insurance companies are seldom able accurately to assess the liability to risk of individual policy holders, they charge a 'price' that reflects their past experience with respect to all policy holders. People who are poor risks (poor health, liable to injuries, etc.) will be happy to pay this 'average' price, whereas people who are less at risk will not. This makes the situation worse, since the liabilities of the insurance companies will increase as time goes on and so their prices will rise. The market for low-risk customers becomes even more restricted.

advertising. Most advertising is of individual products, although some relates to institutions, informing us, for example, how much a company is spending on restoring or preserving the environment. The advertising of products, on television, commercial radio, outdoor poster sites, etc., is believed to have both advantages and disadvantages. By providing information about the availability and characteristics of a product, it enables purchasers to make a better-informed choice from a wider range of alternatives. Also, if advertising increases the number of purchasers, the firm will be able to take advantage of ECONOMIES OF SCALE and so sell at a lower price. On the other hand it is argued that advertising can persuade purchasers that the differences between the various brands of a product are greater that they are in fact, and that this PRODUCT DIFFERENTIATION can act as a BARRIER TO ENTRY into the market. Moreover it is argued that advertising of competing brands is largely self-cancelling, with little impact on economies of scale. Since the cost of advertising has to be covered by the price of the product, the overall effect is higher prices. In view of these conflicting arguments it may not be surprising that governments have seldom sought to regulate the overall volume of advertising, preferring instead to restrict only the advertising of products with proven harmful effects, e.g. cigarettes.

advertising levy. A tax paid by independent television franchise holders. The levy is a (variable) percentage of advertising revenue.

Advisory, Conciliation and Arbitration Service. ACAS was established in 1975 to give advice to industry on industrial relations matters and to provide, on request, conciliation and arbitration services.

affirmative action. Measures designed to improve the job prospects of minorities. For example in the USA federal contractors are required to set goals and timetables for minority employment in job categories where these minorities have been under-represented.

African Development Bank. Originally established in 1964 to assist the economic growth of African countries by the provision of loans at a low rate of interest, the Bank opened its membership to other countries in 1982. It has a number of associated institutions, the best known being the African Development Fund, which provides interest-free loans to the poorest member countries.

after-sales service. Suppliers may offer a range of services to purchasers, including the provision of advice and the maintenance, servicing and repair of machinery and equipment. The service may be provided free or at a fixed cost specified in a service contract. After-sales service can be an important form of PRODUCT DIFFERENTIATION.

age-earnings cycle. Most people earn more when middle-aged than when young or elderly, since productivity and hours worked are normally greatest in middle age.

agency theory. *See* PRINCIPAL–AGENT RELATIONSHIP.

agglomeration. The larger the population in a given area, the larger is the range of skills in the labour force and the larger is the market for goods and services. These advantages help to explain the geographical concentration of industry in towns, cities, regions and even countries.

aggregate concentration. *See* CONCENTRATION.

aggregate demand. Aggregate monetary demand is the total spending on goods and services in a given period. In simple models of the economy spending is undertaken by households (CONSUMPTION) and firms (INVESTMENT). In more comprehensive models spending is also undertaken by the GOVERNMENT and by the overseas sector (EXPORTS).

aggregate demand curve. This shows what the total planned spending (volume of goods and services) would be at various average price levels. The lower the average price, the greater the volume of spending (D_1, Fig.1).

aggregate demand shock. Anything that causes a change in aggregate demand, as shown by a shift in the aggregate demand curve, e.g. a fall in interest rates which causes the demand curve to shift up to the right (D_1 to D_2, Fig.1).

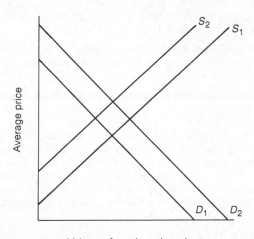

Figure 1 Aggregate demand and supply curves

aggregate supply. The total supply of goods and services in a given period. In simple models of an economy goods and services are supplied by domestic firms. In more comprehensive models goods and services are also supplied by the GOVERNMENT and by overseas firms (IMPORTS).

aggregate supply curve. This shows what the total planned supply (volume of goods and services) would be at various average price levels. The higher the average price, the greater the volume supplied (S_1, Fig. 1).

aggregate supply shock. Anything that causes a change in aggregate supply, as shown by a shift in the aggregate supply curve, e.g. an increase in wages which causes the supply curve to shift up to the left (S_1 to S_2, Fig. 1).

aggregated rebate. *See* DEFERRED REBATE.

aggregates. Total amounts or quantities, e.g. AGGREGATE DEMAND.

allocation of resources. *See* RESOURCE ALLOCATION.

allocative efficiency. *See* ECONOMIC EFFICIENCY.

altruism. Concern for the interest of others at the expense of one's own interests. Since the efficient ALLOCATION OF RESOURCES through the market requires that individuals always try to further their own interest, the market process cannot maximize altruistic concern for partners in market transactions. Altruism conveys benefits on individuals, and it has been argued, e.g. by Fred Hirsch, that a free market system will lead to a lower supply of altruism than would be socially desirable.

amalgamation. *See* MERGER.

American Depository Receipts. Issued by US banks against shares deposited with the banks, ADRs circulate as bearer documents, in effect giving title to the corresponding shares.

amortization. When a firm incurs a debt, it may set up a sinking fund into which regular payments are made. These sums, plus accumulated interest, are available to repay the debt when it becomes due. Amortization is also used as a synonym for DEPRECIATION when regular sums are put aside towards the cost of replacing plant or equipment.

animal spirits. A term used by J.M. Keynes to denote the fact that businessmen's optimism or pessimism about the future state of the economy could have a marked impact on investment decisions.

annual allowances. *See* CAPITAL ALLOWANCES.

annual percentage rate. The true cost of a loan.

annuity. A guaranteed series of future payments purchased now for a lump sum. Where payment is for a fixed number of years, the annuity is said to be 'certain'. A 'life' annuity payment continues until the death of the person for whom it was purchased. Annuities are sold by insurance companies who invest much of the proceeds in interest-bearing securities. The higher the rate of interest when the annuity is sold, the lower the price at which the insurance company is able to sell an annuity with a given value.

anticipated inflation. The inflation rate that individuals believe will occur. These EXPECTATIONS can influence people's behaviour.

anti-competitive practices. *See* COMPETITION ACT.

anti-trust. A term applied, particularly in the USA, to policies and legislation aimed against practices which might restrict competition. The most important pieces of US legislation are the Sherman Act (1890) which made MONOPOLY or the restraint of trade illegal, the Clayton Act (1914) which prohibited PRICE DISCRIMINATION, EXCLUSIVE DEALING and INTERLOCKING DIRECTORATES, the Robinson-Patman Act (1936) which strengthened the existing provisions against price discrimination, and the Celler-Kefauver Act (1950) which prohibited MERGERS which might lessen competition. US policy is intended to be NON-DISCRETIONARY.

appreciation. An increase in the value of an asset. During inflationary periods, an increase occurs in the nominal but not necessarily the real value of monetary assets. *See also* CURRENCY APPRECIATION.

appropriation account. A statement showing how a company's net profit is apportioned between dividends, reserves, pension funds, etc.

appropriation accounts. *See* PUBLIC EXPENDITURE.

Arab Fund for Economic and Social Development. The capital of AFESD, which began operations in 1972, is held by twenty-one Arab countries plus the Palestine Liberation Organization. It grants SOFT LOANS to Arab countries.

arbitrage. When the price of an asset varies between different geographical markets. For example, if the pound sterling could be bought for $2.50 in New York and sold for $2.51 in London, it might be possible (depending upon the costs incurred) to make a profit by buying in the cheaper and selling in the dearer market, a process known as arbitrage. Although arbitrage often involves dealing in very large quantities, the profit per unit is extremely low and so for arbitrage to be worthwhile, dealing or transactions costs must also be low. Moreover, communications between the two markets must be fast and efficient, otherwise the price differential might change before the transaction is completed, thus introducing a considerable element of risk. Arbitrage eliminates, or at least reduces, price differentials between geographical markets.

arbitraticn. When employers and workers cannot agree during wage negotiations, the differences may be resolved by arbitration; a third party makes a decision, e.g. an increase in the hourly wage rate, which is accepted by both sides. The arbitrator frequently chooses a figure between those proposed by the two sides, but under pendulum, or final-offer arbitration, either the offer of the employer or the demand of workers must be chosen. The intention of this method is to encourage both sides to propose reasonable figures, acceptable to the arbitrator, and thus reduce the scope for conflict.

arc elasticity. The average elasticity over a range of a demand or a supply curve. The notation of arc elasticity of demand (e) is:

$$e = \frac{Q_1 - Q_o}{P_1 - P_o} \times \frac{P_1 + P_o}{Q_1 + Q_o}$$

where P_o is the original price, Q_o the original quantity demanded, P_1 the new price, and Q_1 the new quantity demanded.

arithmetic progression. A sequence having the form a, $a+r$, $a+2r$, etc., where a is the original amount and r is the amount added each time. A sequence of this form shows a linear relationship, and applies to many areas in economics, e.g. simple interest on loans.

articles of association. Rules adopted by a company which govern its internal working. They cover such matters as the issue and transfer of the company's shares, the procedures for convening general meetings, and shareholders' voting rights.

Asian Development Bank. Established in 1966 to foster economic growth in Asia and the Pacific. It has thirty-three member countries in Asia and the Pacific and fourteen elsewhere. Through its affiliate, the Asian Development Fund, it provides SOFT LOANS to the poorer countries in the region.

aspiration levels. *See* BEHAVIOURAL THEORY OF THE FIRM.

asset bundling. When assets previously owned by the state in a command economy are returned to the private sector, decisions have to be made concerning the assets to be grouped or bundled together.

asset motive. *See* MONEY, DEMAND FOR.

asset stripping. Purchasing a company and selling-off at least some of its assets. Asset stripping is undertaken because the company's current market value is less than the value when the assets have been separated and sold (in total or in part).

asset structure. The proportion of various types of ASSET as shown in the firm's balance sheet. The asset structure can influence the financing of the firm, e.g. a firm with a high proportion of fixed assets is likely to rely more on long-term borrowing than a firm with a high proportion of current assets.

assets. Those things which an individual or organization owns, or has title to, and which are of value. The assets of a company are normally classified as FIXED ASSETS (including INTANGIBLE ASSETS), TRADE INVESTMENTS and CURRENT ASSETS.

Assisted Areas. Areas which receive assistance as part of the government's REGIONAL POLICY.

associated company. A company in which another company or group has a significant but not a majority shareholding, i.e. 20 to 50 per cent of the voting shares.

Association of South East Asian Nations. The Association, whose members are Indonesia, Malaysia, the Philippines, Singapore and Thailand, has undertaken a number of joint industrial projects and introduced some TARIFF concessions on trade between members.

assumptions. *See* ECONOMIC MODEL.

assurance. An agreement to pay a capital sum when a future event occurs. Strictly speaking the term assurance should be applied only to events that are bound to occur, e.g. a specified year arrives or a person dies, while INSURANCE applies to events that may or may not occur, e.g. fire, theft. However insurance is now also applied to events that are certain. The capital sum guaranteed is supplemented under some forms of contract, e.g. under a 'with profits' contract the policy holder shares in the profits earned by the insurance company.

asymmetric information. *See* INFORMATION.

atomistic competition. Atomistic competition exists when a market is supplied by a large number of firms selling identical or very similar products.

auction. Selling by competitive bidding, the sale being made to the highest bidder (subject to any reserve price being attained).

audit. (1) Companies are legally required to have their accounts reviewed by an external auditor who must certify that these accounts present a true and fair view of the company's affairs. (2) An account, usually including quantitative measures, of aspects of a firm's operations, e.g. audits of the EFFICIENCY of nationalized industries, or environmental audits indicating the impact of a firm's operations on the environment.

Austrian economics. The Austrian school of economics had its origin in the publication in 1871 of Carl Menger's *Principles of Economics*, in which he proposed the marginal utility theory of value as an alternative to the then dominant labour theory of value. But contemporary Austrian economists believe that more important to subsequent economic thought than the technical development of marginalism, has been Menger's insistence on the subjective character of utility (one consequence of which is the impossibility of deriving an objective SOCIAL-WELFARE FUNCTION). In recent times the Austrian tradition has been developed most vigorously by F.A. Hayek. Hayek wrote at length about what he saw as the inapplicability of the objectivism and historicism which stem from the 'scientific' approach to social phenomena. He also developed Menger's ideas about the significance of imperfect INFORMATION and knowledge about the future; for Hayek, the MARKET was primarily an information-gathering process. These ideas also underlie the theory of ENTREPRENEURSHIP developed by Hayek, Von Mises and, more recently, I.M. Kirzner. Austrian economists have little faith in the COMPARATIVE STATICS approach and in theories which emphasize equilibrium to the exclusion of the study of the processes which tend to result in equilibrium. They emphasize the inherent unpredictability and indeterminacy of human preferences, expectations and knowledge. This emphasis leads them to regard 'empirical proofs' with scepticism, and to regard econometric measurement procedures as resulting in misleading conclusions.

authorized capital. The amount of share capital specified in a company's MEMORANDUM OF ASSOCIATION. If a company initially issues less than its authorized capital, it can subsequently issue more, up to the specified figure, without applying again to the Registrar of Companies.

auto-correlation. *See* REGRESSION ANALYSIS.

automatic stabilizers. Mechanisms which reduce the response of the economy, or part of the economy, to a shock. If unemployment increases (a shock or disturbance), loss of income will cause a fall in CONSUMPTION and therefore in GROSS DOMESTIC PRODUCT. However the payment of unemployment benefit, an automatic or built-in stabilizer, reduces the loss of income and hence the fall in consumption.

autonomous consumption. That part of consumption that does not depend on the level of disposable income. Changes in autonomous consumption shift the CONSUMPTION FUNCTION.

autonomous investment. That part of investment that is not induced by a change in output, sales, or gross domestic product.

Autumn Statement. The Chancellor of the Exchequer's Autumn Statement includes a survey of current, and a forecast of future, economic conditions. It forms the background to the BUDGET in the following Spring, and has occasionally been accompanied by a 'mini-budget', minor changes in government economic policy. With effect from 1993, the Autumn and Budget Statements were combined and presented in December.

average. A single number which summarizes and represents the values of a number of items in a set. The most common measure is the mean; this is calculated by aggregating the values of all the items and dividing by the number of items. For example if the value of imports in five months was (£ million) 300, 300, 370, 400 and 900, the average would be 2270 ÷ 5, which is 454 millions. Variables whose average is represented by the mean include COST, REVENUE and PRODUCTIVITY. The median is the value that comes mid-way in a series, having as many values above as below it. The median is less influenced than the mean by extreme values. In the above example the median is £370 millions. If the final import figure of £900 millions was very much out of the ordinary, e.g. because of the import of expensive, infrequently purchased items, the median would be the better measure. The median is often applied to the distribution of income and wealth. The mode is the value that occurs most frequently in the set. In the above example the mode would be £300 millions, which would not seem to be a good measure in this instance. The mode would be a more useful measure in a situation in which a supplier wished to set a price for its product that was in line with the price that customers were most used to paying.

average-cost pricing. Producers set their prices by calculating the average cost at the expected output and adding a MARK-UP. Empirical evidence shows that average-cost or full-cost pricing is a common method of pricing.

average propensity to consume. The proportion or percentage of income (usually PERSONAL DISPOSABLE INCOME), that is spent on goods and services, other than for investment. It can be applied to an individual, a household or a country (Table 1).

Table 1   Average propensity to consume

	Personal disposable income (£ million)	Expenditure (£ million)	Average propensity to consume
1971	38 849	36 010	0.93
1976	86 118	76 881	0.89
1981	177 720	155 412	0.87
1986	265 824	243 030	0.91
1991	407 646	367 853	0.90

Source: *United Kingdom National Accounts*

average propensity to save. The proportion or percentage of income (usually PERSONAL DISPOSABLE INCOME) that is saved, i.e. not spent on goods and services. It can be applied to an individual, a household or a country. The average propensity to consume plus the average propensity to save equals one.

average tax rate. The proportion of total income paid in tax. The term is sometimes defined more narrowly as the proportion of income paid in income tax.

avoidable costs. *See* COSTS.

B

back door. *See* LENDER OF LAST RESORT.

backwardation. The amount by which the SPOT PRICE of a commodity (including the cost of stocking the commodity) exceeds the FORWARD PRICE.

backward integration. A form of vertical integration in which a firm expands by taking over or merging with another firm from which it previously might have bought inputs, e.g. a firm making tyres takes over a firm producing rubber.

balance of payments. A record of all the financial transactions between one country and other countries in a given period. Transactions involving an inflow of money are known as credit transactions; those involving on outflow of money are known as debit transactions. When the sum of credits (money inflows) exceeds the sum of debits (money outflows) the country is said to have a balance of payments surplus, or a favourable balance. When the opposite occurs it is said to have a balance of payments deficit, or an unfavourable balance.

Table 2   UK balance of payments 1990

	£ million
Visible balance	-18 675
Invisible balance	4 295
Current balance	-14 380
net transactions in UK external assets and liabilities	12 081
Balancing item	2 299

As shown in the table, transactions are grouped under several broad headings. Transactions in goods, e.g. food, machinery, are entered in the visible account. It is this account that is usually referred to when people speak of EXPORTS and IMPORTS although, strictly speaking, these terms have a wider application, since services are also exported and imported. The balance of transactions in goods is known as the visible balance, although the less appropriate term balance of trade is sometimes used. The invisible account includes transactions relating to: imports and exports of services, e.g. tourism and insurance; transfers, e.g. military and other assistance provided by the government of one country to another; interest, profits and dividends received from, and paid, abroad. The balance of these three sets of items is known as the invisible balance. Adding together the visible and invisible balance gives the balance on current account. The current balance is often a good indicator of whether a country is 'paying its way' internationally, and is sometimes spoken of as 'the balance of payments'. In fact the accounts contain further items, net transactions in UK external assets and liabilities, popularly known as the capital account. The accounts are so constructed that in principle the balance on current account equals, but with opposite signs, the balance on capital account. In the example given in the table, more money was invested in the UK by overseas residents than UK residents invested abroad. This net inflow of money is recorded with a positive sign. As noted above, in principle the current and capital accounts should balance. But in practice this equality does not occur because of errors and deficiencies in the provision and collection of information. Consequently the final entry in the accounts is a balancing item. Unfortunately this may be substantial, even exceeding in some years the current or capital balance, a fact which makes it very difficult to gain an accurate picture of how the country's payments and receipts have been brought into balance.

balance of trade. *See* BALANCE OF PAYMENTS.

balance sheet. A statement of an organization's assets and liabilities at a certain date, normally the end of its financial year. As shown in Table 3, the balance sheet has two sections: assets are listed at the top (or alternatively on the left hand side), the liabilities at the bottom (or on the right hand side). By definition assets must equal liabilities.

Table 3   A simplified balance sheet

The company balance sheet	Dec. 31st		£ million
Fixed Assets			
Buildings	55		
Machinery	45		
Fixtures	5		
	105		105
Trade investments			5
Current assets			
Stocks	7		
Trade debtors	10		
Bank	25	42	
Current liabilities			
Trade creditors	12		
Corporation tax	10	22	
Working capital			20
Net assets			130
Less 10% debentures			30
Net worth			100
Assets			
Issued share capital			75
Reserves			5
P.& L. credit balance brought forward			20
			100

Adding the organization's FIXED ASSETS, TRADE INVESTMENTS and CURRENT ASSETS, and subtracting CURRENT LIABILITIES gives the organization's net assets. Subtracting from net assets any long-term loans to the organization, e.g. DEBENTURES, gives the net worth or equity. The net worth is also represented by the sum of three items: the issued share capital, reserves and the balance brought forward from the PROFIT AND LOSS ACCOUNT.

balanced budget. *See* BUDGET.

balanced budget multiplier. Refers to the fact that equal changes in government expenditure and tax revenue lead to an overall increase in AGGREGATE DEMAND and hence in NATIONAL INCOME. This conclusion depends upon three assumptions. The first is that all the government expenditure feeds into an increase in aggregate demand, i.e. it ignores the possibility that the expenditure might include TRANSFER PAYMENTS which are partly saved. The second is that the increase in government expenditure does not cause a fall in any other form of expenditure, i.e. that there is no CROWDING-OUT. The final assumption is that the SAVINGS RATIO is positive, meaning that taxpayers react to the increase in tax rates by reducing both spending and saving, so that their expenditure falls by less than their disposable income. Under these assumptions, with a savings ratio of, say, 10 per cent, an increase in government expenditure and taxation of £100 millions would cause an increase in aggregate demand of £10 millions, the amount by which the increase in government expenditure (£100 millions) exceeds the fall in spending by taxpayers (£90 millions).

balanced growth. Economic growth in which consumption, investment and employment grow at the same rate as national income.

balancing allowance. *See* CAPITAL ALLOWANCES.

balancing item. *See* BALANCE OF PAYMENTS.

bank. An institution which acts as a FINANCIAL INTERMEDIARY, usually performing three functions: the acceptance of deposits from customers, the transfer of these deposits from one account to another (or their withdrawal in the form of notes and coin), and the lending of money by way of loans and overdrafts to customers. (However, the Banking Act 1979 did not regard the transfer function as essential to qualification as a bank. Under this Act the BANK OF ENGLAND has the right to decide which institutions are entitled to designation as 'recognized banks'.)

bank, commercial. A financial intermediary licensed by the government or the CENTRAL BANK to accept DEPOSITS, including deposits against which cheques can be written, and to make LOANS. Commercial banks are sometimes known as joint-stock banks. In the UK the largest commercial banks, e.g. Barclays, have an extensive network of branches, a system known as branch or retail banking. As with other companies, banks' balance sheets list their assets and liabilities, but these differ considerably from the assets and liabilities of most other companies. About 90 per cent of banks' liabilities comprise deposits. (Other liabilities, in common with other companies, include loans made to the bank, issued share capital and reserves.) The banks try to use the money deposited with them so as to yield a profit above the cost of the deposits and the costs of running the business. But they also have to ensure that they can meet the demands of all depositors who might wish to withdraw their money. Their assets therefore include some which are highly LIQUID but have a low YIELD, and some which are less liquid but have a higher yield. A typical list of assets, in order of decreasing liquidity, would be: CASH (notes and coin), balances with the BANK OF ENGLAND, MONEY AT CALL AND SHORT NOTICE (included in market loans), BILLS, INVESTMENTS and ADVANCES.

Table 4   Assets of banks in the UK, June 1992

	Percentages
Notes and coin	0.3
Balances with Bank of England	0.1
Market loans	44.3
Bills	1.1
Advances	42.9
Investments	7.6
Miscellaneous	3.7
Total assets (sterling and other currencies)	100

Source: *Bank of England Quarterly Bulletin*

bank advances. There are two main forms of bank advances: overdrafts and loans. (The discounting of BILLS is sometimes considered to be a form of advance, but it is identified as a separate type of asset in the banks' balance sheets.) With an overdraft, the most common form of advance, the customer is permitted to overdraw a CURRENT ACCOUNT into debit up to an agreed amount. Interest is charged on a daily basis on the amount overdrawn, which makes the overdraft especially appropriate for customers whose need for credit constantly varies, e.g. small shopkeepers and tradesmen. The interest charge is set in relation to the BASE RATE, e.g. base rate + 4 per cent, and so varies as the base rate varies. With a loan, the bank lends a given amount at a fixed rate of interest, and the loan is repaid within an agreed time, say one or two years, normally in regular instalments. Bank loans were introduced primarily to help with lump-sum payments such as the purchase of a car, but forms of loan introduced more recently, such as the REVOLVING CREDIT scheme, are used for less expensive purchases. For many years the aim of banks was to 'borrow long and lend short' and thus minimize their risks. But in the 1970s banks began to make more medium-term loans, from two to ten years, especially to companies, and since then even longer-term lending has become accepted. A form of lending that became increasingly common in the 1980s was mortgage lending for house purchase. Bank advances are the least liquid form of asset but the most profitable (assuming, of course, that the proportion of bad debts does not become too great).

bank bill. *See* BILL OF EXCHANGE.

bank deposits. The great bulk of the banks' liabilities consists of the deposits of their customers. Two main types of account are available to depositors, the current and deposit account. With a current account the balance standing to a customer's credit is repayable on demand (which is why these accounts are sometimes known as sight deposits), and there is a right to draw cheques (which is why they are sometimes known as chequing accounts). Until fairly recently current account balances did not attract interest but now about one-third do so. With a deposit account (or time deposits), the amount standing to a customer's credit is in principle repayable upon personal application after a stated period of notice, usually seven days, although in practice the period of notice is often waived. Moreover the customer has no, or a very limited, right to draw cheques. To compensate for these limitations, a higher rate of interest is paid on deposit accounts. The interest rate often relates to the banks' BASE RATE, although sometimes to other rates, e.g. MONEY MARKET rates.

Bank for International Settlements. An institution whose board is made up of representatives of the central banks of a number of countries, including the UK. Its main purpose is to promote central bank co-operation, including the provision of short-term liquidity to central banks in need. The bank has acted as a clearing-house for inter-bank transactions in European Currency Units.

bank loans. *See* BANK ADVANCES.

Bank of England. The CENTRAL BANK in the UK banking system, established in 1694 and brought into public ownership in 1946. The Bank of England has several major areas of responsibility. First, it directs and supervises the activities of the institutions comprising the country's banking and financial system to try to ensure the stability and efficient functioning of the system. It has the right to decide which organizations are entitled to designation as RECOGNIZED BANKS, which as LICENSED DEPOSIT-TAKING INSTITUTIONS, and which are not entitled to either designation. It vets the accounts of both sets of institutions four times a year and is in regular contact with senior management, so the Bank should have early warning of any trouble that may be developing. (However the collapse in 1991 of the Bank of Credit and Commerce International showed that supervision is not always adequate.) The stability of a banking system depends heavily upon the confidence of depositors that the banks will always have adequate liquidity, i.e. will be able to repay deposits when required. The Bank of England helps to maintain this confidence in several ways. Through the DISCOUNT MARKET it acts as LENDER OF LAST RESORT to the COMMERCIAL BANKS. If any bank is in trouble the Bank will attempt to organize support. When in the 1970s a number of 'secondary' banks had difficulty in meeting their obligations because they had loaned too much money to the property markets, where prices had fallen drastically, the Bank persuaded the commercial banks not to call in their loans to the secondary banks and to take over the responsibility for some of the secondary banks' debts. The Bank also administers the DEPOSIT PROTECTION FUND. Second, the Bank acts as the government's banker, and as such it ensures that the government always has sufficient money to meet its planned expenditure. Since public expenditure frequently exceeds revenue from taxation, this implies that the Bank is responsible for managing the government's borrowing programme. It arranges for the government to borrow by the issue of GILT-EDGED SECURITIES and it may itself lend directly to the government, but only overnight through WAYS AND MEANS ADVANCES. Third, the Bank is responsible, together with the Treasury, for the conduct of the government's MONETARY POLICY. (The Bank and the Treasury together are known as the monetary authorities.) The Bank is obliged by law to accept directives from the Treasury, although the governor of the Bank has the right to be consulted, and indeed acts as a channel of communication between the Treasury and the financial institutions. The fact that the Bank acts as banker to the commercial banks (see below) helps it to fulfil this responsibility. One of the objectives of monetary policy is to maintain the stability of the exchange rate and the Bank manages the EXCHANGE EQUALIZATION ACCOUNT. The Bank is divided into two departments. The issue department is responsible for the issue of BANK-NOTES. Against these liabilities it holds government and other securities, including a small amount of gold. The banking department's liabilities include bankers' deposits or balances (arising from the Bank's role as bankers' bank), deposits of government departments and a small number of private customers, and reserves. Its principal assets are government securities, discounts and advances.

Table 5   Bank of England balance sheet, 24 June 1992, £ million

ISSUE DEPARTMENT

Liabilities		Assets	
Notes in circulation	15 990	Government securities	10 589
Notes in banking department	10	Other securities	5 411

BANKING DEPARTMENT

Liabilities		Assets	
Public deposits	84	Government securities	1 234
Bankers' deposits	1 518	Advances, discounts, etc.	2 317
Reserves, etc.	3 602	Premises, etc.	1 657
		Notes and coin	10

Source: *Bank of England Quarterly Bulletin*

bankers' balances. *See* BANK, COMMERCIAL.

banker's draft. A CHEQUE drawn by a bank at the request of a customer, whose account is debited when it is drawn. It cannot be returned unpaid and is used when a creditor is unwilling to accept a personal cheque in payment.

banking. Accepting deposits and lending money. These activities are characteristic of banks, but are also undertaken by other financial institutions, e.g. building societies.

banking system. The mechanism through which the money supply of a country is created and controlled. The UK banking system is normally understood to include COMMERCIAL BANKS, through which the process of CREDIT CREATION occurs, secondary banks, the CENTRAL BANK, MERCHANT BANKS or ACCEPTING HOUSES, and the DISCOUNT HOUSES, but to exclude other financial institutions.

banknote. A note issued by a bank undertaking to pay the holder the face value on demand. In the UK banknotes are issued by the Bank of England and the Scottish and Irish commercial banks. Since banknotes ceased to be convertible into gold, the 'promise to pay' has in reality been a 'promise to exchange' into another banknote; the promise is now simply a guarantee that banknotes are LEGAL TENDER.

bankruptcy. When individuals or companies are declared by a court of law to be unable to pay their debts. A company declared bankrupt goes into LIQUIDATION. An undischarged bankrupt cannot, without the consent of the court, serve as a director of a limited company or take an active part in its management.

bargain. A transaction on the STOCK EXCHANGE.

bargaining. (1) Negotiations between employers and workers about such matters as rates of pay, hours of work and other conditions of service. All aspects of the relationship between employer and employee may be subject to bargaining, and if agreement is reached on all aspects, the CONTRACT between the two sides is said to be complete. But if some aspects are not subject to bargaining or if agreement is not reached, an incomplete contract is said to exist. Wage bargaining may be collective, where representatives of the employer or employers meet representatives of the workers, and the contract relates to more than one worker, or it may be individual, where each worker agrees a contract with the employer. Collective bargaining may be centralized or decentralized. Centralized bargaining might determine the national rates of pay in a particular industry, and would be conducted by a body representing all, or many, employers in the industry, e.g. the Engineering Employers Federation, and representatives of many of the workers in the industry, e.g. the Amalgamated Engineering and Electrical Union. In the Civil Service centralized bargaining might determine the rates of pay in all regions of the country. Bargaining can be decentralized organizationally or geographically. If the management of an engineering company negotiates rates of pay with unions representing the workers in that company, bargaining is decentralized organizationally. If pay in each region of the Civil Service is determined by negotiations between management and staff in the various regions, bargaining is decentralized geographically. Workplace bargaining is a further stage of decentralization to the individual production unit. It is possible to have a combination of organizational and geographical bargaining. The post-war period has seen a very clear trend towards decentralized collective bargaining. In the mid 1950s there were only a few hundred distinct bargaining units with separate agreements. Now there are over 30 000 bargaining units covering twenty-five or more employees. (2) In the BEHAVIOURAL THEORY OF THE FIRM bargaining is seen as involving various individuals and groups: managers, workers, shareholders, suppliers and customers. The bargaining is concerned with a wide range of issues, including pay, prices, output, investment and profits.

bargaining theory of wages. Wages in an occupation are assumed to be determined by the relative strength of unions and employers and by the strategies that they adopt. Factors affecting the outcome might include the UNION DENSITY, the costs that a stoppage would impose on employers and workers, and the current level of unemployment. Some models utilizing GAME THEORY assume that employers and unions wish to divide the firm's profits but also to maximize them.

barometric price leadership. *See* PRICE LEADERSHIP.

barriers to entry. Factors which make it difficult for a firm to enter a market, i.e. to begin supplying goods or services in competition with existing suppliers. Barriers may be 'natural' or 'innocent', as when existing producers have lower costs, e.g. because of access to superior technology or because of the LEARNING EFFECT, and set a price too low to allow higher-cost producers adequate profits. They may be 'artificial' as when existing producers engage in PRODUCT DIFFERENTIATION. Finally, barriers may result from government intervention as when private sector producers are prevented from competing with NATIONALIZED INDUSTRIES or when licences are granted to only a limited number of private sector producers.

barriers to trade. *See* TRADE BARRIERS.

barter. Selling or buying products in exchange for other products rather than for money.

base period. The reference date from which an INDEX NUMBER in a TIME SERIES is calculated. For example at present the RETAIL PRICE INDEX is calculated with January 1987 as its base.

base rate. The rate of interest in relation to which the COMMERCIAL BANKS normally set the interest charged on ADVANCES and paid on DEPOSITS.

base-weighted index. *See* INDEX NUMBER.

basing point price system. A system under which, although a product is made in a considerable number of locations, its price is related to a single or small number of locations. Customers pay a price that includes the transport cost from the base location even though many customers might have been supplied from other locations. This gives rise to CROSS-SUBSIDIES. Moreover if all producers use the same basing point it inhibits competition from plants located near to customers.

Basle Accord. This agreement, made by the G10 group of countries, and implemented in the UK by means of the Banking Act 1989, was a response to the globalization of banking. All member countries agreed to adopt similar regulatory systems. This is intended to establish equal treatment of all banking systems and hence encourage effective competition among these systems. All bank regulation is to be conducted on the basis of a bank's global portfolio, rather than its domestic portfolio as had normally been the case. Banks will be expected to maintain a uniform capital ratio of 8 per cent of attributable assets.

batch production. Production of articles in small quantities, usually because the products are non-standardized. Markets supplied by batch production usually have a low level of seller concentration.

bear. Someone who expects the price of securities on the STOCK EXCHANGE to fall and sells those securities in the hope of being able to re-buy at a lower price. If he has the securities which he sells he is described as a covered or protected bear; if not he is said to have 'sold short'.

bear market. A market in which the price of securities is falling.

bearer bonds. Bonds which can be transferred from one person to another without the change of ownership having to be registered.

17

behavioural economics. Economics which constructs theories and models on the basis of the observed behaviour of individuals.

behavioural theory of the firm. A theory developed, especially by R. Cyert and J.G. March, on the basis of observation of how people in organizations, and especially managers, behave. Firms are believed to have goals relating to production (stable output, adequate cost performance), stock levels (sufficient to meet demands of customers), sales and market share (maintain or increase), and profit (sufficient to meet the demands of shareholders and the future needs of the business). If it is not possible to achieve all these goals at the same time, the resulting conflicts must be resolved. Conflict resolution is helped by the fact that objectives are stated in terms of 'aspiration levels' and that those taking decisions do not attempt to maximize but to 'satisfice', i.e. they aim for a satisfactory aspiration level. This means that bargaining between managers can have a co-operative, 'give and take' element, often characterized by the formation of temporary coalitions. Moreover it implies that if a problem, in the shape of an unfulfilled objective, occurs, the firm is able to concentrate on solving that problem without worrying too much at this time about the impact on other objectives. The theory assumes that in many firms there is organizational slack; more resources are available than are necessary to meet the current demands of the firm. If performance becomes inadequate in terms of a particular objective, the firm is generally able to increase efficiency by utilizing slack resources, and so achieve that objective without detracting from others. Finally, conflict is less likely to occur when standard operating procedures are in place. For example if it is understood that a fall in profits below a certain level, due to an increase in costs, will lead to a rise in price, this will be accepted when it occurs despite the possible impact on the volume of sales and market share.

below the line. Items entered in a statement below the line at which a total is made, i.e. items excluded from that total. This contrasts with items entered ABOVE THE LINE.

below-the-line promotion. The promotion of goods and services by such means as direct mailing and in-store displays.

benefits principle of taxation. People who receive more than their share of public spending should pay more than their share of tax revenues, e.g. people with cars should pay more towards the cost of road provision than people without cars.

Bertrand model. A model of DUOPOLY developed by J. Bertrand, a French nineteenth century economist. Bertrand showed that if both firms start by charging the MONOPOLY price, but each firm believes that the other will not react to a small price cut, the price will eventually settle at the competitive level.

betas. Beta is a measurement of the extent to which a particular SHARE'S return changes with changes in the whole stock market. A share with Beta = 1 moves exactly in line with the market. The higher the betas of the shares in an investor's portfolio the more risky is that portfolio, since the value of the portfolio will fluctuate more than the market as a whole.

Beveridge Report. This report, published in 1942, has been the foundation of UK anti-poverty legislation. No attempt was made at a comprehensive overhaul of the Beveridge system until the Social Security Act 1986. The primary aim of the Beveridge Plan was to eradicate all want by concentrating on its causes: loss of work through unemployment or sickness, cessation of work through retirement, and the drain on household resources created by a large number of dependants. The main instrument of the system was a programme of social or national insurance, giving flat-rate benefits to the unemployed and sick, and flat-rate retirement pensions (financed mainly by weekly contributions from those covered by the scheme). These benefits were supplemented by allowances to mothers (initially called Family Allowance and paid in respect of all children except the first), and a minimum income guarantee (initially called National Assistance) for those whose needs could not be met by the insurance scheme. The role of National Assistance was expected to be minimal, largely because it was assumed that government policy would be able to ensure that unemployment remained at a low level.

Big Bang. This term refers to changes made in the operation of the London STOCK EXCHANGE in 1986. The separation of STOCKBROKERS from stockjobbers was ended, and many of these firms now act as MARKET MAKERS, quoting a price to investors which includes a profit margin. Other changes included the abolition of a common scale of commissions on sales, the removal of the regulation which prevented non-members of the stock exchange, e.g. banks, from acquiring control of member firms, and an extension of electronic trading off the floor of the exchange.

bilateral monopoly. A product or labour market in which a single seller (a MONOPOLIST) faces a single buyer (a MONOPSONIST). Price is indeterminate in such markets.

bilateralism. A trading agreement between two nations. In the former COMMAND ECONOMIES numerous agreements were made between two governments for the exchange of goods, frequently in the form of BARTER deals. Bilateralism may refer to other forms of agreement, e.g. two countries may apply preferential TARIFFS or QUOTAS to each other's trade. Since under bilateralism trade does not take place in accordance with the principle of COMPARATIVE ADVANTAGE, it is said to reduce overall economic welfare.

bill. A short-term financial asset which takes the form of a document giving evidence that the holder will receive repayment of a debt on a specified date (normally less than one year from the date on which the bill was issued). Bills which are issued or endorsed by reputable institutions, as is the case with TREASURY BILLS and BILLS OF EXCHANGE, may be sold by the institution making the initial loan to another institution before the MATURITY date.

bill broker. An individual or institution (normally a DISCOUNT HOUSE) that deals in TREASURY BILLS and BILLS OF EXCHANGE on the London MONEY MARKET.

bill of exchange. The main functions of bills of exchange are to enable exporters to obtain cash as soon as possible after exporting their goods, and importers to defer payment at least until they have received, and possibly until they have sold, the goods. The drawer of the bill makes a promise to pay a specific sum at a future date, normally three months from the date of issue. However the drawee does not need to wait until the maturity date. Once the bill has been 'accepted' (endorsed) it becomes negotiable and can be sold on the MONEY MARKET at a small discount. The acceptance function is normally undertaken by an ACCEPTING HOUSE, but bills may also be accepted by a bank (bank bills) or a trader (trade bill).

binomial distribution. A distribution showing the probability of obtaining a given number of successes out of a particular number of trials.

birth rate. The number of births in a year for every 1000 population.

black economy. Economic activity which cannot be counted in the GROSS DOMESTIC PRODUCT because it is not declared for taxation purposes. Although it cannot be identified, such activity is estimated to account for 3-5 per cent of gross domestic product.

black market. When the price of a product is officially controlled but some trading occurs at a higher price.

Blue Book. Popular name for the UNITED KINGDOM NATIONAL ACCOUNTS.

blue chip. Highly regarded, low risk, shares.

board of directors. The group responsible to the shareholders for the running of a company. The board often contains a mix of full-time executive directors and part-time non-executive directors.

Bolton Committee. A committee of inquiry which reported in 1971 on the small-firm sector of the economy. This was found to be in decline, mainly because of increasing taxation, increased importance of marketing economies, the increasing role of the State, and improved transport and communications. The committee concluded that small firms were a breeding ground of new industries and a source of dynamic competition, and they recommended that the government should grant concessions to small firms by reducing tax rates and lessening their obligations in connection with training, the provision of information, and planning controls. In recent years the decline of the small-firm sector has been reversed.

bond. (1) A longer-term financial asset than a BILL. Bonds, which may be issued by central or local government, companies, banks or other institutions, usually have a fixed rate of interest. A bond may have a specified MATURITY date or it may be irredeemable, e.g. Consols (Consolidated Stock) issued by the UK government. (2) Goods stored in a warehouse until customs duty has been paid are said to be held in bond.

bonus issue. *See* SCRIP ISSUE.

book value. The value at which assets appear in the firm's BALANCE SHEET. These assets are often valued at their purchase price minus DEPRECIATION, and this may well be below the market price.

boom. A rapid rate of increase in economic activity leading to a high level of capacity utilization and low unemployment. For a more technical definition see BUSINESS CYCLE.

borrowing ratio. The amount of money borrowed by the PERSONAL SECTOR as a proportion of PERSONAL DISPOSABLE INCOME.

bottlenecks. A lack of capacity in one sector of the economy which prevents the expansion of output not only in that but also in other sectors. For example if component suppliers cannot recruit the skilled labour required to increase output, a lack of components could reduce growth in other parts of the engineering industry.

bounded rationality. People and institutions are said to behave rationally when they choose what they consider to be the best course of action to achieve a specified objective. But in many situations rationality is bounded. It may not be possible, because of time or cost considerations, to identify all possible courses of action; moreover people may be uncertain about the outcome of some courses of action.

Box-Jenkins method. A method of forecasting which uses time-series analysis to extrapolate values of a variable.

Brady Plan. A plan adopted in 1989 with the aim of reducing levels of international debt in those severely indebted countries with INTERNATIONAL MONETARY FUND or WORLD BANK programmes in place. Debt reduction would occur by means of debtors using resources from the IMF or World Bank to buy back debt at a discount. Little progress had been made by the end of 1992.

branch banking. *See* BANK, COMMERCIAL.

branding. Differentiating, by advertising or other means, the product supplied by a given firm from physically identical or similar products supplied by other firms. Successful branding causes the demand for each brand to become less price ELASTIC.

brand loyalty. Denotes that BRANDING has been effective.

break-even point. The output at which total revenue equals total cost. It is usually assumed in break-even analysis, that the cost and revenue functions are linear. This is illustrated in Fig. 2 in which X is the break-even output.

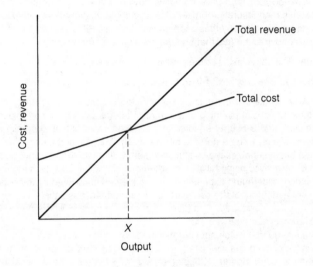

Figure 2 Break-even output

break-up value. (1) Tangible assets minus liabilities, as shown in the firm's balance sheet. (2) When the firm engages in a number of distinct operations, the value of these operations might be greater when run as separate operations, i.e. if the firm was broken up.

Bretton Woods system. The system of exchange rates agreed at a conference held at Bretton Woods in 1944, that operated for a quarter of a century after the Second World War. Countries other than the USA fixed their exchange rates in terms of the dollar and therefore, by implication, in terms of each other. Other currencies could be converted into dollars and it was sometimes necessary for central banks to buy or sell dollars in order to defend the fixed exchange rates. Since countries were allowed to change their exchange rates occasionally, the system was known as the 'adjustable peg' system. The Bretton Woods conference also established the INTERNATIONAL MONETARY FUND and the INTERNATIONAL BANK FOR RECONSTRUCTION AND DEVELOPMENT.

Bridlington Rules. Procedures established by the Trades Union Congress to prevent trade unions from poaching members from each other.

British Overseas Trade Board. An agency of the Department of Trade and Industry whose function is to promote British exports. It does this by providing information about overseas markets, conducting overseas market research, running trade fairs, etc.

British Technology Group. BTG was established by the government to develop new ideas from universities and companies for commercial exploitation. It has taken out patents on various products, e.g. the hovercraft, and has a portfolio of around 1700 innovations. Plans are currently in hand to privatize the Group.

broad measures (money). *See* MONETARY AGGREGATES.

broker. An intermediary between a buyer and seller in a market. For example on a stock exchange a STOCKBROKER transmits buying and selling orders from investors to MARKET MAKERS. An insurance broker acts as an intermediary between INSURANCE COMPANIES and people who buy those companies' policies. Bill brokers act on their own behalf, an exception to the rule that brokers act as agents for others.

brokerage. The commission or fee charged by a BROKER.

bubble policy. *See* EMISSIONS TRADING PROGRAMMES.

budget. An estimate of income and expenditure for a future period. Budgets are an essential tool in financial planning and control. Patterns of income and expenditure seldom coincide, and a budget enables an institution or individual to predict in advance when there is likely to be a need to borrow or an ability to lend money. Moreover constructing a budget enables the institution to see whether its existing policies are likely to result in its objectives being fulfilled, or whether a change in policies is required. Finally, by monitoring income and expenditure during the period covered by the budget, the institution will again be able to see whether its performance is satisfactory or whether a change in policy is required. This process of monitoring, and where necessary correction, is known as budgetary control.

The national budget which sets out estimates of central government expenditure and income in the coming financial year, was presented by the Chancellor of the Exchequer to Parliament each Spring. (Supplementary 'mini-budgets' have occasionally been presented in Autumn when it was felt that a policy change needed to be made at that time.) However, the date of presentation will be switched to December with effect from December 1993. The budget is mainly concerned with CONSOLIDATED FUND revenue, and not with national insurance or local authority finance.

In economic models, government expenditure includes both central and local government spending, and taxation includes central and local taxes plus national insurance. If planned expenditure equals planned revenue from taxation the budget is said to be balanced. If expenditure is planned to exceed revenue there is a planned budget deficit. If revenue is planned to exceed expenditure, there is a planned budget surplus. The balance between expenditure and revenue from taxation affects AGGREGATE DEMAND and hence the level of economic activity. If expenditure and revenue are equal, aggregate demand will increase because of the BALANCED BUDGET MULTIPLIER. It follows that a budget deficit will give rise to an even bigger increase in aggregate demand. We cannot say in principle how a budget surplus will affect aggregate demand, but a large surplus is likely to cause demand to be less than it would otherwise be. If the government were concerned only with aggregate demand we would expect to find budget deficits when the government wished to boost demand, e.g. to reduce UNEMPLOYMENT, and budget surpluses when it wished to moderate demand, e.g. to bring down the rate of INFLATION. (In fact the budget may also serve other government objectives, e.g. to change the DISTRIBUTION OF INCOME and WEALTH.)

budget, balanced. *See* BUDGET.

budget constraint. The constraint imposed on spending opportunities by the resources available to the individual, household or firm.

budget deficit. *See* BUDGET.

budget line. A graphical representation of the BUDGET CONSTRAINT, (most commonly applied to the consumer). When one product is plotted on one axis and another product on the other axis, the budget line joins all the combinations that could just be purchased, given the consumer's income. A budget line can also be drawn with income on one axis and a product on the other. It then shows combinations of that product and income available to be spent on other products.

budget share. The amount spent on a product as a percentage of total consumer spending or income.

budget surplus. *See* BUDGET.

budgetary control. *See* BUDGET.

buffer stock. An organization established, by a group of producers or the government, in order to stabilize the price of a product and hence the incomes of producers. It does so by entering the market as buyer when the quantity supplied exceeds the quantity demanded at the TARGET PRICE, and as seller when the reverse applies. The term is also applied to the products taken off the market and held in store by the organization.

building society. An institution whose main business is making loans for house purchase on MORTGAGE. (Societies are limited in the proportion of their assets that can be devoted to other uses.) Its liabilities mainly comprise deposits which can be withdrawn on demand or upon a specified period of notice, and shares. Both attract interest, a slightly higher rate often being paid on shares as compensation for slightly more restrictive withdrawal conditions. (However even higher rates are payable on deposits which are made for longer periods, such as a year.)

built-in stabilizers. *See* AUTOMATIC STABILIZERS.

bull. Someone who expects the price of securities on the STOCK EXCHANGE to rise and buys the securities in the hope of being able to re-sell at a higher price.

bull market. A market in which the price of securities is rising.

bureaucracy. A managerial system found in large organizations in which decisions are taken in accordance with rigid rules and procedures and there is an elaborate authority structure. Co-ordination often involves an extensive use of committees, and this can lead to a lessening of individual responsibility and a lack of responsiveness to market forces. Some models of bureaucracy assume that the bureaucrats attempt to maximize their budget as a source of power and status. Bureaucracy is an element in many MANAGERIAL THEORIES OF THE FIRM.

business cycle. The tendency for output and employment to fluctuate around their long-term trends. The point at which the gap between actual and trend output is at a maximum is known as a slump. The recovery stage of the cycle begins as output rises, coming closer to trend. Eventually output rises above the trend – the point at which this excess of actual over trend is at a maximum is known as a boom. The next stage in the cycle is recession, as output grows less quickly than trend, and perhaps even falls. (The Treasury defines a recession as two successive quarters of negative growth). Eventually recession becomes a slump, completing the cycle.

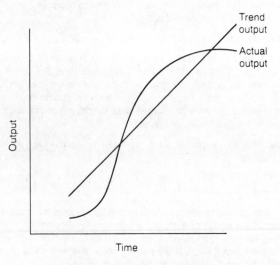

Figure 3   The business cycle

Some economists have attempted to explain the occurrence of business cycles in terms of the interaction between the ACCELERATOR and MULTIPLIER mechanisms. One possible scenario is that after a period of slump, investment eventually increases for some reason, e.g. because as existing capital wears out the CAPITAL-OUTPUT RATIO becomes less than firms desire, or because a fall in INTEREST RATES, possibly initiated by the government, increases the profitability of investment. The increased income generated by the additional investment and magnified by the operation of the multiplier, leads to an increase in AGGREGATE DEMAND which leads, through the accelerator, to a further increase in investment. Or the initial move away from the floor may be caused by an increase in aggregate expenditure, due e.g. to higher government spending, which leads via the accelerator, to an increase in investment. The business cycle may reach a ceiling because aggregate demand begins to grow at a slower rate, e.g. because many of the demands of consumers have been met, or because there is not sufficient spare capacity in the economy to permit a faster growth in expenditure. This slowing in the rate of growth of expenditure may lead, via the accelerator, to a fall in investment and hence, via the multiplier, to a fall in income and demand.

Business Expansion Scheme. A scheme under which tax incentives are given to investors in companies which are not listed on the main STOCK EXCHANGE and which have not been trading for more than five years. These are small businesses whose growth might have been hampered by a lack of finance. The scheme was due to be abolished at the end of 1993.

business finance. Money used to meet the cost of establishing and running a business. Businesses usually use both internal and external finance. When a business is first set up, internal finance may consist of the savings of the proprietor or partners. But once a business becomes established, most internal finance consists of undistributed income, i.e. profits retained within the business. Internal funds account for around two-thirds of the total funds used by large industrial and commercial companies. The sources of external finance that are available depend partly upon the legal form of the business. External finance for SOLE TRADERS and PARTNERSHIPS is largely short-term, comprising bank loans, trade credit, hire-purchase finance, etc. Longer-term credit may sometimes be obtained by means of a mortgage on land or buildings. In addition to having access to all these sources of finance, joint-stock companies are more likely to borrow long-term by the issue of DEBENTURES and can raise permanent capital by issuing SHARES. The relative importance of the different sources varies as changes occur in the financial markets. For example over the period 1988-91 industrial and commercial companies raised more than four times as much by bank borrowing as they did by the issue of ordinary shares. However additional bank borrowing varied from £33 millions in 1989 to a net repayment of over £3 millions in 1991.

business fluctuations. Changes in the level of business activity as denoted by changes in expenditure, output and employment. If the fluctuations are pronounced and follow a regular pattern, the term BUSINESS CYCLE is used.

Business in the Community. A business-support network sponsored by the private sector. It advises member-companies on various aspects of their relationship with the community, including education, the impact of business on the environment, and the social responsibility of business.

business saving. That part of a business's net revenue that is not distributed as interest, dividends or taxation but is retained to help to finance the future running of the business. Also known as retained earnings, retentions and undistributed income. It is an important source of BUSINESS FINANCE.

buy-back agreement. In order to obtain an order to supply plant such as a factory, a firm agrees to buy a specified amount of the output from the plant when commissioned.

buy-in management buy-out. *See* MANAGEMENT BUY-OUT.

buyer concentration. The number of buyers in a market and their relative shares in total purchases. There is some evidence that high buyer concentration, i.e. a relatively few firms account for a large proportion of total purchases, is associated with lower profit-margins for suppliers.

buyers' market. A market in which buyers are currently in a more powerful position than sellers, enabling them to obtain improved terms, e.g. lower prices, extended credit.

buying economies. *See* ECONOMIES OF SCALE.

by-product. A product which is produced by a process set up and operated in order to produce another product. Since its production cannot be avoided as long as the process continues in operation, the OPPORTUNITY COST of a by-product is zero.

C

Cairns Group. A group of thirteen major food-exporting countries, including Australia, Canada, Brazil and Argentina, which has taken part in international negotiations aimed at reducing barriers to trade in agricultural products.

call money. *See* MONEY AT CALL AND SHORT NOTICE.

call option. The right to buy a stated security during a specified period, usually three months, at the price ruling at the time the bargain was struck plus a small commission.

Calmfors-Driffil model. A model which suggests that countries with highly centralized and countries with highly decentralized systems of wage setting both achieve lower rates of inflation than countries with mixed systems such as the UK. Later work suggests that if there is a relationship, the degree of employer co-ordination is more important than the degree of centralization.

Cambridge School. A system of economic thought influenced by economists at Cambridge University, beginning with Alfred Marshall who taught there until 1908. In the post-war period, Cambridge School economics has been most concerned with issues in MACROECONOMICS, being influenced by the inter-war writings of J.M. Keynes. However, models of economic growth constructed by some Cambridge economists assume full employment in contrast to the Keynesian approach which assumes under-employment of resources.

canons of taxation. Adam Smith proposed four canons or principles by which the desirability of taxation could be assessed: (a) the amount paid in tax should be proportional to income; (b) taxpayers should be sure what they are paying in tax; (c) there should be convenience of payment; (d) taxes should not be imposed if their cost of collection would be excessive. These canons would still be considered valid today by most economists, with the exception of the first; a proportional tax system would generally be considered less desirable than a PROGRESSIVE system.

capacity. The maximum output that could be produced in a given period from a given set of resources or inputs. At the national level the potential output can be represented by a PRODUCTION POSSIBILITY FRONTIER. In order to simplify analysis, the traditional THEORY OF THE FIRM ignores many of the questions that exist in practice in identifying the firm's capacity, e.g. how many hours per week machinery is operated.

capacity costs. Costs which depend upon the capacity of the firm, e.g. the cost of plant and equipment, as opposed to the costs of running the firm, e.g. the wages of workers operating plant and equipment. If capacity costs are a high proportion of total costs, the firm may levy capacity charges by means of a TWO-PART TARIFF.

capacity utilization. The output that a firm or economy produces in a given period (actual output) as a percentage of the output that could have been produced (potential output). The unemployment rate is a commonly used indicator of the degree of underutilization of capacity at the national level.

capital. (1) Assets that have themselves been produced and which can be used in the production and distribution of goods and services. When applied to the total productive assets of the economy the term social capital is used, denoting that the assets are used in the production of both marketable and non-marketable outputs. Capital is one of the FACTORS OF PRODUCTION. (2) The money value of real assets. The capital of a business is taken to be its net worth, as recorded in the BALANCE SHEET. In both uses of the term, two forms of capital are normally distinguished: (a) fixed capital, which includes buildings, plant and machinery, and (b) circulating, floating or working capital, which includes components and work in progress. But raw materials would normally be excluded from capital seen as a factor of production, whereas stocks of raw materials held by a firm would be included in working capital.

capital, authorized. *See* AUTHORIZED CAPITAL.

capital, cost of. (1) When capital is defined as physical assets, its cost in any period is the reduction in potential output or CAPACITY in future periods. This cost can have two sources. First, as the assets are used they wear out (loss through use). Second, even if the assets are not used, their value may fall through OBSOLESCENCE. (2) When capital is considered as a factor of production, INTEREST is deemed to be its return or cost. (3) Interest is also sometimes suggested as the cost of capital to the firm. However interest is better seen as one element of the firm's overall COST OF FINANCE.

capital, issued. *See* ISSUED CAPITAL.

capital, sources of. *See* BUSINESS FINANCE.

capital account. *See* BALANCE OF PAYMENTS.

capital accumulation. The growth over time of the stock of real capital. Capital accumulation denotes that CAPITAL FORMATION is positive. Capital accumulation plays a prominent role in MARXIAN ECONOMICS.

capital allowances. Reductions in a firm's tax liability which relate to its capital expenditure. The year-by-year DEPRECIATION of a firm's capital assets is recognized as a cost to be offset against revenue (a writing-down allowance) in calculating the firm's tax liability. But in order to encourage investment the government may allow accelerated depreciation for tax purposes. For instance, in addition to the annual allowances, the firm may be given an initial allowance in the year in which an item is purchased. An extreme example of this procedure is where the initial allowance is 100 per cent, allowing the firm to offset the entire cost of an item in its year of purchase, a system known as free depreciation or depreciation at choice. When assets are sold, a balancing allowance or charge is made, to ensure that the total allowances for an item equal its cost.

capital asset pricing model. A model of the markets for financial assets which seeks to explain their relative prices in terms of the degree of correspondence between the performance of each (especially changes in price) and the performance of the market as a whole. The model suggests that the price of assets whose performance corresponds closely with the market will be relatively low. Conversely the price of assets which are affected very little by movements of the market will be relatively high, since they offer good returns when they are most needed, i.e. when the market is depressed.

capital budgeting. Constructing BUDGETS for capital expenditure.

capital consumption. The reduction in the value of a CAPITAL STOCK that would occur in a given period, due to wear and tear and obsolescence, if no INVESTMENT took place. It is a similar concept to DEPRECIATION, although capital consumption is usually applied to

B

the economy as a whole, as in the UK NATIONAL ACCOUNTS, whereas depreciation is more often applied to the accounts of individual firms.

capital deepening. As a result of investment, an increase occurs in the CAPITAL-LABOUR RATIO.

capital employed. There are several alternative definitions, among the most common being: (a) fixed plus current assets; (b) fixed plus current assets minus current liabilities; (c) fixed plus current assets but excluding trade debtors.

capital expenditure. The purchase of real assets, both fixed, e.g. machines, and current, e.g. components, plus expenditure on TRADE INVESTMENTS. (This last item is excluded from CAPITAL FORMATION.)

capital flows. Movements of money between one sector of the economy and another, or between one country and another.

capital formation. *See* FIXED CAPITAL FORMATION.

capital gains. A gain that is realized when assets are sold for prices above those at which they were purchased.

capital gains tax. A tax levied on capital gains made outside the normal course of business. When the tax was introduced in 1962 it was argued that capital gains should be taxed in the same way as other forms of income. However the tax has gradually been made less onerous since then, and it applies only to gains over a substantial amount (£5800 in 1992/3). (Any capital losses can be offset against gains from other transactions.) Since 1982 the purchase price has been subject to INDEXATION so that only gains above the rate of inflation are taxable. The tax is levied at the marginal rate of income tax of the individual concerned.

capital gearing. *See* GEARING.

capital goods. Following from the economist's definition of CAPITAL, goods which are used in the production of goods and services are classified as capital goods. Note that this definition is not always followed in the UK NATIONAL ACCOUNTS. Cars bought by a manufacturing company for the use of its directors would be classified as capital goods, whereas cars bought by those directors for their own private use would be classified as CONSUMPTION GOODS. But both sets of cars would yield a series of services (transportation) in future years.

capital intensive. A process that uses a large amount of CAPITAL in relation to other FACTORS OF PRODUCTION is said to be capital intensive.

capital-labour ratio. The amount of capital available per worker employed (or, alternatively, per production worker employed).

capital loss. A loss that is sustained when an asset is sold for less than the purchase price. Since most non-financial assets lose value through use, capital loss can only be meaningfully applied to financial assets. Capital losses are taken into account in computing liability to CAPITAL GAINS TAX.

capital market. The market for medium- and long-term loans. The money that is borrowed, e.g. by the issue of DEBENTURES, is often used to finance the purchase of fixed assets. The term is sometimes extended to include the market for permanent capital raised by the issue of SHARES.

capital-output ratio. The stock of CAPITAL required to produce a given output, divided by that output. The incremental capital-output ratio is the increase in the stock of capital needed to produce an increase in output, divided by that increase in output. In certain circumstances, the capital-output ratio has the same value as the accelerator coefficient, a key mechanism in the operation of the ACCELERATION PRINCIPLE.

capital re-switching. It is reasonable to suppose that as the required rate of return on investment falls, firms will switch from less to more capital-intensive methods of production, thus increasing the level of investment. But it can be shown that under quite plausible circumstances the rate of return could reach a level at which firms would switch back (re-switch) from more to less capital-intensive production methods, thus causing the level of investment to fall.

capital services. The services produced over a number of periods by a piece of capital equipment, e.g. the amount of cloth woven each year on a loom. In deciding whether to buy the equipment, the firm will consider its price and the value of the services produced.

capital stock. The total physical ASSETS of a firm or economy.

capital stock adjustment models. Models which seek to explain changes in the capital stock in terms of changes in such factors as the level of output, the relative prices of capital and other factors of production, the rate of interest and retained earnings.

capital structure. The composition of a company's long-term capital, and especially the division between long- term borrowing and equity capital.

capital theory. Theory relating to (a) the process whereby CONSUMPTION is deferred, enabling capital goods to be produced; (b) the role of capital in ECONOMIC GROWTH; (c) the factors influencing the income derived by the owners of capital as a proportion of total income.

capital transfer tax. *See* INHERITANCE TAX.

capital widening. If the LABOUR FORCE increases, an increase in the CAPITAL STOCK is required to maintain the existing capital-labour ratio. This process is known as capital widening.

capitalism. A system in which productive assets are owned privately (i.e. not by the state). The owners are free to use these assets as they wish, subject to certain constraints imposed, for example, to protect citizens from danger. The goods and services produced by these assets are usually allocated by means of the PRICE MECHANISM.

capitalization. (1) The conversion of a company's accumulated profits and reserves into ISSUED CAPITAL. (2) Market capitalization is the stock market's valuation of a company, i.e. the number of shares issued multiplied by their price.

capitalized value. The capital value of an asset which, given the current rate of interest, would yield its current earnings. If an asset earned £100 a year and the rate of interest was 5 per cent the capitalized value would be £2000.

car tax. Until November 1992 new cars, motor cycles, scooters, mopeds and some motor caravans were chargeable with car tax at 5 per cent on the wholesale value. Value added tax was charged on the price including car tax.

cardinal utility. *See* UTILITY.

Caribbean Common Market. Formed in 1973 the Caribbean Common Market has twelve member states in the Caribbean and the American mainland. It has a COMMON EXTERNAL TARIFF and its members co-operate in certain aspects of agriculture, health, education and transport.

cartel. An organization of producers set up to regulate output and sales of a product. The tightest form of cartel is where all the producers supply their output through a central selling organization, an example being De Beers. Handling a substantial proportion of the world's supply of diamonds, De Beers has been able to keep prices steadier than they would otherwise have been. In looser forms of cartel, such as the Organization of Petroleum Exporting Countries, producers agree OUTPUT QUOTAS but each sells its own output. OPEC's quotas were designed to restrict supply and so increase prices and profits, but it has proved very difficult to reach agreement on quotas and to enforce agreements, once made.

cash. Coins and BANKNOTES.

cash discount. A price reduction given for payment in cash or for prompt payment. See also TRADE DISCOUNT.

cash flow. The flow of MONEY to and from a firm (or individual). The term can be given various meanings. Expenditure may be called a negative cash flow, and income or revenue received a positive cash flow; alternatively these terms may be used to denote the balance, an excess of expenditure over income being called a negative cash flow, and an excess of income over expenditure a positive cash flow. Two more precise terms are (a) gross cash flow, defined as gross profit (after the payment of any interest due) plus DEPRECIATION provisions, i.e. the money available for tax payments, dividends and investment; (b) net cash flow, defined as gross cash flow minus tax payments. The net cash flow of individual projects is an important consideration in INVESTMENT APPRAISAL.

cash limits. (1) The expenditure plans of government departments are expressed in terms of current prices and the departments are not allowed, in principle, to overspend. Consequently if the prices of inputs are higher than was expected when the spending was agreed, the volume of spending will be less than planned. (2) The target profit (or loss) set by the government for each nationalized industry.

cash ratio. The ratio of a bank's holdings of cash to its total deposits. A minimum ratio may be maintained either because the bank wishes to ensure that it can always repay deposits when required, or because the CENTRAL BANK or the government says so (i.e. for prudential or for control purposes). At present members of the monetary sector whose ELIGIBLE LIABILITIES exceed £10 millions must keep 0.35 per cent of their deposits at the BANK OF ENGLAND. These deposits are the equivalent of cash, but they are required not for control purposes but as a contribution towards the cost of the Bank's operations, no interest being paid by the Bank.

ceiling price. The maximum price that suppliers are allowed by the government to charge for a product.

Central American Common Market. A common market of four Central American states which has established, for most products, FREE TRADE among members and a COMMON EXTERNAL TARIFF.

central bank. Every country of any size has a central bank, e.g. the BANK OF ENGLAND, Federal Reserve Bank, Bundesbank. Moreover it is proposed that the European Community should have a central bank in the near future. The basic roles of central banks are to act as banker to the government and to the country's COMMERCIAL BANKS, to control the supply of banknotes, and to advise on the formulation, and assist in the implementation, of MONETARY POLICY.

central government. Those departments and other bodies (but not the local authorities) for whose activities a minister of the Crown, or other responsible person, is accountable to Parliament.

central planning. A form of planning, now abandoned in almost all countries, in which the government, on the advice of the body charged with the responsibility for planning, decides what products are to be produced, how they are to be produced, and how the revenue is to be allocated among those contributing to the production process.

Central Statistical Office. The office responsible for the government's statistical services. ,

certificate of deposit. A certificate stating that a specified sum has been deposited with a bank and that the bank will repay on a given date. CDs are purchased for less than their face value and therefore offer a positive yield. The first sterling CDs were issued in 1968 and there is now a flourishing secondary market, comprising the DISCOUNT HOUSES and the banks in the INTER-BANK MARKET.

certificate of incorporation. A document, issued by the Registrar of Companies, certifying the legal existence of a company, the legal requirements for registration having been met.

certificate of origin. A document issued by a customs officer of a country, certifying that the goods have been exported from that country. The certificate is especially important when the exporting country has been granted a preferential TARIFF rate, or when the importing country operates a system of IMPORT QUOTAS.

ceteris paribus. In analysing the effect of a change in an economic variable, it is frequently assumed that no change occurs in other variables that could have affected the outcome, i.e. it is assumed that other things remain equal or constant (ceteris paribus). For example a demand curve shows how the quantity demanded changes as price changes, the conditions of demand (income, etc.) remaining constant.

chain store. A popular term for a MULTIPLE RETAILER.

characteristics space. Characteristics space analysis views products as different combinations of particular qualities or characteristics, e.g. colour, durability. Products are demanded because they incorporate bundles of the characteristics desired by the consumer. A consumer will buy a product yielding bundle A rather than a product yielding bundle B as long as the extra UTILITY of A is greater than the price difference between the two products. This analysis attempts to explain how consumers behave and also throws light on decisions made by firms regarding the introduction of new products.

cheap money. A low rate of interest which makes it cheaper to borrow money. A government is most likely to adopt a cheap money policy when it wishes to encourage spending, and especially investment, in order to increase the rate of economic activity.

check trading. A form of credit trading. A company such as a FINANCE HOUSE sells a check or voucher on credit, the debt being repaid with interest, in regular instalments. The check can be used to purchase goods at shops which have an agreement with the finance house issuing the check. The finance house reimburses the retailer to the value of the check, less a discount. These procedures are not unlike those relating to CREDIT CARDS.

cheque. When a person writes a cheque he is telling his bank to pay the amount specified on the cheque to the person named (the payee). The money must be paid on demand provided, of course, that the drawer has enough in his current account to cover the cheque.

Chicago School. A number of economists who have worked at the University of Chicago. They have made important contributions in a number of areas of enquiry, including the CONSUMPTION FUNCTION, the theory of REGULATION, and the QUANTITY THEORY OF MONEY. Chicago economists tend to be very sceptical of government intervention in the economy, believing that its consequences are often adverse. For example George Stigler has argued that regulations designed to benefit consumers end up by benefiting producers, while Milton Friedman has claimed that attempts to increase employment via higher expenditure will eventually fail but will cause an increase in the rate of inflation.

Chinese walls. Barriers, physical or otherwise, between different departments of a bank or other financial institution, designed to prevent the exchange of price-sensitive information that could cause a conflict of interest within the institution.

chi-square distribution. A probability distribution used in formulating tests of significance in order to decide whether observed proportions in samples may reasonably be attributed to chance.

circular flow of income. *See* THEORY OF INCOME DETERMINATION.

circulating capital. *See* CAPITAL.

City. The term City refers to the institutions situated within the City of London which together constitute the hub of the UK's financial system: the Bank of England, the head offices of the major commercial banks, merchant banks, discount houses, stock exchange, etc.

City code. A self-regulatory system governing behaviour in TAKEOVER bids and MERGERS. The main purposes of the code are to ensure that all shareholders (in each company) receive equal treatment and that insider information is not abused. The code is administered by the City Panel on Takeovers and Mergers.

classical economics. Classical economics was dominant for about a hundred years, until roughly the middle of the nineteenth century. But the views of classical economists have continued to be influential and have received increased attention, especially as incorporated in the NEW CLASSICAL ECONOMICS, during the past two decades. The MACRO-ECONOMIC models of classical economics assumed that prices, including wages, were fully flexible, leading to the conclusion that involuntary unemployment cannot persist. This supposed outcome leads to the conclusion that government intervention to reduce unemployment is not required. In fact, classical economists were more concerned overall with MICROECONOMIC issues, the operation of markets, the distribution of income, etc. But again the implications of their analysis was that only limited government intervention was required. Although Adam Smith was fully aware that producers were prone to adopt anti-competitive practices, he believed that in general society would benefit most by allowing people to pursue their own advantage, via the operation of the so-called INVISIBLE HAND.

classical unemployment. *See* UNEMPLOYMENT.

claw-back. The claw-back principle relates to the taxation of state benefits, e.g. unemployment benefit, retirement pensions. With a progressive system of taxation, claw-back means that the real value of benefits falls as income rises.

clearing banks. Members of the CLEARING HOUSE.

clearing house. An institution where mutual indebtedness between institutions is settled. A well known example is the London Bankers' Clearing House, where CHEQUES drawn against member banks are set off against each other. At the end of each working day a series of balances between banks is struck, and a bank that is indebted to another settles the debt by drawing a cheque on its balance at the BANK OF ENGLAND. Standing orders are cleared through the Bankers' Automatic Clearing Service and large cheques through the Clearing House Automated Payments System.

clearing system. The procedures by which mutual debts are offset and net indebtedness is settled.

close company. A company effectively controlled by five or fewer shareholders.

close-down point. When the price that would maximize the firm's profits is less than average VARIABLE COST at the corresponding level of output, the firm will cease operations.

closed economy. An economy which has no transactions with other countries.

closed shop. A firm in which all employees must belong to a union. In a pre-entry closed shop only existing union members are recruited. In a post-entry closed shop any non-union members recruited must join a union on starting work. The justification of the closed shop is that it avoids the free-rider problem, with non-unionists enjoying the same wages and conditions as unionists who have fought for these things. On the other hand the closed shop can be seen as infringing personal freedom and as reducing the flexibility of the LABOUR MARKET. Consequently closed shops have been forbidden or controlled by some governments. In the UK, under the Employment Act 1990, people cannot be refused a job because they do not belong to a union. The European Court ruled that a group of railway workers who had been dismissed because they had refused to join a union had been dismissed unfairly.

closing prices. The prices of commodities or securities ruling at the end of a day's trading.

Club of Rome. An international group of academics and civil servants which has produced reports drawing attention to the fact that economic growth could be brought to a halt by the exhaustion of finite resources. The group advocates that greater attention be given to the conservation of resources and suggests that governments may need to take steps to modify the rate of growth.

coalition. *See* BEHAVIOURAL THEORY OF THE FIRM.

Cobb-Douglas function. *See* PRODUCTION FUNCTION.

cobweb model. A model of a market which assumes that producers' output decisions respond with a lag to price changes. So for example farmers would decide what crops to grow in the light of the prices ruling in the previous year. Because producers' decisions are not co-ordinated, they result in large changes in supply and hence in price. If the price changes get bigger over time we have a divergent cobweb, if they get smaller we have a convergent cobweb.

coefficient of determination. Measures the proportion of the variance of a dependent variable that is explained by the linear influence of an independent variable. The values of the coefficient (which is usually denoted r^2) lie between 0 and 1. If two variables are strongly related, with a CORRELATION COEFFICIENT (r) of, say, 0.9, the coefficient of determination (r^2) would be 0.81.

cohesion. The term given to the demand for a transfer of resources from the richer to the poorer members of the European Community. To meet this demand it is proposed that between 1993 and 1997, £7 billions should be transferred to those members whose per capita incomes are less than 90 per cent of the Community average.

coincident indicators. *See* ECONOMIC INDICATORS.

collateral security. A security provided by the borrower when a loan is made. Shares and other company securities are often provided as collateral for bank loans, but property is often the collateral for very large loans. In the early 1990s banks and building societies made losses because of falling property values. The market value of property acquired from borrowers who could not repay was sometimes less than the value of the loan.

collective bargaining. *See* BARGAINING.

collective restrictive practices. Practices restricting competition that involve an agreement between two or more firms. If two producers agreed to supply only a limited number of retailers, this would constitute a collective restrictive practice. If a single producer limited its supply in this way it would not be a collective restrictive practice (although it might restrict competition and might be deemed to be illegal). These practices are subject to the government's COMPETITION POLICY.

collectivization. Usually practised in particular in agriculture in the former COMMAND ECONOMIES, collectivization involves taking assets such as land and livestock away from individual owners and putting them in the hands of state-owned collectives. Despite the promise of increased ECONOMIES OF SCALE, collectivization in agriculture led to huge falls in PRODUCTIVITY.

collusion. Agreements or understandings between firms, and especially between producers, whereby they accept limitations on their freedom of action. Collusion may take many forms ranging from PRICE LEADERSHIP to CARTELS. Most forms of collusion are now illegal.

command economy. An economic system in which RESOURCES are ALLOCATED by means of decisions taken by the state planning authority. These decisions concern what is produced, how it is produced, for whom it is produced and the rewards obtained by those involved in production. A command or planned economy is not compatible with widespread private ownership of the means of production or with a flexible price system.

commanding heights of the economy. Industries such as the fuel, power and transport industries were NATIONALIZED in the early post-war period, since it was felt that state ownership would not only benefit these industries, but would have an influence on the economy as a whole. As many of the reputed benefits of state ownership failed to materialize, and as the balance of political power shifted, many of the nationalized assets were returned to the private sector.

commercial banks. *See* BANK, COMMERCIAL.

commercial bill. *See* BILL OF EXCHANGE.

commercial economies. *See* ECONOMIES OF SCALE.

commercial policy. Government policy that influences international trade through TAXATION, the granting of SUBSIDIES, or by the imposition of direct controls on IMPORTS and EXPORTS.

commodity. (1) In economic theory commodity can be used as another term for product. (2) In everyday use the term usually refers to a primary product, such as wheat or tin.

commodity agreements. Agreements designed to stabilize, or reduce fluctuations in, the prices of primary commodities. The prices of these products fluctuate more than the prices of manufactured goods for several reasons. Changes in climatic conditions can lead to big changes in the output of agricultural products. Many primary commodities are produced by a large number of independent firms who do not co-ordinate their production decisions, again leading to wide swings in output. (Changes in output as lagged responses to price changes underlie the COBWEB MODEL.) Changes in price following changes in supply are sometimes (but by no means always) accentuated by SPECULATION. The main elements in commodity agreements are limitations on output (designed to increase rather than stabilize price), and the operation of a BUFFER STOCK. Commodities subjected to agreements have included tin, natural rubber, coffee and cocoa. However, most agreements have collapsed or operated very imperfectly after a few years, for two main reasons. First, at least some producers have failed to abide by the agreed OUTPUT QUOTAS. Second, there have been disagreements about the TARGET PRICE and the financing of the buffer stock. If the only aim of the agreement was to stabilize price, the target price should equal the average expected free market price. At this price the buffer stock's purchases (made to keep the price up to target) should, over a number of years, equal its sales (made to keep the price down to target). In practice producers have often insisted on a higher target price, leading to an increase in the amount of the commodity taken off the market. It has been especially difficult to agree on the financing of the additional costs of purchasing and storing the commodity when the agreement has involved countries which import the commodity.

commodity exchange. A MARKET in which commodities, and especially primary commodities, are bought and sold. For many products a well established grading system allows trading to take place without even samples of the commodity being inspected at the exchange.

commodity market. *See* COMMODITY EXCHANGE.

commodity money. Ordinary goods which serve as MONEY. Commodity money is used either when people have lost confidence in the official currency (usually because it is losing its value as a vast quantity is printed), or because official currency is very scarce, e.g. cigarettes have functioned as money in prisons.

Common Agricultural Policy. The system of agricultural support operated by the EUROPEAN COMMUNITY. The objectives of the CAP are to stabilize the price of commodities, protect producers' living standards and encourage structural improvements in farming (although expenditure on structural aspects accounts for only a small proportion of expenditure). Under the price-support mechanism a target price is set which reflects the price in the area where the product is in shortest supply and which takes account of the costs of production and transport. A threshold price is then set which, when transport costs are added, equals or slightly exceeds the target price. If world prices are below the threshold price, an import levy equal to the difference is imposed. If domestic supply exceeds demand at the target price, support buying becomes necessary. This buying takes place at the slightly lower intervention price. Some of the commodities taken off the market are sold in the world market, a SUBSIDY normally being paid equal to the difference between the intervention and world prices. The CAP has failed to protect the REAL INCOMES of many farmers in recent years. Nevertheless it has required increased expenditure and this has been a source of complaint, especially from countries with a small agricultural sector, e.g. the UK. Subsidized selling in the world market has also led to complaints, and the threat of retaliation, from other producer countries. In 1992 a change of policy was agreed, whereby support prices would be reduced, but more farmers would be compensated for land taken out of production. Although these changes would not reduce the overall cost of the CAP, they were expected to lead to a reduction in output, storage costs and subsidized exports.

common external tariff. A tariff applied, at a rate agreed by all the members of a COMMON MARKET, on goods imported from non-member countries.

common market. A common market is in principle characterized by a COMMON EXTERNAL TARIFF, and by an absence of restrictions on internal trade. In practice some members of a common market may insist on retaining some restrictions on trade with other members. In a well developed common market, such as the EUROPEAN COMMUNITY, members may agree to abandon other restrictions relating, for example, to the mobility of labour and capital.

common property resource. A resource whose ownership is vested in a defined group of users, each of whom agrees to abide by a set of rules about the use of the resource. For example an agreement has been reached to limit the rate of production and consumption of CFCs, which deplete the ozone layer. This agreement in effect recognizes that the ozone layer is a common property resource, owned by all the nations of the world.

Commonwealth Development Corporation. A British organization which provides aid to LESS DEVELOPED COUNTRIES. Aid was initially confined to the Commonwealth but can now be provided to other LDCs. The CDC makes direct investments and also buys shares and makes loans to companies in these countries.

community charge. Until replaced by the council tax in 1993, the community charge was the main source of local authority finance (apart from central government grants). The community charge was known popularly as the poll tax since it was levied on all adults. But unlike a true poll tax, the amount paid varied between local authority areas. Moreover, rebates were given to people on low incomes.

company saving. As defined in the UK NATIONAL ACCOUNTS, company saving is the income of companies that remains after deducting tax, profits due abroad, transfers and payments of interest and dividends. The money that companies spend on FIXED INVESTMENT and STOCKS is not deducted from income, but DEPRECIATION is.

company taxation. *See* CORPORATION TAX.

comparability. A principle used in determining wages and salaries. It has been applied particularly in the public sector, where wage awards have been made in the light of wages in comparable private sector jobs. It is, however, difficult to find jobs that are comparable in every respect. Moreover comparability tends to maintain the existing structure of wages and so hinders the changes in relative wages which help to reallocate resources.

comparative advantage. Assume that with a given combination of resources country A can produce either 10 000 units of food or 5000 units of machinery (its opportunity cost ratio between food and machinery is 1 : 0.5), and that country B can produce either 4000 units of food or 4000 units of machinery (its opportunity cost ratio is 1 : 1). Country A has an absolute advantage in the production of both products. However it has a comparative advantage in the production of food, while B has a comparative advantage in the production of machinery. Total output will be maximized if specialization and international trade take place in accordance with the principle of comparative advantage, i.e. if each country specializes in those products which it can produce at a lower relative cost (in terms of opportunity cost) than other countries. (This conclusion depends on the assumption that transport costs are negligible and that differences in opportunity costs would persist over time, i.e. it ignores the INFANT INDUSTRY argument.) Table 6 compares the output without specialization (each country devotes half its resources to food and half to machinery) with the output under specialization (A devotes

80 per cent of its resources to food and 20 per cent to machinery, B devotes all its resources to machinery).

Table 6   Comparative advantage

	Food	Machinery
Without specialization		
A	5 000	2 500
B	2 000	2 000
Total	7 000	4 500
With specialization		
A	8 000	1 000
B	–	4 000
Total	8 000	5 000

comparative statics. A method of analysis in which we start from an EQUILIBRIUM situation and assume that a disturbance occurs which leads to a new equilibrium, which is then compared with the initial situation. For example we can analyse the effect of a change in demand in a MARKET by comparing the EQUILIBRIUM price and quantity (output) before and after the change. Comparative statics has the advantage of simplicity, but at the cost of ignoring many important questions. For example, given the assumption that in PERFECT COMPETITION the short run SUPPLY CURVE slopes up, it is easy to show by comparative statics that an increase in demand will cause an increase in price. But we are left with the question as to how the price increase occurs, given that no firm is able to influence the market price. Generalizing we can say that comparative statics has little to say about the path or speed of movement from equilibrium to equilibrium.

compensating wage differentials. Higher wages paid to compensate employees for bearing greater risk, e.g. of injury, redundancy.

compensation principle. Many changes cause some people to gain but others to lose, e.g. if a cheaper version of an existing product was introduced we might expect consumers and the producers of the new version to gain, but producers of the old version to lose. The compensation principle states that total welfare has increased if the gainers could fully compensate the losers and still be better off. Although the principle may provide some guidance to decision-makers at the national level, it has a serious weakness. Since in practice compensation is seldom made voluntarily, it becomes necessary to evaluate the welfare effects of a change by estimating the monetary gains and losses, a rather daunting requirement. Moreover, subtracting losses from gains would give a valid measure only if the MARGINAL UTILITY of money is the same for gainers as for losers, a proposition for which there is no evidence.

competing group. *See* MONOPOLISTIC COMPETITION.

competition. This term can be given meanings which are quite different and even contradictory. Some economists confine the term competition, and allied terms such as competitive supply and competitive outcome, to PERFECTLY COMPETITIVE markets. It is argued that the performance of this form of market, in terms of cost, prices and profits, tends to be superior to the performance of other market forms. Other economists, however, point out that in perfect competition the only form of competition that exists is price competition and, moreover, that the form of analysis used, COMPARATIVE STATICS, does not explain how price competition actually operates. Many other forms of competition, found in other markets, such as the introduction of new products and processes, make a substantial contribution to economic welfare and should be taken into account in evaluating market performance.

Competition Act. *See* COMPETITION POLICY.

Competition and Credit Control. A system of monetary control which operated from 1971 to 1981. The system made a number of changes, including the abandoning of the clearing banks' interest rate cartel, the specification of a 12½ per cent RESERVE ASSET RATIO for all banks, and the introduction of a SPECIAL DEPOSITS scheme. Quantitative lending ceilings were abolished, although the monetary authorities reserved the right to offer qualitative guidance. The main objectives of the system were to increase competition among the clearing banks, to extend the authorities' influence with other financial institutions, to make those institutions compete with the banks for reserve assets, and to improve the authorities' control over the money supply. However the system could at best be considered only a partial success and was soon modified, in particular by the introduction in 1973 of the supplementary special deposits scheme which attempted to control the growth of bank deposits. CCC was effectively abandoned in 1981.

competition policy. Policy to increase the level of competition in the economy, usually by preventing firms from operating in an anti-competitive manner. The Monopolies and Mergers Act 1965 was the first serious attempt to control MERGERS in the UK. Any proposed merger that would result in at least one third of the market being in the hands of a single supplier could be referred to the MONOPOLIES COMMISSION. If the Commission found the merger to be against the public interest, the relevant government minister, the Secretary of State, was empowered to stop the merger, lay down conditions on which a merger could proceed, or break up a merger that had already taken place. Under the Fair Trading Act 1973, the market-share criterion for reference to the renamed Monopolies and Mergers Commission was reduced from one third to one quarter. Of the mergers referred to the MMC only about a third have eventually gone ahead. However only about 3 per cent of mergers that could be referred are referred. Consequently the criteria for reference are very important. The Office of Fair Trading, which is responsible for administering policy, has specified the indicators of MARKET CONDUCT and MARKET PERFORMANCE that are most likely to lead to a reference. The Fair Trading Act gave both the DIRECTOR-GENERAL OF FAIR TRADING and the Secretary of State the power to refer MONOPOLIES (including COMPLEX and LOCAL MONOPOLIES) to the MMC. (Merger references can be made only by the Secretary of State, although he normally acts on the advice of the Director-General.) If the Commission finds that the monopoly has acted against the public interest, it can recommend that the government order the monopoly firm to change its behaviour. The criteria to be taken into account by the Commission in reaching a decision are very wide (some would say too wide to act as a clear guide). They include maintaining and promoting effective competition in the supply of goods and services, promoting the interests of consumers, purchasers and users of goods and services, maintaining and promoting a balanced distribution of industry and employment. Under the Competition Act 1980, the Secretary of State may refer to the MMC the nationalized industries and other enterprises operating in markets where competition is limited by statute. The Commission may be asked to examine the enterprise's efficiency and costs, standards of service, and possible abuses of monopoly power. The Act also made it possible for certain specific anti-competitive practices to be referred to the Commission without a full-blown monopoly investigation. These practices include FULL-LINE FORCING, EXCLUSIVE DEALING agreements and PREDATORY PRICING. UK firms are also subject to EUROPEAN COMMUNITY competition policy. (There has been considerable discussion about the Community's sphere of influence, e.g. which proposed mergers should be investigated by the national authorities and which by the European Commission.) Article 86 of the Treaty of Rome states that any abuse of a dominant position within the Common Market or in a substantial part of it shall be prohibited. This is a wider ranging provision than the corresponding UK one. For example it has been used to force British firms to abandon the practice of DUAL PRICING. Legislation has not prevented a continuing increase in the level of CONCENTRATION in British industry, and it has been estimated that mergers have accounted for about half of this increase. This has led to suggestions for a more restrictive policy. At present a merger is allowed to proceed unless the MMC finds that it is expected to operate against the public interest. The chances of a merger being allowed to succeed would be reduced if the possibility of its operating against the public interest was sufficient grounds for its being blocked. Another approach would be the incorporation into policy of NON-DISCRETIONARY RULES.

Another important area of competition policy relates to collective restrictive practices. The Restrictive Trade Practices Act 1956 required all RESTRICTIVE AGREEMENTS to be registered. Since 1973 the Office of Fair Trading has been responsible for the implementation of this legislation and the Director-General is able to refer any registered agreement to the RESTRICTIVE PRACTICES COURT. The agreement can continue to be operated only if the Court can be convinced that its benefits outweigh the detriments that the 1956 Act assumes all such agreements to have. An agreement can be defended only on certain specified grounds (gateways), the most important of which have been: that the restriction is reasonably necessary to protect the public against injury; that the removal of the restriction would deny to the public, as purchasers, consumers or users of any goods, specific and substantial benefits; that the removal of the restriction would be likely to have an adverse effect on employment or on exports. Relatively few registered agreements have come before the Court. But since in the majority of the early cases the verdict went against the parties to the agreement, most registered agreements have been abandoned. (However it is clear that some agreements which were stated to have been abandoned have actually continued.) Article 85 of the Treaty of Rome, which deals with agreements and practices which hinder competition, is similar to UK legislation, but tougher in a number of respects. It covers a wider range of agreements, imposes heavier penalties (fines of up to 10 per cent of the company's turnover), and has more limited grounds for exemption.

Agreements whereby a single producer seeks to enforce the prices at which its products are sold by distributors are subject to the provisions of the Resale Prices Acts. A producer may seek to justify an agreement on certain specific grounds, namely, that in the absence of the agreement, a reduction would occur in the quality and variety of goods, in the number of retailers stocking the goods, or in the services provided in connection with the sale of goods; goods would be sold under conditions likely to cause danger to the public because of mis-use of the goods; the price of the goods would increase. Further, producers have to convince the Restrictive Practices Court that any advantage that they demonstrate outweighs the disadvantage of restricting the freedom of distributors. Only the producers of books, maps, and certain medicaments have satisfied the Court in this respect. The Resale Prices Act 1976, which replaced the 1964 Act of the same name, forbids manufacturers from trying to evade the intention of the legislation by REFUSAL TO SUPPLY.

competitive fringe. In some models of OLIGOPOLY, the market is assumed to comprise a large DOMINANT FIRM and a number of much smaller producers – the competitive fringe.

complementary demand. Denotes that two goods are bought together. Examples of complementary goods, or complements, are cricket bats and balls, gas fires and gas. When the price of one good goes up the quantity demanded of that good, and therefore of the complement, will fall, i.e. complements have a negative CROSS PRICE ELASTICITY OF DEMAND. However since, as illustrated by the above examples, complements need not be bought in fixed proportions, it may not be easy to identify the value of the cross elasticity.

complex monopoly. *See* MONOPOLY.

compliance costs. The costs incurred in complying with government legislation and regulations. They include the expenditure of time and money in completing forms and keeping records, licence fees, and capital expenditure required to meet regulations regarding safety, health and the environment.

composite demand. A product demanded for more than one purpose, e.g. wool is used in the manufacture of shirts and blankets. If the demand increases for, say, shirts and this causes a rise in the price of wool, less wool is likely to be used in the manufacture of blankets.

compound interest. The total interest due is calculated by applying the rate of interest to the sum of the capital invested plus the interest previously earned and re-invested. For example if £100 is invested at 10 per cent per annum the interest due in the first year is £10, and in the second year £11 (i.e. 10 per cent of £110).

comprehensive income tax. An ideal against which the structure of an income tax can be judged. The comprehensive income tax is based on an accretion concept of income, and measures income by reference to the increase in value of an individual's assets. Under a comprehensive income tax all capital gains would be taxed, as would accumulations of income on behalf of households and individuals, such as life assurance funds.

computable general equilibrium models. Models of the economy that can be manipulated with the aid of computers. Because CGEMs are very complex they are associated with a narrow class of models; generally these assume perfectly competitive markets, constant elasticity of substitution demand functions and constant elasticity of supply production functions.

concealed unemployment. Another term for DISGUISED UNEMPLOYMENT.

concentration. The distribution of a market among the firms supplying that market. The two theoretical extremes of concentration are represented by the models of MONOPOLY (highly concentrated, single seller) and PERFECT COMPETITION (unconcentrated, many sellers). In practice most markets fall between these two extremes. Both the traditional THEORY OF THE FIRM and the STRUCTURE-CONDUCT-PERFORMANCE PARADIGM recognize that the level of concentration can affect prices, outputs, profits, the rate of innovation, etc. Consequently there has been considerable interest in measures of concentration such as the CONCENTRATION RATIO and the HERFINDAHL INDEX. Empirical studies show that concentration has increased in both the USA and the UK. In the USA, MERGERS, internal growth and exit from the industry appear to be of roughly equal importance in increased concentration, while in the UK mergers appear to be the most important explanation. Less attention has been paid to buyer concentration, but it is believed that a high degree of buyer concentration is likely to lead to lower profits for producers. In addition to the market or industry, concentration is sometimes measured with respect to sectors of the economy, e.g. manufacturing, and the economy as a whole (aggregate concentration).

concentration ratio. A measure of the distribution of a market among the firms supplying that market. Concentration ratios usually measure the combined market share of the few largest firms, say three, four, five or eight. These ratios usually relate to output or sales but they have also been calculated for other variables, e.g. capital employed. A more comprehensive measure of concentration than the concentration ratio is the HERFINDAHL INDEX.

concert party. A group of individuals who act together in order to facilitate a takeover bid. For example they may each buy shares on the understanding that all these shares will be pledged to the individual mounting a bid. Concert parties usually operate in secret and may infringe the CITY CODE on takeovers.

condition of entry. The ease or difficulty with which new firms can enter a market. At the two extremes are free entry into perfectly competitive and contestable markets, and blocked entry into monopolies.

conditionality. A term associated especially with the operations of the International Monetary Fund. It refers to the provision of assistance by the Fund on condition that the country concerned adopts certain policies intended to strengthen its economy.

conditions of demand. All the factors that influence the demand for a product, but excluding the price of the product. For most products the most important conditions of demand include some combination of: the level of income, the distribution of income and wealth, the price and availability of substitutes and complements, the promotional activities of suppliers, tastes, the cost and ease of borrowing.

conditions of supply. All the factors that influence the supply of a product, but excluding the price of the product. These include the cost of producing and distributing the product, the desired profit margin, and indirect taxes.

conduct regulation. *See* REGULATION.

Confederation of British Industry. An organization that represents the interests of British firms, e.g. in discussions with the government.

confidence interval. The range of values or interval within which we can say, with a given degree of probability, that the MEAN of a POPULATION will lie.

conglomerate. A firm which has several distinct, unrelated businesses. The businesses often have a high degree of autonomy, and they may even be organized as a number of subsidiaries of a HOLDING COMPANY. Conglomerates can take advantage of RISK-BEARING ECONOMIES OF SCALE.

conglomerate merger. A merger between two companies with dissimilar activities, e.g. cigarette manufacturing and life insurance.

conservation of resources. Policies or procedures to reduce the quantity of resources used for a given level of output. Resource conservation will be affected by the nature of the PROPERTY RIGHTS in those resources, and by the existence or absence of markets in FUTURE GOODS. RECYCLING is making an increasing contribution to resource conservation.

consolidated accounts. The aggregate accounts (e.g. balance sheet, trading and profit and loss account) of a group of companies.

Consolidated Fund. A government account held at the Bank of England, used for the receipt of tax payments and for public expenditure.

consolidated stock. An unredeemable government stock, popularly known by its abbreviation, Consols. Most Consols bear 2½ per cent interest, although there was also a 4 per cent issue.

Consols. *See* CONSOLIDATED STOCK.

consortium. A temporary grouping of independent firms which pool (some of) their resources for a particular purpose, e.g. to undertake a major civil engineering project such as the Channel Tunnel.

41

consortium banks. Independent banks jointly owned by other banks and/or financial intermediaries located in a variety of countries, with no single parent having a majority share in the consortium. There are around twenty such banks in London, the majority being set up because individual small banks could not afford a London operation, and the combined status of the parents could be expected to attract more business than if they acted independently.

conspicuous consumption. The purchase of products at least partly because they are acknowledged as status symbols, e.g. diamonds, Porsche cars. An implication of this motivation is that if the price of the product fell it might be seen to convey less status and so the quantity demanded would not necessarily increase and might even fall.

constant. A term which takes only a single number value (as opposed to a variable which can take different values).

constant cost industry. *See* CONSTANT RETURNS TO SCALE.

constant natural assets rule. A suggested guide for policy makers, namely that they might permit individual environments to be lost provided that the overall stock of environmental assets available to future generations is not reduced.

constant prices. The prices of products corrected to take account of a general change in prices. If between two years the CURRENT PRICE of cars increased from 100 to 106 and the RETAIL PRICE INDEX increased from 100 to 102, the constant price of cars would have increased by 3.9 per cent. Another way of expressing this is to say that constant prices give a measure of REAL VARIABLES.

constant returns to scale. It may be possible to increase the SCALE OF ORGANIZATION by increasing all INPUTS by the same proportion. If as a result OUTPUT increases by the same proportion, returns to scale are said to be constant. An implication of constant returns to scale is that the firm's long-run average cost curve is horizontal. If all the firms in an industry experience constant returns to scale, we can speak of a constant-cost industry.

consumer behaviour. Models of consumer behaviour often draw upon the insights of psychology and sociology as well as economics. Consumers' decisions are intended to satisfy their wants, but these decisions often have to be taken on the basis of imperfect information and in the light of UNCERTAINTY, factors not taken into account in the elementary theory of CONSUMER CHOICE.

consumer choice. Consumers choose that bundle of goods that maximizes their satisfaction from a given level of income. Models of consumer choice may incorporate INDIFFERENCE-CURVE ANALYSIS, may adopt the REVEALED PREFERENCE approach, or may be based on the theory of DIMINISHING MARGINAL UTILITY.

consumer credit. Short-term lending to consumers for the purchase of specific goods. Credit may be provided by retailers, by banks in the form of personal loans, by hire-purchase companies and by credit card agencies, e.g. Visa. Under the Consumer Credit Acts, traders offering credit have to be licensed by the Office of Fair Trading. Consumers are also protected by regulations governing the content and style of advertising material, the calculation and explanation of the rate of interest, and the provision of a 'cooling-off' period during which consumers have a right to withdraw from a contract.

consumer discrimination. This exists when consumers refuse to purchase goods or services from minority suppliers, e.g. suppliers from a minority ethnic group, unless they are cheaper than comparable goods and services from majority suppliers. Consumer discrimination seems to be strongest where professional services are offered, e.g. lawyers, doctors.

consumer good. Any good purchased by a consumer, whether a non-durable good, e.g. a breakfast cereal, or a durable good, e.g. a car. All consumer goods (and also SERVICES bought by consumers) are included within CONSUMERS' EXPENDITURE in the UK NATIONAL ACCOUNTS with the single exception of new dwellings, which are included within INVESTMENT.

consumer optimum. *See* OPTIMUM.

consumer protection. Measures taken by public sector and private sector bodies to protect the interests of consumers. These measures include the provision of information to consumers, e.g. through product labelling; controlling the information provided by suppliers, e.g. relating to the status of price reductions; establishing standards for, e.g. quality; providing consumers with the means of redress, e.g. for purchases of articles of sub-standard quality; providing for a cooling-off period during which consumers have the option of withdrawing from certain contracts, e.g. the purchase of life assurance.

consumer sovereignty. By deciding how to spend their incomes, consumers ultimately determine what goods and services are produced. The American economist, J.K. Galbraith, has questioned the existence of consumer sovereignty in an economy dominated by large firms insulated from competition.

consumer surplus. (consumers' surplus, consumer's surplus). A downward sloping MARKET DEMAND CURVE implies that different consumers would receive different levels of satisfaction from, and therefore would be willing to pay different prices for, the product. Assuming no PRICE DISCRIMINATION, all consumers pay the same price. For some consumers this price is less than they would have been willing to pay; the difference denotes the surplus satisfaction obtained by these consumers.

consumers' expenditure. As defined in the UK National Accounts, consumers' expenditure includes all items purchased by consumers with the exception of expenditure on the purchase of new dwellings. As people's incomes have increased they have spent a lower proportion on necessities (food accounted for 12.0 per cent of spending in 1991 as compared to 16 per cent in 1981) and a greater proportion on services (services, other than rates etc., accounted for 35 per cent of spending in 1991 as compared to 26 per cent in 1981).

Table 7   Consumers' expenditure 1991

	Percentages
Durable Goods:	
Cars, motor cycles, other vehicles	4.5
Furniture, floor coverings	1.7
Other durables	2.6
Other Goods:	
Food	12.0
Alcoholic drink	6.4
Tobacco	2.6
Clothing, footwear	5.7
Energy products	6.8
Other goods	11.0
Services:	
Rents, rates and water charges	11.6
Other services	35.1
Total	100

Source: *United Kingdom National Accounts*

consumers' surplus. *See* CONSUMER SURPLUS.

consumption. (1) A term used in economic models, being a short form of CONSUMERS' EXPENDITURE. (2) The satisfaction derived from a consumer's ownership of a good. Durable goods provide a series of services which are enjoyed over a period of time, e.g. a television set provides entertainment. Consumption in this sense tends to appear in more advanced economic models.

consumption bundles. Combinations or bundles of goods and services which a consumer might consider purchasing.

consumption externalities. *See* EXTERNALITY.

consumption function. In economic models the consumption function shows the level of planned consumption at each level of income. When statisticians estimate consumption functions they relate actual consumption (CONSUMERS' EXPENDITURE) to PERSONAL DISPOSABLE INCOME. The consumption function incorporated in simple economic models usually takes the form:

$$C = a + b(y)$$
where C is consumption
        a is a constant
        b, a constant, is the MARGINAL PROPENSITY TO CONSUME, i.e. the proportion of additional income (y) that is spent.

A function of this form implies that the AVERAGE PROPENSITY TO CONSUME declines as income rises, a proposition that receives some support from empirical studies. However these studies also show that the marginal propensity to consume is far from stable on a year-to-year basis. Three hypotheses which may help to explain the variability in MPC are the PERMANENT INCOME, LIFE-CYCLE and RELATIVE-INCOME HYPOTHESES.

consumption good. *See* CONSUMER GOOD.

consumption possibility line. Another term for BUDGET LINE.

contestability. *See* CONTESTABLE MARKET.

contestable market. A market in which there are no BARRIERS TO THE ENTRY of new firms or to the exit of existing firms. In contestable markets only NORMAL PROFITS are earned. SUPERNORMAL PROFITS would be competed away by the entry of new firms. If SUBNORMAL PROFITS were earned, some firms would leave the industry, allowing the remaining firms to earn normal profits. The level of profits is not associated with the number of firms in the market, as suggested by the traditional THEORY OF THE FIRM. An important influence on the ease of entry and exit is the degree to which COSTS are SUNK, i.e. are irretrievably committed to that market. An example would be a machine that can be used in the manufacture of only one type of product. The higher the proportion of sunk costs, the more risky entry becomes. Similarly, the higher the proportion of sunk costs, the more reluctant will existing firms be to leave the market. The theory of contestability has important implications for the conduct of COMPETITION POLICY and the REGULATION of industry.

contingent markets. Markets for dealing with risk, e.g. markets for INSURANCE and for FUTURE GOODS.

contract. Any agreement governing or influencing the relationship between two (or more) parties, e.g. workers and employers. A contract may be explicit, perhaps in writing, or IMPLICIT, depending on custom and usage. Economic theories have explored in some detail the implications of contracts that are incomplete, i.e. do not fully specify the relationships between the two parties.

contract curve. A line joining points at which the MARGINAL RATES OF SUBSTITUTION of two traders for the two products being traded are the same. Only if exchange takes place at one of these points will the total welfare of the two traders be maximized.

contracting out. (1) When a public body such as a central government department or local authority employs an outside agency to perform work previously done by itself, e.g. a hospital which begins to employ outside caterers. This is a form of PRIVATIZATION. (2) Denotes that members of a union declare that they are unwilling to pay a political contribution. (3) An arrangement by which members of an occupational pension scheme obtain rights under the scheme in place of under the state earnings-related pension schemes. Contributions to the national insurance fund are reduced for these employees.

contractionary policy. Government policy to reduce the level, or the rate of increase, of economic activity, a policy usually adopted in an attempt to reduce the rate of INFLATION.

contribution. Sales revenue minus VARIABLE COST. If total contributions equal total FIXED COSTS, the firm breaks even.

convergence hypothesis. The hypothesis that all economic systems are tending to move towards a similar form of MIXED ECONOMY.

conversion. A new issue of securities to replace an existing one. The two issues may be of the same type of security or they may differ. It is quite common for a firm to borrow money by the issue of DEBENTURES and to offer lenders the opportunity to convert the debentures into SHARES at a later date.

conversion rights. The option of converting debentures into shares at a later date.

convertibility. Convertibility between currencies exists when there are no exchange controls on CURRENT or CAPITAL ACCOUNT transactions. Some economists add a further condition, namely that the government, acting through the central bank, undertakes to buy or sell as much of the currency as people wish to trade at the fixed exchange rate.

co-operative. A grouping of like-minded people who establish a business enterprise. Producer co-operatives are owned, and often run, by the workers, although they may employ salaried managers. Profits not retained in the business are shared out among the workers. Consumer co-operatives, most common in retailing, are owned by the customers but usually run by salaried managers. The UK retail co-operative societies used to pay shareholders a dividend based on the value of their purchases.

core inflation. *See* INFLATION.

corporate control, market for. The market for corporate control consists of the SHARES in a company with voting rights (this will often be all the shares). An effective market for corporate control is an important means of ensuring management's efficiency. An inefficient management faces the risk of losing their jobs following a change of control of the company, especially if it is the result of a TAKEOVER. If any shareholders expect a takeover bid to succeed they may prefer to keep their shares so as to participate in the higher profits expected to follow the change of control. However if all shareholders behave in this way the bid will fail. This would constitute an imperfection in the market.

corporate planning. The formulation by businesses of long-term objectives. These might relate to profits, sales, market share, etc. These plans form the basis for decisions on INVESTMENT, including investment in HUMAN CAPITAL.

corporate sector. *See* SECTORS OF THE ECONOMY.

corporation. A term sometimes used to refer to a company, especially in the USA.

corporation tax. A tax levied on the assessable profits of companies, currently at a rate of 33 per cent, falling to 25 per cent below a certain profit threshold. Assessable profits are calculated after the payment of INTEREST and after CAPITAL ALLOWANCES, but before the distribution of DIVIDENDS. Companies 'impute' to shareholders a tax on their dividends and this is remitted to the Inland Revenue as advance corporation tax (ACT). Shareholders are considered to have pre-paid income tax at the standard rate on their dividends. Since companies deduct ACT in computing their liability to mainstream corporation tax, shareholders, who own the profits, are in the same position after tax regardless of the amount of profits distributed as dividends.

correlation. A measure of the extent to which two variables change together. If there is perfect correspondence between the variations in the variables the correlation coefficient (r) will have the value +1 if the values move in the same direction, or –1 if they move in opposite directions. If there is a complete absence of correspondence the value of the correlation coefficient is zero.

correlation coefficient. *See* CORRELATION and REGRESSION ANALYSIS.

correspondent bank. A bank which acts as a clearing agent for another which is not a member of the country's clearing system.

cost. The cost of any action is what is foregone, given up, as a result of taking that action. For a firm, the cost of using its resources to produce more of one good is the value of other goods that could have been produced by those resources. For a consumer the cost of purchasing one product is the satisfaction from another product that could have been purchased. For students the cost of a visit to the cinema might be the time that they would have spent studying in order to increase their chances of passing an examination. The term given to these foregone alternatives is OPPORTUNITY COST. Opportunity cost is an immensely powerful idea with many applications in economics, but in the THEORY OF THE FIRM the terms cost and COSTS usually mean the amount of expenditure incurred.

cost accounting. The branch of accounting concerned with identifying and measuring a firm's COSTS. These measurements are used in PRICE and INVESTMENT decisions. Estimates of future costs can also be used for control purposes, by providing a benchmark against which the actual costs of the firm can be compared. If actual costs exceed estimated costs, the firm will try to identify the reason for, and correct, the deviation.

cost benefit analysis. Analysis of an investment project which takes into account the SOCIAL (PRIVATE plus EXTERNAL) COSTS and BENEFITS. Firms are mainly interested only in private costs and benefits, and would not undertake a project for which costs exceeded benefits (revenue). But the social benefits of the project might exceed the social costs, implying that the project would increase total WELFARE. When London Transport built the Victoria Line, it was known that the revenue would not cover the costs. However it was decided to build the line, with government financial assistance, because of the additional benefits that would arise, including a saving of passengers' time and a reduction in congestion. The principle underlying most cost-benefit analysis is known as the Kaldor-Hicks test, the hypothetical compensation test, the potential PARETO improvement criterion, or the willingness-to-pay test. Estimates are made of the money value of the benefits or gains of a project and of the losses, defined as the minimum sum that people adversely affected by the project would require in order to agree to the project proceeding. If the gains outweigh the losses, the project passes the test. Those people who gain from the project could fully compensate those who lose, without becoming losers themselves. Putting the matter another way, it would be possible, by linking the project with an appropriate set of money transfers, to make some people better off, without making anyone worse off, a Pareto improvement.

cost centre. A section of a firm for which costs can be identified and used for cost control purposes.

cost curve. A line which shows the cost of production at different levels of output. The curve might relate to average cost and marginal cost (Fig. 4), or (especially in break-even analysis) total cost.

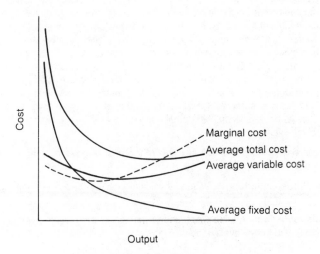

Figure 4   Cost curves

cost, insurance, freight. In international trade when goods are sold cif the price is: the price as the goods leave the factory or warehouse, plus the cost of delivery to the port (docks or airport) to which the goods are to be consigned, plus insurance to that point, plus any charges or dues imposed there (but excluding the cost of transport from the port to the buyer's premises). In the UK BALANCE OF PAYMENTS ACCOUNTS, IMPORTS are recorded cif, but EXPORTS fob (FREE ON BOARD), and an allowance must be made for this difference in estimating the balance on current account.

cost minimization. *See* MINIMIZATION.

cost of capital. *See* CAPITAL.

cost of finance. Firms' investment programmes are funded by three broad types of finance: money borrowed, e.g. by the issue of DEBENTURES, permanent (equity) capital obtained by the issue of SHARES, and RETAINED EARNINGS. As a general rule, after taking tax into account, borrowed money is cheapest and equity capital the most expensive, with retained earnings in between. (Attaching a cost to retained earnings can be justified because of the OPPORTUNITY COST; if they were not used to finance the firm's investment programme, they could be used to earn income in other ways.) Firms' use of the cheapest type of finance, borrowing, is limited by the risks attached to high GEARING. The firm's overall cost of finance can be estimated by taking a weighted average of the

47

costs of the three sources. If the firm used 25 per cent borrowed money at a cost of 8 per cent, 25 per cent equity capital at 12 per cent and 50 per cent retained earnings at 10 per cent the overall cost of finance would be 10 per cent.

cost-of-living index. A popular term for the RETAIL PRICE INDEX.

cost-plus pricing. A procedure whereby the firm sets its price by estimating its AVERAGE COST at its expected level of output and adding a profit margin. An alternative procedure is to estimate the PRIME COSTS and add a margin to cover SUPPLEMENTARY COSTS and profit. Cost-plus pricing has been criticised on two grounds. It is said to involve circular reasoning because price itself will affect the output on which cost estimates are based. While this is true, past experience is often a good guide to future output provided that prices and other market conditions do not change drastically. Moreover average costs (and prime costs) are often constant over quite a wide range of output, meaning that even if output is not as expected, average cost may be. Thus the profit margin will be as expected, (although total profit would be either higher or lower than expected). The second criticism is that cost-plus pricing takes no account of demand conditions, but this ignores the fact that the margin added to cost may well vary as demand changes.

Cost-plus pricing is often used for government contracts. If the contract involves a great deal of uncertainty, e.g. about the costs of a new manufacturing process, the contractor is protected. On the other hand there is no incentive for the contractor to reduce its costs. Indeed, if the profit margin is a percentage of costs, there is an incentive to inefficiency.

cost price. A price which just covers the cost of production and distribution, with no margin for profit added.

cost-push inflation. Inflation that is initially caused by a rise in the costs of inputs, e.g. wages, imported raw materials.

cost schedule. A table which shows the cost of production (average, marginal or total cost) at different levels of output.

Table 8 Cost schedule

Output (units)	Fixed cost	Average fixed cost	Variable cost	Average variable cost	Total cost	Average total cost	Marginal cost
	(£)	(£)	(£)	(£)	(£)	(£)	(£)
1	10	10	4	4	14	14	4
2	10	5	6	3	16	8	2
3	10	3.3	8	2.7	18	6	2
4	10	2.5	18	4.5	28	7	10
5	10	2	35	7	45	9	17

costs. Expenditure incurred; applied especially to the production and distribution of goods and services. The costs of a firm can be classified in many ways, partly because of the different conventions adopted by accountants, economists and corporate planners, and partly because different types of decision may require different ways of looking at costs. Costs are most commonly broken down into fixed and variable costs (an intermediate category, semi-variable, is sometimes added). Variable costs change as output changes with a given SCALE OF ORGANIZATION or in the SHORT RUN. Fixed costs change only when a change in output requires a change in organization, or in the LONG RUN. (Viewing the situation from a different angle, the long run is defined as that period within which all costs are variable.) The costs of raw materials and some forms of labour are usually classified as variable, the costs of plant and equipment as fixed. (The purchase price of plant and equipment is assumed to be spread over its life.) Semi-variable costs might include such items as fuel, power and transport. The change in cost that results from a change (increase or decrease) in output of one unit is known as marginal cost. The increase in cost that results from an increase in output of one or more units is known as incremental cost. Accountants distinguish between prime and overhead, indirect or supplementary costs. Prime costs are those costs, mainly direct labour and materials, that can be allocated to a particular type of product. Costs which cannot be so allocated (sometimes called joint costs) e.g. equipment and workers used to produce several types of product, are included in overhead costs. Prime costs are clearly much more likely than overhead costs to vary as the output of one type of product changes. When a decision has to be made as to whether to reduce output, it is important to know which costs are escapable or avoidable, and which are sunk or unavoidable. When a machine is purchased, its price represents a sunk cost. If, because of a reduction in output, the machine is taken out of operation, its operating costs would be avoided, but the capital cost of the machine (spread over its expected life) would continue. The level of costs at different levels of output can be shown by means of a COST CURVE or a COST SCHEDULE.

Council for Mutual Economic Assistance (Comecon). A council designed to extend planning from the national to the international sphere, especially within Eastern Europe. It collapsed along with the collapse of national planning in its member countries. It was subsequently claimed that the USSR had obtained through Comecon very favourable terms of trading with other members.

council tax. A source of local authority finance introduced in 1993 as a replacement for the community charge. The tax is based on the estimated sale price of the house on 1 April 1991, houses being grouped into eight valuation bands for ease of administration. The tax payable on a house in the lowest band, A, is two thirds of that payable in the fourth band, D, and one third of that in the highest band, H. Discounts are available in certain circumstances, e.g. a 25 per cent discount on a house occupied by only one adult. Council tax benefit up to 100 per cent is available for people on Income Support and other people on low incomes.

counter-cyclical policy. The use of FISCAL and MONETARY POLICY to counteract SLUMPS and BOOMS.

counterpurchase. *See* COUNTERTRADE.

countertrade. The term covers several mechanisms including: BARTER; counterpurchase, which requires an exporter to accept part payment for exports in goods; BUY-BACK agreements; offset, a mechanism frequently used in large transactions, especially relating to defence or aerospace equipment, which requires the exporter to make investments in the client country in terms of plant or components, to offset the cost of the goods sold. In a report issued in 1985 the OECD estimated that countertrade accounted for 5 per cent of total world trade, while other estimates have suggested a higher figure. Partly because of its bilateral nature, the growth of countertrade has caused considerable concern in GATT and other international agencies.

countervailing duty. An additional import duty imposed to counteract a fall in price following the granting of a subsidy by an exporting country.

countervailing power. If one group of economic agents achieves market power, other agents will re-organize to counteract this power. The growth of unions can be seen as a reaction to the power exerted by large employers. Large retailers or associations of retailers such as VOLUNTARY GROUPS are able to limit the power of large manufacturers.

49

cover. The ratio of total profit to profit distributed as dividends.

craft union. A trade union whose members engage in a particular craft or skill.

crawling peg. *See* EXCHANGE RATE.

cream-skimming. In multi-product industries entrants target the profitable lines of business, leaving the incumbents with the loss-making rump.

credentialism. Discrimination in the labour market based on education, i.e. where education, although not necessary for the job, is required by the employer.

credible threat. In GAME THEORY a credible threat is one which, after the event, the player would then feel it optimal to carry out.

credit. (1) Granting the use of goods and services without immediate payment. The main types of credit are CONSUMER CREDIT, TRADE CREDIT and BANK ADVANCES (bank credit). (2) One part of the DOUBLE ENTRY system of accounts. The procedure is to 'credit the giver', e.g. the seller of materials bought by a firm.

credit account. An account allowing purchases to be made on credit, which is usually to be settled monthly. (CREDIT CARDS can be seen as a form of credit account.) With an instalment credit account the customer makes regular payments and is granted credit up to a multiple of these monthly payments.

credit cards. A form of credit that has become increasingly important in recent years, although the imposition of a charge to all card-holders by the banks, the main issuers, led to a fall in the number of holders. The card enables holders to obtain several weeks' free credit on purchases, interest only being charged on accounts not settled on the due date. The issuers also charge the retailers of the goods and services a small percentage of the price.

credit control. Part of the government's MONETARY POLICY.

credit creation. When banks extend loans, credit is created. The amount of credit that can be created is determined by the amount of money initially deposited with the banks (the MONETARY BASE), and the value of the CASH RATIO desired by, or imposed upon, the banks. If they are to maintain a 5 per cent cash ratio, and £1 million were deposited with them they would be able to lend £20 millions. This assumes that all the money loaned comes back to the banks as deposits. When the process is complete, to match their assets (loans) of £20 millions the banks have liabilities of £20 millions, comprising £1 million initial deposits and £19 millions created deposits. Looking at the loans we can say that the credit multiplier has a value of twenty. Alternatively, since bank deposits are seen by depositors as money, we can say that the money multiplier has a value of twenty. This process also operates in reverse. A reduction in the monetary base or an increase in the desired cash ratio results in a multiple contraction of deposits.

credit guarantee. An insurance against default given to a lending institution. It is not unusual for individuals to act as guarantor for their relatives or friends. Government guarantees are provided under the loan guarantee scheme and by the EXPORT CREDITS GUARANTEE DEPARTMENT.

credit multiplier. *See* CREDIT CREATION.

credit squeeze. Government restrictions designed to make credit more difficult to obtain and more expensive.

creditor. Anyone to whom money is owed.

creeping inflation. A persistent but low rate of increase in the average price of goods and services.

critical-path analysis. A planning technique which identifies the sequence of steps which minimizes the time required to undertake a project. The critical path influences decisions regarding the time at which materials are purchased, the recruitment of labour, etc.

cross-price elasticity of demand. The percentage (or proportionate) change in the quantity of one product demanded, divided by the percentage (proportionate) change in the price of another product. A high positive value usually indicates that the products are good substitutes for each other.

cross-rates. Bilateral exchange rates between one country and another.

cross-section analysis. Statistical analysis of members of the POPULATION at a given point in time. For example estimates of the CONSUMPTION FUNCTION have been made by investigating the expenditure, in a given period, of people with differing incomes.

cross-subsidy. When a business enterprise subsidizes loss-making activities out of the profits made from other activities. The Post Office charges a uniform rate for letters delivered anywhere within the UK, knowing that the service to outlying rural areas will make a loss, to be met out of the profits from the service to more densely populated areas. (Nationalized industries sometimes receive government grants to compensate them for providing loss-making 'social' services.)

crowding. The crowding hypothesis states that because women and ethnic minorities are excluded from, or have restricted entry to, higher-paying occupations, they are crowded into other occupations. In these other occupations the enforced abundance of supply lowers marginal productivity and hence wages.

crowding-out. The proposition that additional government expenditure (or activity) will leave total expenditure (activity) unchanged because it will cause a compensating fall in private sector expenditure (activity). Several mechanisms might be involved in crowding-out. If the government expenditure is financed by the issue of bonds, the INTEREST RATE will rise which will cause a reduction in private-sector spending, especially on INVESTMENT. The fall in the price of bonds will reduce the WEALTH of existing bond holders, which may lead to a fall in their expenditure. In addition to these financial crowding-out mechanisms, there may be real-resource effects. J.M. Keynes thought that increased government spending might reduce businessmen's confidence and lead to a cut-back in investment (what might be called the EXPECTATIONS effect). Finally it has been argued, especially by R.W. Bacon and W.A. Eltis, that much government expenditure is directed to the NON-MARKET sector, and that an expansion of this sector may divert capital and labour from the firms which produce 'marketable' output. They suggested that the long-term effect had been to reduce the rate of growth of the economy and to weaken the balance of payments, since the market sector provides the nation's productive investment and exports. It has been impossible to produce firm evidence about the degree of crowding-out that has occurred. This is hardly surprising given the number of mechanisms, some of which are short-term and others very long-term in nature.

cum dividend. The purchaser of a security cum (with) dividend is entitled to the next dividend that becomes payable.

cumulative preference shares. *See* SHARES.

currency. Notes and coin that are used as a medium of exchange. International currency is any currency used in settling international debts, e.g. the dollar, sterling, gold.

currency appreciation. A rise in the value of one currency in terms of another. If £1 could be exchanged for $1.50 at one time and for $2.00 subsequently, we would say that sterling had appreciated. If the rise in value was the result of a government decision, rather than the interplay of market forces, we speak of a REVALUATION or UP-VALUATION of the currency.

currency crisis. A situation in which a country's FOREIGN EXCHANGE RESERVES are insufficient to support the current exchange value of its currency. This would lead under a floating exchange rate to the depreciation of the currency or, under a FIXED EXCHANGE RATE system, to DEVALUATION.

currency depreciation. A fall in the value of one currency in terms of another. If £1 could be exchanged for $2.00 at one time and for $1.50 subsequently, we would say that sterling had depreciated. If the fall in value was the result of a government decision, rather than the interplay of market forces, we speak of a DEVALUATION of the currency.

current account. *See* BANK DEPOSITS.

current account balance. *See* BALANCE OF PAYMENTS.

current assets. Short-term or liquid assets, e.g. stocks of goods for sale, the trade debts of customers, bank deposits and cash.

current-cost accounting. One of several systems of accounting that attempt, by allowing for INFLATION, to present a truer picture of the firm's real financial position. The Sandilands Committee, set up by the accounting profession, recommended the use of this system, and it has been adopted on a voluntary basis, although few firms use it for their published accounts. A feature of the system is that operating profit 'is struck after charging the "value to the business" of assets consumed during the period, thus excluding holding gains from profit and showing them separately'.

current costs. Prices that would be paid for assets today. When assets have a long life and are entered in a firm's accounts at the prices at which they were bought (HISTORIC COSTS), a misleading picture of the firm's financial position can be given during periods of inflation. If the prices of the firm's output have increased in line with inflation, but historic costs have been applied to assets, money or nominal profits will overstate real profits.

current liabilities. Short-term liabilities, e.g. amounts owing to suppliers, wages and salaries unpaid at the date of the balance sheet, bank overdrafts.

current prices. *See* NOMINAL PRICES.

current purchasing-power accounting. A system of accounting that attempts to allow for the effects of INFLATION by expressing accounts in terms of 'purchasing units', modifying changes in money values by means of a RETAIL PRICE INDEX.

current ratio. The ratio of CURRENT ASSETS to CURRENT LIABILITIES. The current or acid-test ratio is the most commonly used balance sheet ratio, being a measure of LIQUIDITY and of the margin of safety that management maintains to allow for the unevenness in the flow of funds through the current asset and liability accounts.

current-weighted index. *See* INDEX NUMBER.

customs duties. Taxes on imports that are imposed for reasons other than raising revenue, and especially to protect domestic producers.

customs union. The two essential features of a customs union are (a) that there are no barriers, such as TARIFFS and QUOTAS, to trade between member countries, (b) all members impose a COMMON EXTERNAL TARIFF on imports from non-member countries. In some customs unions, e.g. the European Community, the abolition of internal barriers extends beyond trade to encompass movements of capital and labour. It is impossible to say whether a customs union will lead to an increase or a decrease in total economic welfare. Within the union itself, the abolition of barriers will lead to an increase in specialization and trade in accordance with the principle of COMPARATIVE ADVANTAGE, i.e. TRADE will be CREATED. On the other hand the common external tariff will militate against the operation of this principle. TRADE will be DIVERTED from low-cost to higher-cost producers. The net welfare effect will depend upon the balance of these two opposing forces.

cyclical unemployment. *See* UNEMPLOYMENT.

D

dampened accelerator. *See* ACCELERATION PRINCIPLE.

dated securities. Securities with a stated date for redemption, i.e. for repayment.

dawn raid. The purchase of a large number of shares in a company in a short period of trading, often to lay a foundation for a takeover bid.

deadweight debt. A debt not covered by a real asset. Most of the NATIONAL DEBT is deadweight debt because it was incurred to finance war or other current PUBLIC EXPENDITURE.

deadweight welfare loss. The reduction in CONSUMER SURPLUS arising from the monopolization of a competitive industry, minus any resource savings accruing to the monopolist.

dear money. A high rate of interest which makes borrowing more expensive. The government is most likely to adopt a dear or tight money policy when it wishes to discourage expenditure in order to counteract INFLATION.

death rate. The number of deaths in a year for every 1000 of population.

debentures. Fixed interest securities issued by companies in return for long-term loans. Mortgage or fixed debentures are secured by a mortgage on specific assets of the company, whereas floating-charge debentures are not. The claims of debenture holders have priority over the claims of shareholders in two respects. First, debenture interest is paid before profits are declared and dividends distributed. If the company is unable to pay the interest, debenture holders can force the company into liquidation. Second, if for this or any other reason liquidation occurs, debenture holders' claims on the assets of the company are met in full before any payment is made to shareholders. In view of these privileges, the rate of interest on debentures is less than that on preference shares.

debit. One part of the DOUBLE ENTRY system of accounts. The procedure is to 'debit the receiver', e.g. the purchaser of the firm's output.

debt. Money or other assets owed by one party to another.

debt conversion. *See* CONVERSION.

debt deflation. A reduction in the level of economic activity resulting from a high level of debt. An extreme example is when the prices of houses fall to a level below that of the mortgage debt, preventing occupiers from purchasing new houses.

debt finance. Money borrowed to finance business activities.

debt management. The management of debt by making arrangements for the payment of interest and the refinancing of maturing bonds. In managing the NATIONAL DEBT the authorities can have several objectives (which may not always be compatible): to minimize the cost of government borrowing, to avoid disrupting the financial markets, and to influence the level of interest rates.

debt ratio. A country's external debt relative to the value of its EXPORTS.

debt rescheduling. If a debtor is unable to meet its liabilities to pay interest or, more especially, to repay maturing loans, it may be allowed to reschedule its debts. Creditors may make new loans in order to enable the old to be repaid or, more commonly, the repayment date may be delayed. Several least and less developed countries have been allowed to reschedule debt in recent years.

debt restructuring. Reducing the overall size of a country's international debt by mechanisms such as those suggested in the BRADY PLAN. Debtors would use funds provided by the World Bank or the International Monetary Fund to buy back their debt at a discount, or as collateral for the issue of new obligations to be traded against existing discounted debt.

debt-service ratio. The ratio of the payments due in a given year on a country's debts (interest payments plus repayment of maturing debt) to the total volume of those debts.

debt servicing. The cost of servicing debt comprises interest payments plus scheduled repayments of the principal plus administrative costs.

debtor. One who owes money or other assets to another.

decentralized wage bargaining. *See* BARGAINING.

decision tree. A procedure for setting out alternative courses of action, together with the probabilities of alternative outcomes and expected pay-offs along each branch of the tree.

declining block pricing. Charging customers lower prices for each successive 'block' of the product or service bought. Used by some nationalized industries in price negotiations with large customers.

de-coupling. Modification of the impact on the environment of economic and population growth. This can be best achieved by improved CONSERVATION OF RESOURCES and by technological change which reduces resource use and the production of waste at given levels of output.

decreasing cost industry. *See* INCREASING RETURNS TO SCALE.

decreasing returns to scale. Decreasing returns to scale exist if, when the SCALE OF ORGANIZATION is increased by increasing all INPUTS by the same proportion, OUTPUT increases by a smaller proportion. An implication of decreasing returns to scale is that the long run supply curve is upward sloping. If all firms in an industry experience decreasing returns, we speak of an increasing cost industry.

deductive method. A method of analysis in which assumptions are made about motivations, e.g. that consumers wish to maximize their satisfaction or utility and firms their profits. Given these assumptions it is possible to deduce how consumers and firms will behave. If the assumptions made about motivations are incorrect, the conclusions reached may also be incorrect.

deferred compensation model. A variant of models of effort-motivating wage contracts. The basic deferred compensation model was formulated by G.S. Becker and G.J. Stigler. They envisaged a payment system in which the individual is initially paid less than his marginal productivity and only subsequently, having proved to be hard working, is paid more. Such a system requires a long-term relationship between employer and workers, with stable workers self-selecting into the firm, a process which makes supervision easier. Given that firms may default at the point where higher wages become due, fair terminations would require severance payments.

deferred rebate. Price rebates based on the quantity bought in a given period, e.g. a year, rather than on the size of a single order. This process of aggregation means that the rebate is deferred, and in some instances there is a further delay, with the purchaser receiving the rebate only when another order is placed in the following year. Deferred rebates, especially of this latter form, have been criticized as a barrier to competition from other suppliers.

deficiency payments. If it is felt that market prices give producers an inadequate income, the government may set a guaranteed price. The subsidies given to cover the difference between the market and the guaranteed price are known as deficiency payments. Before joining the European Community the UK operated this system for a number of agricultural products.

deficit. An excess of EXPENDITURE over INCOME or of LIABILITIES over ASSETS.

deficit financing. Deficit financing or spending means an excess of planned EXPENDITURE over INCOME. Income is defined to exclude borrowing, and a government BUDGET DEFICIT means that expenditure exceeds tax revenue.

deflation. (1) A sustained fall in the price level, often accompanied by a fall in output and employment. (2) Government policies to reduce the level of aggregate demand and so counteract inflation. The government might use fiscal policy (increases in taxation and reductions in government expenditure) or monetary policy (high interest rates and a reduction in the supply of money). (3) An adjustment to an index number by the change in the retail price index to give an index in real terms.

deflationary gap. The difference between the actual expenditure required to maintain full employment and planned expenditure at the full employment level of income.

de-industrialization. A decline in the share of manufacturing in the national income. There is debate as to whether de-industrialization in the UK is simply part of the shift from manufacturing to services seen in most countries, or whether it is partly due to a loss of international competitiveness by UK manufacturers.

delivered prices. Prices which include the cost of transporting the goods to the customer.

demand. The desire for a product backed up by the ability to pay, i.e. effective demand. (*See also* AGGREGATE DEMAND.)

demand, joint. *See* JOINT DEMAND.

demand curve. A line showing the quantities of a product that would be bought at various prices. A market demand curve is obtained by adding horizontally the demand curves of all the individuals who would buy the product. It is conventional to plot price on the vertical, and quantity demanded on the horizontal axis. Since price and the quantity demanded are normally inversely related, the demand curve for most products slopes down from left to right.

demand-deficient unemployment. *See* UNEMPLOYMENT.

demand function. In principle the demand function could relate the quantity of a product demanded to any factor influencing its demand. In practice the term usually refers to demand as a function of price or, less often, income.

demand management. Government policies and especially FISCAL POLICY, aimed at influencing AGGREGATE DEMAND. NEW CLASSICAL ECONOMICS suggests that demand management policies are ineffective and even harmful, and in the 1980s more attention was paid to SUPPLY-SIDE POLICIES. However there has been a slight swing back of the pendulum in the 1990s.

demand price. The price an individual would be willing to pay for a specified quantity of a product.

demand-pull inflation. When AGGREGATE DEMAND exceeds AGGREGATE SUPPLY, producers take advantage of the situation to increase the price of their products.

demand schedule. A table showing the quantities of a product that would be demanded in a given period at various prices.

demand theory. Theories advanced to explain the relationship between price and quantity demanded. Explanations using either the proposition of DIMINISHING MARGINAL UTILITY, or INDIFFERENCE-CURVE ANALYSIS, or the REVEALED PREFERENCE approach, or OPPORTUNITY COST all reach the conclusion that as price falls the quantity demanded increases, i.e. the demand curve slopes down from left to right.

demerit good. A good whose consumption the government discourages, e.g. by high taxes, or forbids, because of the disbenefits of the goods, e.g. cigarettes, heroin. Some economists argue that if the disbenefit is purely private, state intervention is not justified. But in practice consumption often gives rise to EXTERNAL COSTS or disbenefits, e.g. crime or the use of scarce medical facilities.

department store. *See* RETAIL TRADE.

dependence effect. A term coined by J.K. Galbraith to denote the fact that in an affluent society wants are increasingly created as part of the process by which they are satisfied.

dependent population. The dependent population refers to those people of an age at which it is uncommon to have paid employment. This age may vary from one country to another; of men aged 55 and over, only a tenth work in Italy as compared to a third in Britain and 60 per cent in Japan. It may also change over time because of changes in legislation and custom.

dependent variable. A variable whose value changes in response to a change in the value of an independent variable or variables. For example the demand for a product may change as income changes.

depletable resources. Materials that can be used only once, e.g. oil that is used to fuel a machine.

depletion theory. The branch of economics concerned with the rate at which natural resources are consumed over time. If future consumption is valued more highly than current consumption, profits will be made by deferring consumption and depletion. Deferral of consumption is a form of INVESTMENT, and in theory the rate of consumption should be such that the profits to be made by not depleting resources are equal to those on other forms of investment. However, difficulties in measurement and uncertainty about future changes in costs and prices reduce the theory's value in decision-making.

deposit account. *See* BANK DEPOSITS.

Deposit Protection Fund. A fund, administered by the Bank of England, to protect depositors in the case of a bank's defaulting.

deposits. *See* BANK DEPOSITS.

depreciation. (1) The fall in the value of an asset through time. This loss of value is due mainly to the use of the asset, e.g. machines gradually wear out, but it can also occur because the asset deteriorates physically over time. Finally the value of an asset may fall because of obsolescence; as time goes on, more efficient or cheaper alternatives are produced, bringing down second-hand prices of existing assets. When a firm purchases a capital asset, it normally allocates the cost over the expected life of the asset, usually allowing a margin for error. If a machine was expected to last for twelve years and then to have no scrap value, the firm might charge one tenth of its cost against profits for the first ten years. This is known as the straight-line method of depreciation. Another common method is the reducing-balance method, in which the depreciation charge is a constant percentage of the cost of the asset. If the asset cost £1 million and the depreciation charge was 20 per cent, the charge would be £200 000 in year 1, £160 000 (20 per cent of £800 000) in year 2, and so forth. Depreciation is taken into account when a firm's liability to corporation tax is calculated. But firms have to follow the guidelines laid down by the Inland Revenue, and the depreciation charge for tax purposes may not be the same as that in the firm's internal accounts. Sometimes governments grant CAPITAL ALLOWANCES which allow a faster rate of depreciation (accelerated depreciation) than would be adopted for internal purposes. In the examples above the depreciation charge or expense related to the actual purchase price of the asset. This HISTORIC COST approach has the advantage of precision. However it can be argued that if the price of assets is rising, the firm's costs will be understated, and consequently it may charge too little for its output. To avoid this danger the firm might value its assets, and hence set its depreciation charge, on the basis of the expected REPLACEMENT COST. If too much uncertainty surrounds the replacement cost, another alternative is to revalue assets each year in line with the changes in their price. This CURRENT COST approach has much to commend it in principle, but it requires considerably more work to administer than the other methods. (2) Depreciation of a currency, *see* CURRENCY DEPRECIATION.

depression. A period of reduced economic activity and prolonged high unemployment.

deregulation. A removal or slackening of any restrictions imposed by the government in its REGULATION of economic activity. Examples of deregulation include granting licences to new operators of bus services, allowing building societies to put some of their assets to additional uses, and the various measures discussed under PRIVATIZATION and the stock exchange BIG BANG.

derivatives. A term covering FUTURES and OPTIONS.

derived demand. The demand for a FACTOR OF PRODUCTION that is derived from the demand for the output produced by that factor.

deseasonalization. *See* SEASONAL ADJUSTMENT.

destocking. A reduction in a firm's stocks or inventories of raw materials, components, etc. Destocking is sometimes involuntary, due to demand being higher than expected. In other instances firms reduce their stocks deliberately, because a shortfall in demand has caused stocks to rise above the target level, because of pessimism about the future state of the economy, or because cutting back expenditure on stocks improves the firm's LIQUIDITY. Regular destocking, and subsequent restocking, gives rise to an INVENTORY INVESTMENT CYCLE.

detrending. In a given period a variable may change in response to a number of factors. Some of these factors may affect the variable in a regular way over many periods, others may operate in that period only. Detrending removes the effects of the first set of factors, so that the effect of the second set can be isolated. For example if the sales of a firm's product grows by 2 per cent in a certain year but trend factors (changes in income, technology, etc.) would have resulted in an increase in sales of 5 per cent, the firm may need to consider whether it is becoming less competitive in the market and, if so, take corrective action.

devaluation. A reduction in the official rate at which a country's currency is exchanged for other currencies. Whereas currency depreciation is the result of market forces operating on a floating exchange rate, devaluation occurs via government edict in a FIXED EXCHANGE RATE SYSTEM. When a currency is devalued, (or depreciates), exporters can reduce their prices without losing revenue in terms of the domestic currency. For example if a UK car manufacturer sold in the USA at a price of $30 000 with an exchange rate of £1 = $2, it would receive £15 000 per car. If sterling was then devalued to £1 = $1.50, the manufacturer could afford to reduce its price to $22 500, since that would now yield £15 000. The manufacturer would, of course, expect to increase the number of cars sold at the lower price, and therefore to increase employment. If firms selling into the UK market are to receive the same amount per unit sold, in terms of their domestic currencies, they will have to raise their prices. As import prices rise, consumers will substitute domestic for imported goods, giving a further boost to employment. However, the implications for employment of higher import prices are not entirely favourable. Higher prices of imported capital goods will increase the costs of UK manufacturers. Higher prices of imported consumer goods may lead to claims for higher wages. If these two factors give rise to COST-PUSH INFLATION, the initial improvement in UK competitiveness could be lost. The effect of devaluation on the current account of the BALANCE OF PAYMENTS would depend upon the PRICE ELASTICITY OF DEMAND for imports and exports. If the sum of the elasticities is greater than unity (ignoring the negative signs) the balance will improve; if less than unity, the balance will worsen. There is some evidence that the effect of devaluation might be an initial worsening of the current account balance, followed by a subsequent improvement. This reaction is summarized in the J-CURVE.

developing countries. See LESS DEVELOPED COUNTRIES.

development, economic. See ECONOMIC DEVELOPMENT.

Development Areas. Areas of the UK that receive assistance as part of the government's REGIONAL POLICY.

differentiated products. Products perceived as different by consumers. This perception may be due to the physical characteristics of the products, e.g. size, colour, durability, or to the image conveyed by ADVERTISING and BRANDING. As far as the individual producer is concerned, DEMAND will be less PRICE ELASTIC for a differentiated than an undifferentiated product.

diffusion. The spread of an INNOVATION from the innovating firm to other firms. The rate of diffusion, which can have a marked impact on ECONOMIC EFFICIENCY, may be affected by many factors including the existence of PATENTS, the amount of capital required for the innovation, and the complexity of the technology embodied in the innovation.

diminishing marginal product. See DIMINISHING RETURNS, LAW OF.

diminishing marginal rate of substitution. See MARGINAL RATE OF SUBSTITUTION.

diminishing marginal utility. Each additional unit of a product consumed in a given period yields less utility or satisfaction to the consumer than the previous unit. This assumption or 'law' is used in demand theory and is derived from personal introspection;

C

it cannot be tested empirically by an observer since utility is subjective. Demand theory makes the further assumption that consumers buy products only if they expect them to yield more utility than alternative products requiring the same outlay, i.e. if expected utility exceeds OPPORTUNITY COST. If the price of a product falls, more of this product will be bought; although the utility of the additional unit is less than than that of the previous unit bought, at the lower price the opportunity cost of buying this product is also less than previously. Price and quantity demanded are inversely related; the DEMAND CURVE slopes down from left to right. Consumers are in EQUILIBRIUM when the ratio of marginal utility to price is equal for all products (this is known as the equimarginal principle). If the equilibrium is disturbed by a fall in the price of a product, it will be restored by a fall in its marginal utility; as we have seen, this requires an increase in consumption. An assumption that the marginal utility of aggregate consumption diminishes, implies that the marginal utility of money, required for consumption, also diminishes. This assumption is used to justify a PROGRESSIVE SYSTEM OF TAXATION.

diminishing returns, law of. The additional output obtained from additional units of a FACTOR OF PRODUCTION (the marginal product) diminishes if no change is made in other factors. One person operating a machine might produce 100 units an hour, two people 150 units, three people 170 units. (This example assumes that the additional workers are of some benefit. In other instances the technology may be such that there is no benefit from having more than one worker.) If the price of the variable factor is unchanged, it follows that the cost of that factor per unit of output will rise as output increases.

direct costs. *See* COSTS.

direct labour. Workers who are directly concerned with the manufacture of a good or the provision of a service, and whose wages tend to vary in line with output.

direct materials. Materials which are incorporated in a product and whose quantity used varies in line with output.

direct tax. *See* DIRECT TAXATION.

direct taxation. Taxation of the income or assets of individuals and organizations. Direct taxes include INCOME TAX, CORPORATION TAX, CAPITAL GAINS TAX and INHERITANCE TAX. NATIONAL INSURANCE contributions are also a form of direct taxation.

directional effects. The impact on the pattern of demand resulting from the imposition of indirect taxes at different rates on different products.

Director-General of Fair Trading. The person responsible for administering many aspects of the government's COMPETITION POLICY.

dirty floating. *See* MANAGED FLOATING.

discount. (1) A reduction in price given for specified reasons or in specified circumstances. Suppliers often give discounts to organizations which settle their accounts within a specified period, e.g. seven days. QUANTITY DISCOUNTS are offered by many firms. Retailers of products such as tools and paint often give discounts to approved tradesmen. Retailers' sales sometimes take the form of a percentage discount on their normal prices. (2) A security whose price is less than its face value is said to be selling at a discount.

discount factor. In undertaking INVESTMENT APPRAISAL it is often necessary to apply a discount factor or rate to future sums of money, in order to obtain their present value.

discount houses. Companies which buy, at a discount from face value, CERTIFICATES OF DEPOSIT, BILLS OF EXCHANGE and TREASURY BILLS. The discount house may re-sell the bills or hold them to maturity. The discount houses finance most of their purchases with money borrowed at very short notice from the commercial banks, using bills as security. Should the banks recall or refuse to renew their loans, leaving the discount houses short of funds, they may need to borrow from the BANK OF ENGLAND. The Bank, acting as LENDER OF LAST RESORT, will always meet their needs. However if the authorities wish to encourage a move to higher interest rates, they may impose a penal rate of interest on the money borrowed. The discount houses are the only institutions which are able to call upon the Bank of England as lender of last resort. In return it is understood that, if required, they will tender for all the Treasury bills on offer, ensuring that the government's short-term borrowing needs are always met. In this way the discount houses act as a buffer between the monetary authorities and the commercial banks.

Table 9   Assets of the discount houses, average, 1990

	Percentages
Treasury bills	2.7
Other bills	36.0
UK banks' certificates of deposit	38.8
Building societies' certificates of deposit, etc.	11.6
Other assets	10.9
Total	100

Source: *Annual Abstract of Statistics*

discount market. The market for BILLS OF EXCHANGE, TREASURY BILLS and short-dated BONDS. The market comprises BANKS, ACCEPTING HOUSES and DISCOUNT HOUSES. The discount market is sometimes known as the MONEY MARKET, although the terms are not actually synonymous.

discount rate. *See* DISCOUNT FACTOR.

discount store. A shop which sells at low prices, and normally stocks a narrow range of goods.

discounted cash flow. *See* INTERNAL RATE OF RETURN.

discounting. (1) Applying a DISCOUNT FACTOR to future sums of money. (2) When expected future events lead to buying or selling of a security, currency or commodity and hence to a change in its price before those events occur.

discouraged workers. Workers who, because of the unemployment situation, leave the labour force.

discretionary fiscal policy. Policy, legislated by Parliament, which involves a change in taxation or public expenditure designed to alter the level of AGGREGATE DEMAND or NATIONAL INCOME.

discretionary income. The amount of a household's income remaining after meeting basic needs and commitments, i.e. food, clothing, accommodation, tax and national insurance.

discriminating duty. A tax on imports of some products or from some countries at a different rate from the tax levied on other products or other countries.

discriminating monopoly. *See* PRICE DISCRIMINATION.

discrimination. Differences in wages and other conditions of employment that are not due to differences in productivity represent discrimination. Employers may discriminate with regard to workers' age, sex, race or colour. Governments may legislate to counteract discrimination, e.g. the SEX DISCRIMINATION ACT. But some economists have argued that in the absence of legislation, competition from employers who do not practise discrimination will eventually force other employers to bring wages into line with productivity. (Although discrimination is usually felt to reflect prejudice by employers, some studies have found employee discrimination to be stronger than employer discrimination.) Some writers adopt other definitions of discrimination which may not take into account differences in productivity or in the attitudes and tastes of workers, e.g. women may prefer jobs which offer shorter hours and better working conditions, even though this means a lower wage rate than in jobs occupied mainly by men. An example of these other definitions is PARTICIPATION DISCRIMINATION.

diseconomies of scale. If, following an increase in the SCALE OF ORGANIZATION, the minimum point on a firm's average cost curve is higher than it was previously, diseconomies of scale exist. The most likely reason for diseconomies in production is the existence of INDIVISIBILITIES. Different pieces of plant and equipment often have different capacities, and an increase in output may require the installation of some equipment which does not operate at the point at which average cost is minimized. Average cost may also rise because of an increase in marketing or transport costs per unit as firms seek to extend their market in order to sell the higher output. (This lack of perfect fit between departments is in principle the same as that between different machines.) But probably the most important source of diseconomies is the management and organization of the firm. Large firms, and especially those operating large plants, may become very impersonal and bureaucratic. This in itself can lead to higher costs. It can also cause a loss of job satisfaction, reflected in high turnover, absenteeism and strikes. The diseconomies listed above are internal. External diseconomies arise when the expansion of an industry causes the average cost of each firm to rise, e.g. because of congestion.

disguised unemployment. Disguised or hidden unemployment can take two forms. First, some people who would like to work do not register as unemployed because they do not believe that this will increase their chance of finding employment. This applies especially to people who do not qualify for unemployment benefit and who can exist without a job, e.g. students during the vacation, prematurely retired people. Second, in PLANNED ECONOMIES and some of the LEAST DEVELOPED COUNTRIES the PRODUCTIVITY of some workers is extremely low. The same output could be produced with far fewer workers, a situation known as disguised (hidden) unemployment or underemployment.

dishoarding. The running down of stocks of goods or money previously accumulated by hoarding.

disinflation. A reduction in the rate of inflation.

disintermediation. Flows of funds between lenders and borrowers without the use of financial intermediaries. Disintermediation usually occurs because the monetary authorities restrict the activity of intermediaries, e.g. by limiting their lending or the growth of their deposits. When this happens disintermediation can break the link between the MONEY SUPPLY and AGGREGATE DEMAND and can frustrate the aims of MONETARY POLICY.

disinvestment. Disinvestment occurs when CAPITAL CONSUMPTION exceeds GROSS INVESTMENT, (i.e. net investment is negative).

disposable income. *See* INCOME.

dissaving. In simple models of the economy, investment is undertaken by firms, and saving by households. Dissaving occurs when consumption exceeds disposable income. In more complex models, where saving by other agents, e.g. firms, is identified, dissaving is defined as an excess of expenditure over income.

distortions. A distortion exists whenever society's MARGINAL COST of producing a good does not equal society's MARGINAL BENEFIT from consuming that good. Distortions can be due to imperfections in MARKET STRUCTURE or to government intervention, e.g. the imposition of taxes.

distribution. The link between production and consumption, comprising wholesalers and retailers of various types.

distribution, theory of. See THEORY OF DISTRIBUTION.

distribution of income. How income is shared among different individuals or groups. National income (gross domestic product at factor cost) can be broken down on a functional basis into income from employment (accounting for two-thirds of the total), income from self-employment, gross trading profits of companies, gross trading surplus of public corporations and government enterprises, and rent.

Table 10 Functional distribution of income, 1991

	Percentages*
Income from employment	66.4
Income from self-employment	11.5
Gross trading profit of companies	11.7
Gross trading surplus of public corporations and general government enterprises	0.6
Rent	9.0
Imputed charge for consumption of non-trading capital	0.9
Total: Gross domestic product at factor cost	100

Source: *United Kingdom National Accounts*

(*Figures have been rounded to nearest decimal place.)

Official figures are also published showing the share of household income going to different income groups, and the impact of government measures to redistribute income. Even after redistribution, the highest 20 per cent of income earners accounted for 44 per cent of total income, as compared to 7 per cent for the lowest earners.

Table 11 Shares of household income, 1988

Quintile	Percentages	
	Before tax	After tax
Bottom fifth	2	7
Next fifth	7	11
Middle fifth	16	16
Next fifth	25	22
Top fifth	50	44
	100	100

Source: *Social Trends*

distribution of wealth. How wealth is shared among different individuals or groups. The distribution of wealth can be affected by government policy, especially in relation to wealth transferred at death, but in most years distribution is affected more by changes in the market value of securities, property, etc. Depending on how wealth is defined, the most wealthy 1 per cent of the population owned from 11 to 28 per cent of the total. The least wealthy 50 per cent owned from 6 to 17 per cent of the total.

Table 12   Distribution of wealth, 1989

Percentage owned by:	Marketable Wealth (A)	A minus dwellings	A plus occupational and state pension rights
Most wealthy 1%	18	28	11
5%	38	53	26
10%	53	66	38
25%	75	81	62
50%	94	94	83

Source: *Social Trends*

disutility. (1) Negative UTILITY. The law of DIMINISHING MARGINAL UTILITY implies that increased consumption would eventually give rise to disutility. (2) Production and consumption can cause disutility, or EXTERNAL COSTS, to third parties.

diversification. (1) The production of goods and services (by a firm or in a region) which are related only slightly or not at all to the goods and services already produced. Firms usually diversify either because of poor prospects for growth and profitability in existing markets or to reduce the risk that is inherent in supplying only a few markets. (2) In choosing a portfolio of shares and other securities, diversification is designed to reduce risk by purchasing assets which behave differently from each other, especially with regard to changes in price.

divestment. Selling part of a firm or group.

dividend. The payment made by companies to SHAREHOLDERS. It is normally paid in two parts, an interim dividend, mid-way through the company's financial year, and a final dividend, at the end of the year. A dividend is usually paid as so many pence per share, but in comparing the performance of companies, it is expressed as a percentage of the price of the share. If the nominal or FACE VALUE of a share was £1 and a dividend of 10p was declared, this would represent a dividend of 10 per cent. But this would be the yield only if the current price and the nominal value were the same. If the market price of the share was £2 the yield of a 10p dividend would be 5 per cent. Dividends are paid out of (after-tax) profits and so reflect the changing fortunes of a company. However dividends normally fluctuate less than profits, since most investors dislike fluctuations in their income. If profits are insufficient to meet the dividend that the company would like to pay, it may meet the shortfall out of its reserves (in such instances the dividend is said to be uncovered). Nevertheless ORDINARY SHARES remain a risky form of investment, and some investors prefer to buy the less risky PREFERENCE SHARES on which a fixed dividend is paid.

dividend cover. The after-tax profits of a company divided by the amount distributed as dividends.

dividend yield. *See* DIVIDEND.

division of labour. The breakdown of work processes into small units so that each worker can specialize in a limited range of tasks. Adam Smith noted that specialization speeds up the learning process and so increases workers' proficiency. In assembly line production specialization is combined with the principle of bringing the work to the workers, leading to big increases in PRODUCTIVITY. However in recent years more attention has been given to the disadvantages of specialization such as monotony, boredom and a lack of concern for quality. Ways have been sought of giving workers more control over their activities, including widening the range of tasks undertaken.

domestic absorption. CONSUMPTION plus INVESTMENT plus GOVERNMENT EXPENDITURE.

domestic credit expansion. The PUBLIC SECTOR BORROWING REQUIREMENT minus purchases of public sector debt by the UK non-bank private sector, plus sterling lending by banks and building societies to the private sector at home and overseas. This measure of monetary growth is no longer published, but it remains one of the indicators used by the INTERNATIONAL MONETARY FUND in assessing the progress of an economy. It shows how the increase in credit can exceed the increase in the money supply because of overseas funding through a BALANCE OF PAYMENTS deficit. It also shows how much the credit granted by the private banking system is being augmented by the public sector and is thus a composite indicator of the effect of monetary and fiscal policies.

domestic expenditure. Total domestic expenditure comprises consumers' expenditure, general government final consumption, gross fixed capital formation, and the value of the physical increase in stocks.

domestic mortgage indemnity. Agreements whereby insurance companies take over mortgagees' repayments to building societies, etc. when they are unable to meet their commitments due, e.g., to redundancy.

domestic resource cost. Average domestic resource cost is total VALUE ADDED at domestic prices divided by total value added at world prices. It is an indicator of the degree to which the EXCHANGE RATE is overvalued (if positive) or undervalued (if negative).

dominant firm. A firm which is large enough to influence price.

dominant strategy. In GAME THEORY there is said to be a dominant strategy when a player's best strategy is independent of the strategies chosen by other players.

double coincidence of wants. For trading by BARTER to take place, there has to be a double coincidence of wants, e.g. a tailor wishes to buy food and a farmer wishes to buy a suit of clothes.

double counting. The OUTPUT APPROACH calculates national income on the basis of the value of the outputs of producers. But since the output of some producers goes to other producers, simply aggregating their outputs would result in double counting, resulting in an over-estimation of national income. This danger is avoided by aggregating the VALUE ADDED by each producer. (This principle is equally valid for the INCOME APPROACH to the calculation of national income.)

double-entry bookkeeping. An accounting procedure whereby every transaction gives rise to a credit and a corresponding debit entry. This procedure determines the form of many financial statements, including BALANCE SHEETS and the BALANCE OF PAYMENTS ACCOUNTS.

double taxation. Taxation in two countries of a given income or asset. This arises when companies or individuals have interests in the two countries, e.g. a multinational enterprise with factories in two countries, an individual investor with shares in two countries. To avoid the unfairness of double taxation, numerous double-taxation agreements have been made, allowing tax paid in one country to be offset against tax liability in the other country.

Dow-Jones industrial average. *See* STOCK EXCHANGE.

downswing. A period of falling economic activity.

dual-capacity trading. Following the BIG BANG firms were established which combine the functions previously undertaken by stockbrokers on the one hand and stockjobbers on the other. These firms deal directly with investors, trade on their own account and make markets in securities.

dual labour markets. The dual labour market theory hypothesises that the labour market can be divided into two distinct sectors: a primary market where 'good' jobs and majority workers, e.g. whites, males, predominate and secondary markets where minority workers (blacks, females) predominate. The theory has received little support from empirical evidence.

dual pricing. Selling a product at different prices in different countries. The European Commission has declared the practice to be anti-competitive if the price differences are not due to differences in the costs of supplying the different countries.

dumping. Exporting at a loss, i.e. at a price below MARGINAL COST. Because dumping is likely to threaten domestic producers, the importing countries may seek to retaliate, e.g. by imposing additional TARIFFS. Moreover they may define dumping more widely, to include imports whose price exceeds marginal cost but is less than FULL COST. If the authorities do not have access to information on costs, they may act on the basis of their own estimates, or on a comparison of prices in different markets.

duopoly. A market with two suppliers. Depending on the assumptions made about the duopolists' behaviour, the EQUILIBRIUM price may be anywhere between (or at) the extremes of MONOPOLY and PERFECT COMPETITION.

durable goods. Goods that supply a stream of services over a period of time. They may be owned by producers (capital or investment goods) or by consumers (consumer durables).

dynamic efficiency. *See* ECONOMIC EFFICIENCY.

dynamic peg. *See* EXCHANGE RATE.

dynamics. Analysis of the process of change, often in terms of the path of the movement from one EQUILIBRIUM position to another.

E

earned income. Income from employment and self-employment.

earnings. (1) The income of wage and salary earners. Earnings may change at a different rate from wage-rates because of changes in the number of hours worked and in premium payments, e.g. for overtime working. (2) The income of firms. Earnings may be distributed as DIVIDENDS or may be RETAINED within the business. Earnings per share, a measure of the financial performance of a company, is obtained by dividing the number of ordinary shares issued into earnings, calculated after the deduction of depreciation, interest, preference share dividends and tax.

earnings drift. Another term for WAGE DRIFT.

earnings per share. *See* EARNINGS.

earnings yield. *See* YIELD.

econometrics. Mathematical modelling of economic relationships and the testing of hypotheses concerning those relationships.

economic activity rate. The proportion of the population in each age group that is available for work.

Economic and Social Council. The economic and social policy-making body of the United Nations, which co-ordinates the work of other specialized UN agencies.

economic bads. Outputs of the productive process which give rise to EXTERNAL COSTS, e.g. pollution.

economic convergence. In the move towards EUROPEAN MONETARY UNION the Council of the European Community, in deciding whether it is appropriate to enter stage 3, has to take account of the progress made towards sustainable economic convergence. The progress of a member will be deemed satisfactory if (1) prices have not risen over one year more than 1.5 per cent above the average of the best three members; (2) the Council of the European Commission has not declared the country to have had an excessive budget deficit (i.e. if the planned or actual general government deficit is not more than 3 per cent of gross domestic product at market prices, and government debt does not exceed 60 per cent of GDP at market prices); (3) for at least two years the currency has experienced normal EXCHANGE RATE MECHANISM fluctuations without severe tensions, and there has been no DEVALUATION within ERM on the member's initiative; (4) for at least one year interest rates (on long-term government bonds) have been not more than 2 per cent above those of the best (in terms of price stability) three countries.

economic data. Data can be used in economics to: (a) describe in quantitative terms an economic phenomenon, e.g. the rate of inflation might be described in terms of the change in the retail price index; (b) suggest areas for futher investigation, e.g. the behaviour of two series might suggest that the variables concerned were correlated; (c) test economic theories (including theories relating to previously observed data) by means of simple or complex mathematical, statistical and operations research methods;

(d) assess the impact of policy changes, e.g. if the government introduced measures to encourage investment, levels of investment before and after the introduction of these measures could be observed; (e) form the basis of a quantitative prediction relating, e.g., to an (actual or hypothetical) policy change.

economic development. A similar idea to ECONOMIC GROWTH but applied especially to LESS DEVELOPED COUNTRIES. Measures that receive relatively more attention in discussions of economic development include health and literacy.

economic efficiency. Economic efficiency requires: (a) productive or technical efficiency, so that, given the state of technology, output is produced at the lowest possible cost; (b) allocative efficiency, which means that resources are devoted to the production of goods and services desired by society; allocative or Pareto efficiency is said to exist when it would be impossible to make someone better off without making someone else worse off. (Some writers, taking productive efficiency as given, equate Pareto and economic efficiency.) It is possible to show that, on certain assumptions, economic efficiency will be achieved when all markets are PERFECTLY COMPETITIVE. However the assumptions required to demonstrate this are highly limiting, and the analysis is static, ignoring the dynamics of the process of economic change. Given the existence of ECONOMIES OF SCALE, productive efficiency may involve concentrating production in the hands of fewer firms than is consistent with the perfectly competitive model. Other factors which may contribute to economic efficiency include innovation, in both products and processes, and advertising, none of which features in the model of perfect competition.

economic forecasting. Economic forecasting, the prediction of changes in economic variables, is undertaken by governments, research organizations and firms. At one extreme we have forecasts derived from models containing hundreds of variables, the relationships between variables being expressed by mathematical formulae or equations. These models generate forecasts on macroeconomic variables such as prices, unemployment and the balance of payments. At the other extreme a small firm may conduct occasional back-of-an-envelope exercises predicting sales on which it bases orders for materials, etc. The values given to relationships between variables in large models are usually based on past experience, but there is no certainty that these values will hold for the future, since people's behaviour can change, for many reasons. In fact if, in the light of its forecasts, the government makes a policy change, this may itself cause the past relationships to change and hence make the forecast invalid. This suggests that forecasts should always be treated as highly provisional and liable to modification. Many businesses produce several alternative predictions or scenarios and plan their activities in accordance with the scenario which unfolds.

economic good. Any good or service that is scarce. Scarce goods almost always command a price, although PUBLIC GOODS are often provided without charge, the cost being met from taxation.

economic growth. Economic growth is usually defined as an increase in NATIONAL INCOME. However this definition is not entirely satisfactory since it conceals two sources of the increased income which have different implications. If income increases as EXCESS CAPACITY is used, the process must end as soon as full capacity is reached. On the other hand if income increases because capacity is expanding, the process will continue for as long as the expansion of capacity continues. For this reason some economists confine the term economic growth to the second situation.

economic imperialism. The alleged exploitation of less developed countries by developed countries, especially by the imposition of TARIFFS on imports of cheap manufactured goods.

economic indicators. In predicting changes in economic activity special attention is given to certain key variables, changes in which may be indicative of more widespread changes. Indicators may be leading, changes in the indicators preceding the more widespread change; coincident, the limited and widespread changes roughly coinciding; or lagging, changes in the indicators following the widespread changes. (Lagging indicators confirm rather than predict change.)

economic integration. Economic integration occurs when two (or more) economies become more interdependent. This might happen because, e.g., they become members of a COMMON MARKET.

economic law. The conclusion derived from an ECONOMIC MODEL is sometimes known as an economic law. Since economic models are highly simplified representations of certain aspects of economic life, the term economic law indicates a general tendency rather than a pattern of events or behaviour that will occur in every instance.

economic man. The person whose motivation and behaviour are described in ECONOMIC MODELS. In many models economic man has the following characteristics: he acts as an individual, e.g. consumer, worker; he has solely materialistic objectives which are always pursued in the attempt to maximize satisfaction, regardless of the effect on others; he has perfect information; his tastes are self-determined. Although these assumptions aid the construction of mathematical models, some economists have argued that the models can lead to misleading conclusions, especially in terms of the values of PARAMETERS, since the assumptions are so narrow and unrealistic. These economists have argued that a broader picture of economic man should be presented, one that recognizes that he often acts as part of a group, e.g. a household, a religious organization; has significant non-materialistic objectives; sometimes engages in non-maximizing behaviour; is influenced by the effect that his behaviour may have on others; possesses incomplete information; has tastes which are, in part, socially determined.

economic model. A representation of an economic system, or part of that system. Models are constructed in order to help us to understand how an economy works, and to do so they incorporate only what are believed to be the most significant features of a situation, other features being ignored. In MICROECONOMIC models it is common practice to make assumptions about the motivations of the economic agents, thus making it possible to DEDUCE how they will behave. Although the assumptions made are crucial, there is no agreement as to how one arrives at these assumptions, whether it should be by introspection, observation or experiment. So we can have a divergence of views about the nature of ECONOMIC MAN which can influence models of the behaviour of consumers, firms, workers and markets. MACROECONOMIC models are often constructed by a process of iteration. A model specifying a series of relationships between variables is compared to data relating to these variables. If the data is consistent with the predictions of the model the hypotheses underlying the model are said to be confirmed. If the data is not consistent, the PARAMETERS specifying the relationships between variables may be changed and new variables may be incorporated in the model. The revised model is again compared with the data, and the procedure is continued until a satisfactory fit is obtained. (Consistency of predicted and observed outcome is actually a very weak test of the validity of a model and the underlying hypotheses; the observed outcome might also be consistent with quite different hypotheses.)

economic profit. The revenue derived from the use of resources minus the OPPORTUNITY COST of using those resources. There are several reasons why economic profit may differ from profit as calculated by the usual accounting procedures. First, the economist attaches a cost to the use of RETAINED EARNINGS, since they could have yielded revenue if used outside the business. Second, the economist would value the time of owner-managers in accordance with what they could have earned outside the business, rather than at the salary they pay themselves. Finally the economist's view of the firm as an ongoing entity predisposes them to a CURRENT or REPLACEMENT COST approach, whereas accounting profit is usually calculated on the basis of HISTORIC COST.

economic rent. The difference between the earnings of a factor of production and what would be required to keep that factor in its present use. When the demand for a factor increases and the supply of that factor is relatively price inelastic, a large part of earnings will consist of economic rent. A good example would be the increased earnings of top class football players in recent years. The term economic rent is also applied by some economists to firms which earn SUPERNORMAL PROFITS, i.e. profits in excess of the NORMAL PROFIT required to keep the firm in its existing line of business.

economic sanction. An action designed to damage a country's economy, e.g. a refusal to supply oil, or the imposition of a punitive TARIFF. Sanctions may have a broad political aim, e.g. the cessation of military action, or a narrower economic aim, e.g. a tariff may be imposed to counteract DUMPING.

economic system. A set of institutional arrangements by means of which resources or inputs are converted into outputs to satisfy human needs and wants.

economic union. Implies the integration of the economies of two or more countries. Full economic union would involve freedom of movement of goods, labour and capital and a common fiscal and monetary system.

economics. The study of how people behave in an attempt to satisfy their needs and wants with limited resources. In principle a distinction can be made between positive and normative economics. The aim of positive economics is to explain how decisions are made about production, consumption and the exchange of goods, and to aid predictions about responses to changes in economic circumstances. In order to achieve this aim it uses scientific procedures, especially the formulation of testable hypotheses. Normative economics proposes courses of action based on personal VALUE JUDGEMENTS. In fact this distinction is now less clear-cut than it seemed a few years ago. It has been pointed out that positive economics is not value-free, if only because economists' values influence decisions concerning the parts of economics to be studied, and the hypotheses to be formulated. Moreover although economists adopt some scientific procedures, e.g. the collection and classification of data, they fail to adopt others. Whereas a physicist, say, tests a hypothesis by constructing experiments to try to disprove that hypothesis, an economist seeks to confirm a prediction generated by an ECONOMIC MODEL.

economies of scale. If, following an increase in the SCALE OF ORGANIZATION, the minimum point on a firm's average cost curve is below what it was previously, economies of scale exist. There are several types of scale economies. Technical economies relate mainly to the scale of the production unit. Cost savings may arise because the capacity of plant and equipment increases at a greater rate than the cost of its construction and operation. Technical economies may be enhanced when a larger scale makes it feasible to introduce new technology, e.g. electronic control equipment. Marketing economies may include the savings resulting from the construction and operation of larger warehouses (this could also be seen as a technical economy), the use of larger delivery vehicles, increased specialist knowledge in the sales force due to the greater division of labour, the reduction in invoicing and other costs through selling in bulk, and the ability to use more cost-effective methods of advertising. The most important form of buying economy is the lower cost of bigger orders. There may also be cost savings from a larger buying organization, with greater specialization. (The term commercial economies includes both marketing and buying economies.) Risk-bearing economies arise from the fact that the activities of a firm usually become more diverse at a larger scale of organization. This means that a failure or loss in any one line of activity is less likely to endanger the viability of the whole enterprise. Research and development is an activity which, by definition, yields uncertain rewards. Substantial costs may be incurred before revenue, if any, begins to flow in, and the diversified firm is best able to bear the risk inherent in this situation. (Even if R & D is not important, there may still be a considerable risk in launching a new product or selling into a new market.) Large firms may enjoy financial economies for two reasons. First, they may be able to raise capital on better terms than smaller firms. This may reflect the fact that the providers of capital see large firms, especially if diversified, as less risky. It may also reflect the determination of banks to hold on to large customers. Second, when firms raise capital by means of NEW ISSUES, the costs of advertising, underwriting, etc. decline as a proportion of the sum raised, as the size of the issue increases. There is a final group of economies pertaining to the administration of the firm which can be called administrative or managerial economies. These include the ability to make full use of modern methods of information processing.

All of the above economies are internal to a single firm. External economies arise when the expansion of an industry results in a reduction in the costs of each firm, e.g. when it becomes viable to establish a central unit which trains workers at a lower cost than could each firm acting independently, or when component suppliers set up in a region and so reduce buying costs.

economies of scope. Economies of scope exist when it is cheaper to produce several products together than independently, e.g. hot-rolling of steel (in a single plant or two linked plants) uses less fuel than cold rolling (in two independent plants). Economies of scope can be seen as a special case of ECONOMIES OF SCALE.

economy of high wages. In less developed countries higher wages may lead to better standards of nutrition and therefore to a more efficient workforce, the net result being lower unit labour costs.

Edgeworth box. A device for analysing bilateral trading relationships using INDIFFERENCE CURVES. It can be shown that, assuming perfect information, trading will take place only at points along the contract curve, where indifference curves of the two traders are tangential to each other.

effective demand. The desire for a good, backed by the ability to pay.

effective exchange rate. Sterling's effective exchange rate is an index of its international value in terms of a basket of other currencies, these currencies being weighted by their relative importance in Britain's international trading transactions.

effective rate of protection. The difference between the value added at domestic prices and the value added at world prices, expressed as a percentage of the latter. The effective rate of protection indicates the extent to which protective measures have raised the returns to factors working in that industry, account being taken of the effects on input as well as output prices.

efficiency. *See* ECONOMIC EFFICIENCY.

efficiency audit. The investigation by an outside body of the efficiency of an institution, normally a non-profit making institution. For example the Audit Commission investigates the operations of public-sector institutions. It has been suggested that since nationalized industries are usually sheltered from competition, they should be subject to an audit of their efficiency by an outside body. The investigations of the Monopolies and Mergers Commission might be seen to fulfil this function.

efficiency wage models. These models attempt to explain why firms fail to reduce wages even though there is an excess supply of job applicants. The models are heavily influenced by the fact that firms incur costs in screening or evaluating potential new employees, and in monitoring employees' performance. Given the existence of these costs it is argued that two factors would make it profitable for a firm to pay existing workers a wage which, on average, exceeds that for which they would be willing to work. First, if the firm paid only the average wage required by all workers, the more productive workers would move to employers wishing to pay a wage which reflected their higher productivity. Second, the higher wage would provide a greater disincentive to poor performance, e.g. shirking, because workers would lose more if dismissed on account of a poor performance.

efficient markets hypothesis. A market is said to be efficient if it is impossible to use information to make an abnormal profit by trading in that market. In an efficient market all traders have perfect information. As information about a future change in conditions becomes available it is immediately translated into buying or selling orders which cause prices to change to fully anticipate the changed conditions. The hypothesis is most often applied to financial markets. Since information is assimilated so quickly, changes in the price of shares are independent of one another, and follow a random walk; when a price increases, the next movement could equally well be up or down.

effort, as input. The output produced by workers depends not only upon the hours worked but also upon the amount of effort supplied. This is recognized in the EFFICIENCY WAGE and the X-INEFFICIENCY models.

elastic. *See* ELASTICITY.

elasticity. A measure of the response to a change, elasticity is given by the formula: percentage or proportionate change in the DEPENDENT variable divided by the percentage or proportionate change in the INDEPENDENT variable. The term elastic applies when the value of the formula exceeds one, inelastic when it is between zero and one. Frequently encountered applications include PRICE ELASTICITY OF DEMAND, PRICE ELASTICITY OF SUPPLY, and INCOME ELASTICITY OF DEMAND.

elasticity of substitution. Given a production function with two factors of production, the elasticity or rate of (technical) substitution shows the increase in one factor that is required to keep output constant when the quantity of the other factor is marginally reduced. It can be expressed as:

$$\frac{\text{\% change in the ratio of the quantities of inputs}}{\text{\% change in the ratio of their marginal physical products}}$$

It is defined in terms of percentages so as to be independent of the units in which the inputs are measured. If elasticity is zero, it means that the factors have to be used in fixed proportions; if it is infinity, the factors are perfect substitutes.

electronic funds transfer at point of sale. Immediate payment for goods bought, by electronically debiting the purchaser's bank account.

electronic funds transfer system. The transfer of money, e.g. to settle debts, by electronic means. It is faster than other means of transmission.

eligible liabilities. The banks' eligible liabilities are virtually identical to their sterling DEPOSITS.

eligible paper. Securities which the Bank of England will rediscount or accept as COL-LATERAL for loans to the DISCOUNT HOUSES. Treasury bills, short-term government bonds, and bills of exchange accepted by an accepting house or a British bank are eligible paper.

embargo. A prohibition of imports or exports, usually imposed to further a political aim.

embodied technical progress. TECHNICAL PROGRESS that is incorporated in new machines or other modifications to the production process.

emission reduction credit. *See* ENVIRONMENTAL POLICY and EMISSIONS TRADING PRO-GRAMMES.

emissions trading programmes. These programmes have been established in certain parts of the USA under the Clean Air Acts. The authorities specify for each production unit in a given area (or 'bubble') a maximum permissible quantity of pollutants. Any production unit emitting less than this amount obtains an emission reduction credit, which can be traded with other producers in the bubble. (If a producer has units in several locations, the bubble may be defined as those units as a whole.)

empirical testing. Comparing the predictions of models with data in order to confirm or reject hypotheses.

employee buy-out. The purchase of the assets of a company, or part of a company, by its employees, e.g. the privatized National Freight Corporation.

employees. In common parlance, employees are people who work for a firm. But the official definition is workers who are or wish to be employed, i.e. it includes employees in employment and the registered unemployed (but not the self-employed).

employer discrimination. *See* DISCRIMINATION.

employers' association. A grouping of employers, usually in a given industry. The main functions of employers' associations are to provide a forum for the discussion of issues affecting the industry, lobbying governments and representing members in collective bargaining. Most large employers' associations are affiliated to the Confederation of British Industry.

employment, full. In principle full employment is a situation where everyone who is able and willing to work has a job. (The temporary unemployment of people in the process of changing jobs – frictional unemployment – is ignored.) People's willingness to work is influenced by the REAL WAGE that they are offered, and the flexibility of real wages is thought to be an important determinant of the speed at which an economy approaches full employment.

Employment Act. *See* LABOUR MARKET POLICIES.

Employment Protection Act. *See* LABOUR MARKET POLICIES.

Employment Training. *See* LABOUR MARKET POLICIES.

endogenous variable. A VARIABLE whose value is determined within a set of equations or ECONOMIC MODELS.

Engel's law. In a paper published in 1857, Ernst Engel put forward the economic law that as incomes increase, the proportion spent on food decreases.

engineering approach. The engineering approach to the estimation of cost functions involves the costing of engineering blueprints for different levels of output, using given costs of inputs. The lowest cost estimate at each level of output is taken as the relevant point on the long-run average cost curve.

enterprise. In the census of production, enterprise refers to a single firm or to a group of firms under common control.

enterprise agencies. Government-sponsored organizations whose main function is to advise people engaged in, or wishing to establish, small businesses.

Enterprise Allowance Scheme. *See* LABOUR MARKET POLICIES.

enterprise boards. Organizations financed under the Local Government Act which enables local authorities to spend the product of a 2p rate for any purpose they choose. The boards' funding is used, often in conjunction with private sector finance, in a variety of ways: to finance new firms, to assist the formation of CO-OPERATIVES, to assist MANAGEMENT BUY-OUTS, etc.

enterprise zones. The philosophy underlying the creation of enterprise zones is that a reduction in government interference, e.g. minimizing planning restrictions, together with financial concessions, e.g. exemption from the payment of local authority rates for ten years, will facilitate the growth of companies. Most zones are in depressed inner-city areas.

entrepreneur. Different theories of entrepreneurship emphasize different aspects of the entrepreneur's function. But all the theories recognize that the entrepreneur operates under conditions of uncertainty. Putting this the other way round, perfect information and foresight leave no room for the entrepreneur. This is why the entrepreneur does not feature in models of PERFECT COMPETITION. An economist in whose writings the entrepreneur is prominent is Joseph Schumpeter. Schumpeter stressed the link between entrepreneurship and INNOVATION. Innovation does not necessarily involve new knowledge, and for Schumpeter the distinguishing aspect of successful innovation is that it requires an act of will, of leadership, not of intellect. The entrepreneur is also prominent in AUSTRIAN ECONOMICS, especially in the work of I.M. Kirzner. But whereas Schumpeter saw the entrepreneur as disrupting EQUILIBRIUM, for Kirzner the role of the entrepreneur is to achieve the adjustments necessary to move markets closer to equilibrium. The heart of this adjustment process is the use of a set of inputs to produce a new set of outputs yielding a higher profit than in the previous use. The entrepreneur is characterized by alertness, the ability to perceive and exploit such opportunities, and thus earn supernormal profits. Where the entrepreneur leads, competitors subsequently follow, causing profits to return to normal. There is no general agreement as to where the boundary around entrepreneurship should be drawn. If entrepreneurship is defined as taking advantage of hitherto unexploited profit opportunities, it could apply to a large number of individuals, from Richard Branson, founder of Virgin Airways and Anita Roddick, founder of Body Shop, to the man who occasionally sells surplus produce from his garden to his neighbours. Moreover, even if we narrow the field of observation to firms, it is not easy to precisely locate the entrepreneurial function. It is most likely to be found at the managerial level, but many managers spend at least part of their time on routine, non-entrepreneurial activities. Another area of debate concerns entrepreneurship as a FACTOR OF PRODUCTION. A neat classification of rewards is: wages as the return to labour, rent as the return to land, interest as the return to capital, and profit as the return to entrepreneurship, the factor responsible for combining the other three factors. However in most firms of any size, the bulk of profit distributed as DIVIDENDS goes to shareholders outside the firm who play no part in decisions concerning the use of factors of production. A way round this problem might be to define the function of entrepreneurship as risk-taking, since buying shares is a risky form of investment (more accurately, a form of investment whose rewards are highly uncertain). However, most shareholders are extremely passive as far as the firm's operations are concerned whereas, as we have seen, entrepreneurship is highly active.

entrepreneurship. *See* ENTREPRENEUR.

environmental economics. The analysis of environmental problems and of the contribution of economics to solutions to these problems. A great deal of work has been done in an attempt to find acceptable methods of valuing environmental damage, and of estimating the costs and benefits of environmental improvement. A second broad area of analysis is concerned with identifying the causes of environmental damage. The basic cause is market failure, a lack of incentives to decision makers to take EXTERNALITIES into account. This form of market failure is especially likely to occur when environmental resources are not owned by anyone, e.g. the global atmosphere. It is suggested that environmental damage is less likely when such an OPEN-ACCESS RESOURCE is turned into a COMMON PROPERTY RESOURCE. A third broad area of analysis is concerned with the design of ENVIRONMENTAL POLICY.

environmental policy. Policy designed to reduce environmental damage. Two broad approaches to policy can be distinguished. The so-called command-and-control approach includes such measures as ordering companies generating electricity to install flue gas desulphurization plants in order to reduce emissions of sulphur, and the prohibition of the dumping of sewage at sea. The alternative approach is based on the use of economic incentives, especially via taxes (on the principle that 'the polluter should pay') and subsidies. For example electricity generators could be encouraged to reduce sulphur emissions by taxing the sulphur content of coal. They might install a desulphurization plant (as before), seek increased efficiency in the use of coal, switch to coal with a lower sulphur content, or even switch to another fuel. This approach can be seen to be more flexible (and is often cheaper to implement) than the command-and-control approach. However it does require incentives that are strong enough to elicit a response. Another flexible instrument for controlling pollution is the tradeable permit, such as the emission reduction credit at present being used in the USA. A decision is made about the maximum amount of pollution permitted in an area, or by an industry, and the quota or allowance of each producer. If any producer causes less pollution than its allowance it is given a credit which can be sold to other producers who wish to exceed their allowances. Subsidies may take the form of assistance with research into new technology, e.g. several governments are currently planning to increase their support for research into solar cell generation of electricity, or the provision of facilities for waste treatment and recycling.

environmental tax. *See* ENVIRONMENTAL POLICY.

equalization grants. Grants given by central government to local authorities to reduce inequalities arising from differences in taxable capacity.

equalizing wage differential. Many jobs have important non-monetary advantages or disadvantages, e.g. pleasant or unpleasant working conditions. An equalizing wage differential exactly compensates for these factors, so that there is no overall incentive for workers who wish to remain in a job requiring particular skills and abilities to change employer.

equal pay legislation. At the beginning of the 1970s the average earnings of women in the UK were less than two-thirds that of men. This could have been partly due to differences in occupational distribution, with fewer women in high-paying jobs, and to differences in productivity. But it was believed also to be partly due to DISCRIMINATION. The Equal Pay Act, passed in 1970 and implemented in 1975, attempted to counter discrimination by providing for equal pay where a woman did the same work as a man or where her work was rated as equivalent under a job evaluation scheme. Following the passing of the Act women's pay rose to around three-quarters of men's but there has been little change thereafter. In 1982 the European Court ruled in favour of the European Commission which alleged that the 1970 Act contravened the Treaty of Rome. This led to the passing of the Equal Pay (Amendment) Act, and since 1984 any worker has been able to claim equality of pay with a worker of the opposite sex on the ground that their jobs are of equal value.

equation of exchange. The equation of exchange, also known as the Fisher equation, states that

$$MV = PT$$

where M = the stock of money
V = the velocity of circulation (the number of times the money stock turns over)
P = the average price level
T = the volume of transactions.

The equation tells us that, given the velocity of circulation, an increase in the money stock must be accompanied by an increase in the price level or the volume of transactions (and hence in output and employment), or both. (In practice the velocity of circulation is far from stable.) The less spare capacity there is in the economy, the bigger the impact on prices of a given increase in the money stock.

equilibrium. Equilibrium denotes that a system, or part of a system, is at rest. Any forces acting on a variable are in balance, so that there is no tendency for the variable to assume another value. When applied to a consumer, equilibrium denotes that the consumer's income is spent in a way that maximizes satisfaction. In a market the equilibrium price is the price at which the quantity demanded equals the quantity supplied; the equilibrium quantity is the quantity traded at that price (Fig. 5). Price and quantity may relate to (a) a product; (b) labour, where the real wage denotes the price and employment the quantity; (c) capital, where the rate of interest denotes the price, and the volume of loans denotes the quantity; (d) the foreign exchange market, where the rate at which one currency is exchanged for another denotes the price and the amount of currency exchanged denotes the quantity.

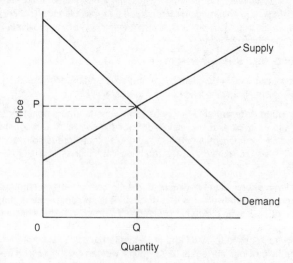

Figure 5   Equilibrium price and quantity

At the macroeconomic level, equilibrium income is where planned expenditure in one period equals income in the previous period. Alternatively it can be defined as the income at which planned injections equal planned withdrawals.

equilibrium business cycle. Since in NEW CLASSICAL ECONOMICS it is assumed that markets clear almost instantaneously, BUSINESS CYCLES must be explained as short-term fluctuations in potential output.

equimarginal principle. *See* DIMINISHING MARGINAL UTILITY.

equities. A popular name for ORDINARY SHARES.

equity. (1) The value of a company's ASSETS after all LIABILITIES, other than to the shareholders, have been allowed for. (2) Fairness, in two possible senses. Horizontal equity is the identical treatment of people whose economic characteristics and performance are identical, e.g. equal pay for equal work. Vertical equity is the different treatment of people who differ in abilities or circumstances in order to reduce the consequences of these innate differences, e.g. taxing the rich more heavily than the poor. It is clear that horizontal and vertical equity may not always be compatible.

equity/efficiency trade-off. The need to sacrifice VERTICAL EQUITY to secure an increase in efficiency, or vice-versa. ECONOMIC EFFICIENCY was defined by Pareto as a situation where it is impossible to make one person better off without making someone else worse off. But such a change may be required in order to increase vertical equity, e.g. by means of fiscal policy to redistribute income.

equity gearing. *See* GEARING.

escapable costs. *See* COSTS.

establishment. The reporting unit in the census of production and census of distribution; an establishment is an operating unit of a business, e.g. a factory.

estimates. Requests to Parliament to provide the money to finance government expenditure, together with the details of that expenditure.

eurobond. A long-term security issued by a government or company and subscribed in a EUROCURRENCY.

eurocurrency. A currency deposited or loaned outside its own country, e.g. dollars deposited in a German bank, sterling loaned to a company in Japan.

eurodollars. *See* EUROCURRENCY.

European Agricultural Guidance and Guarantee Fund. The fund into and out of which payments are made under the European Community's COMMON AGRICULTURAL POLICY.

European Bank for Reconstruction and Development. An institution of the European Community, established to provide financial assistance to aid the development of the former planned economies in Eastern Europe, especially by promoting entrepreneurship. Lending to the public sector cannot form more than 40 per cent of the total. The Bank reported a loss in 1991, after its first year of operation, and it is not yet clear how useful or successful it will be.

European Central Bank. The bank due to be set up in about 1997 as part of the move to EUROPEAN MONETARY UNION. The Bank's president, vice president and four member executive will be appointed by the European Council for eight year terms. (These six executives, plus the governors of the central banks from the participating member states will constitute the governing council.) The Bank's constitution is intended to give it a high degree of independence, being modelled along the lines of the Bundesbank rather than the Bank of England.

European central banking system. The system to be established as part of the move to European monetary union. The system will comprise the EUROPEAN CENTRAL BANK and the participating national central banks, which will act as regional agents in carrying out the policy instructions of the ECB. The Maastricht Treaty requires that national central banks end their present links with their national governments, becoming politically and economically independent before being admitted to the European central banking system. They will be forbidden from seeking or taking instructions from any European Community institution (apart from the European Central Bank), including their national governments. The new banking system is intended to be free of political control, but it is legally bound by the Maastricht Treaty to adopt policies designed to achieve price stability.

European Coal and Steel Community. Under a treaty ratified in 1952 a COMMON MARKET was established in coal, iron ore, steel and scrap, all import duties and quotas on intra-community trade being eliminated. These provisions were subsequently incorporated in those of the European Community common market, but separate provision continues for financial assistance in the form of grants, loans and guarantees to improve economic and social conditions in the coal and steel producing regions of the Community which have suffered particular hardship as a result of industrial decline.

European Communities. The European Community (renamed European Union in 1993) comprises the EUROPEAN ECONOMIC COMMUNITY, the EUROPEAN COAL AND STEEL COMMUNITY, and the European Atomic Energy Community.

European Currency Unit. The European Currency Unit is a composite currency, comprising a 'basket' of currencies of all EMS members, weighted roughly in accordance with their shares in European Community income and trade. The ECU is used as the currency of denomination for all Community transactions and the central exchange rates of the exchange rate mechanism currencies are expressed in ECU. The ECU is becoming increasingly used in commercial transactions, and as part of the proposals for EUROPEAN MONETARY UNION it will become the Community's single currency by the end of the century. The ECU coefficients, which are set every five years, are used daily to calculate the theoretical value of the ECU against all other currencies. The coefficients are based on the relative values of the currencies and their respective weights in the ECU basket.

Table 13   ECU coefficient values

Mark	0.6242
French franc	1.332
Pound	0.08784
Lira	151.8
Florin	0.2198
Belgian franc	3.301
Luxembourg franc	0.130
Peseta	6.885
Krone	0.1976
Punt	0.008552
Drachma	1.440
Escudo	1.393

European Development Fund. A fund established by the European Community to provide loans and non-repayable credits to less developed countries for specific projects such as the building of roads and bridges.

European Economic Area. A free trade zone comprising all members of the EUROPEAN ECONOMIC COMMUNITY and most members of the EUROPEAN FREE TRADE ASSOCIATION, due to be established in 1993. EFTA and the EEC had previously negotiated a FREE TRADE AREA, and this agreement was widened to extend to EFTA members Community provisions relating to freedom of movement for services, labour and capital, together with Community competition provisions. Trade between members of the Area is almost 70 per cent of the two blocs' overall trade, and its establishment is likely to be followed by full membership of the Community of at least some EFTA members.

European Economic Community. Six Western European countries, Belgium, France, Italy, Luxembourg, the Netherlands and West Germany, signed the Treaty of Rome in 1957 for the creation of a CUSTOMS UNION. The Treaty came into force with the establishment of the European Economic Community on 1 January 1958. Since then the Community's membership has expanded to include the Republic of Ireland, the United Kingdom, Denmark, Greece, Portugal and Spain, and further applications for membership are pending. The Community has also extended its sphere of influence and its power in other ways. All import duties on trade between the original members were abolished and a COMMON EXTERNAL TARIFF established by 1968. The concept of free trade among members was extended to services, labour and capital with the formation of the SINGLE MARKET, operative from the beginning of 1993. The budget of the Community has expanded in relation to the combined national incomes of its members, largely because of increased expenditure on the COMMON AGRICULTURAL POLICY. The Community's revenue consists of: (1) duties levied on imports entering the Community under the common external tariff; (2) levies on agricultural imports to bring their prices up to those prevailing under the Community's price support scheme; (3) the yield of a notional value added tax applied to spending on a common basket of goods and services (by far the biggest source of revenue). Originally the ceiling rate of the tax was 1 per cent, but this was raised to 1.4 per cent in 1986 and may be increased again if Community expenditure continues to rise. The Community makes grants through the Structural Funds: the European Social Fund, the European Regional Development Fund, and the Guidance Section of the European Agricultural Guidance and Guarantee Fund (by far the largest). Long-term loans are made to member countries by the European Investment Bank, and to less developed countries by the European Development Fund. Other areas in which the influence of the Community has increased include COMPETITION and ENVIRONMENTAL POLICY, while the forthcoming creation of a EUROPEAN CENTRAL BANKING SYSTEM will severely impinge upon members' MONETARY POLICY. There is a Council of Ministers, comprising heads of states or governments, which initiates policy, and a European Parliament, whose members are elected. But most power is exercised by the European Commission, staffed by civil servants and headed by seventeen Commissioners who are nominated by, but not responsible to, member governments. The Commissioners have portfolios covering major policy areas, e.g. agriculture, competition, the environment. The Community has also established a number of specialist institutions to implement policy, especially by the disbursement of funds.

European economic interest grouping. A legal body, like a company, but with uniform requirements throughout the European Community and with no capital requirements. It provides a legal basis for cross-border joint ventures, the partners in the venture retaining their independence.

European Free Trade Area. A FREE TRADE AREA set up by the members of the EUROPEAN FREE TRADE ASSOCIATION.

European Free Trade Association. The convention setting up the European Free Trade Association was approved in 1959 by the UK, Norway, Sweden, Denmark, Austria, Portugal and Switzerland. Finland and Iceland were subsequently admitted to membership, but the UK, Denmark and Portugal left to join the European Economic Community. Members of EFTA and the EEC plan to establish a EUROPEAN ECONOMIC AREA in 1993.

European Investment Bank. A bank established by the EUROPEAN ECONOMIC COMMUNITY in 1958, its board of governors consisting of the finance ministers of member countries. The principal role of the bank is to make loans for projects that (a) benefit less developed regions of member countries or other countries closely associated with the Community, or (b) are regarded as necessary for the development of the COMMON MARKET, or (c) are of common interest to member countries, e.g. improving cross-border communications. About two-thirds of lending has gone towards meeting the first objective, making the Bank the main source of funds for furthering regional development. About 85 per cent of the funds have been for projects within the Community, with most of the remainder being loaned to African, Caribbean and Pacific countries under the terms of the LOMÉ CONVENTION.

European Monetary Co-operation Fund. *See* EUROPEAN MONETARY SYSTEM.

European Monetary Institute. Under the Maastricht Treaty, the European Monetary Institute is due to be established in 1994. The EMI council will comprise the governors of member central banks, acting independently, plus a president. The EMI's objectives will be to improve co-ordination of monetary policies to ensure price stability and to prepare for a single monetary policy, the establishment of the European Central Banking System, and the creation of a single currency. The EMI is due to be abolished on 30th June 1998, or earlier if the European Central Bank and Banking System have been established.

European Monetary System. In 1978 the members of the European Community agreed to establish a European Monetary System, a scheme for the creation of closer monetary co-operation leading to a zone of monetary stability in Europe. The main provisions of the EMS relate to exchange rates, access to credit facilities, a common currency of denomination (the EUROPEAN CURRENCY UNIT), and a 'divergence' indicator. With regard to exchange rates, the most important provision is the requirement that each country participating in the exchange rate mechanism should intervene to maintain its currency's bilateral exchange rate against every other country within a range of + to − 2.25 per cent of central parity. This obligation applies both to weak and strong currencies. As intervention in the foreign exchange markets is obligatory to prevent a currency from breaking through its bands, corresponding credit provisions are also obligatory. Hard currency countries are required to lend to weak currency countries for purposes of intervention. Moreover the CENTRAL BANKS agreed to pool 20 per cent of their gold and foreign exchange reserves in exchange for European Currency Units in a central fund, the European Monetary Co-operation Fund. The divergence indicator is denominated in ECU and expressed in terms of the permitted deviation of a currency's ECU value from its central parity. The indicator is set to 'flash' when a currency deviates from all the other currencies by three-quarters of 2.25 per cent. The provisions of the EMS place a 'presumption' on the country in question to undertake corrective action, such as central bank buying or selling currency, or a change in fiscal or monetary policy. If none of these measures is sufficient, a realignment of the currency may become necessary. Such an alignment occurred as part of a major shake-up of the ERM in the Autumn of 1992, a shake-up which included the suspension of UK membership of the Mechanism.

European Monetary Union. The proposed coalescing of major parts of the monetary systems of members of the EUROPEAN COMMUNITY. The proposals were contained in the Maastricht Treaty, but the rejection of the Treaty in a Danish referendum, together with the subsequent changes in membership of the Exchange Rate Mechanism, made it unclear how many of the proposals will be implemented. Some may be implemented by some but not all of the signatories. Parts of the timetable may be accelerated, other parts delayed. Major features of the proposals are a single currency and a EUROPEAN CENTRAL BANKING SYSTEM. The agreed timetable for achieving EMU included the following steps: On the ratification of the Maastricht Treaty stage 1 begins. Thereafter the currency composition of the EUROPEAN CURRENCY UNIT shall not be changed. A 28-member advisory Monetary Committee to be created for the period until the beginning of stage 3. By the end of 1993 exchange controls within the Community to end. On 1 January 1994 stage 2 begins. All currencies to be in the narrow (2.25 per cent) band of the EXCHANGE RATE MECHANISM. The EUROPEAN MONETARY INSTITUTE to be established and the Committee of Central Bank Governors to be abolished. The EMI to take over the role of the EUROPEAN MONETARY CO-OPERATION FUND in providing short-term financial assistance to member states. Before the end of 1996 the EMI to specify the framework of the European System of Central Banks, this framework to be submitted to the EURO-PEAN CENTRAL BANK on its formation. The Council of the European Community, comprising heads of state or of government, taking account of progress towards sustainable ECONOMIC CONVERGENCE, to decide whether a majority of member states fulfils the conditions for the adoption of a single currency, whether it is appropriate for the Community to enter stage 3 of EMU and, if so, to set the date for the beginning of the third stage. Between the decision on the date for the start of stage 3 and 1 July 1998, the EUROPEAN CENTRAL BANK and the EUROPEAN CENTRAL BANKING SYSTEM to be established. In 1998 or on 1 January 1999, i.e. whenever stage 3 starts, the European Council, in consultation with the European Commission and the European Central Bank, to decide the conversion rates at which the currencies of the participating countries will be irrevocably fixed, and at which irrevocable fixed rate the ECU shall be substituted for those currencies. The ECU becomes a currency in its own right.

European Regional Development Fund. A fund established by the European Economic Community in 1975 to help to correct regional economic imbalances in member countries. Assistance is provided for both infrastructure and industrial projects.

European Social Fund. Established in 1957 to improve employment opportunities for workers within the European Community, the Fund provides assistance towards the cost of training and retraining schemes, resettling workers and their families who have to move to gain or retain employment, schemes to improve access to employment for disabled and older workers, and job creation schemes for young unemployed people.

ex-ante. The situation before something occurs. The term sometimes has the sense of expected or planned, as in ex-ante or planned saving.

excess capacity. (1) The difference between actual and maximum possible output in a firm, industry or economy. In a firm (and by extension an industry) capacity may be determined by a single input, e.g. the amount of machinery installed. Excess capacity implies that this limiting factor is able to produce a bigger output, although it might be necessary to increase the quantity of other inputs, e.g. labour. Considering the economy as a whole, excess capacity usually implies that some inputs, especially labour, are unemployed. (2) In the traditional theory of the firm, excess capacity is said to exist when the firm produces less than the output at which average cost would be minimized. Persistent excess capacity is a feature of MONOPOLISTIC COMPETITION.

excess demand. Excess demand exists when consumers would choose to buy more of a commodity than is supplied at the prevailing price. In freely functioning markets excess demand would cause price to increase to the EQUILIBRIUM level, i.e. to the price at which the quantity demanded and supplied are equal. Excess demand may persist because the government imposes a maximum price or because suppliers, being satisfied with their existing profit, do not take advantage of the excess demand by raising price.

excess profit. Another term for MONOPOLY or SUPERNORMAL PROFIT.

excess supply. Excess supply exists when producers supply more of a commodity than consumers choose to buy at the prevailing price. In freely functioning markets excess supply would cause price to fall to the EQUILIBRIUM level, i.e. to the price at which the quantity demanded and supplied are equal. Excess supply may persist if there is a minimum price, e.g. a minimum wage imposed by a trade union. The excess supply of labour that may then occur would be defined by some economists, e.g. those of the NEW CLASSICAL SCHOOL, as voluntary unemployment.

exchange. The basis of many economic transactions, e.g. purchasing (exchanging money for goods), working (exchanging leisure for money), dealing in the foreign exchange market (exchanging one currency for another), lending (exchanging command over goods now for command over a different bundle of goods in the future). In the absence of government intervention, exchange will be voluntary, being undertaken only when both parties believe the exchange to be to their benefit.

exchange controls. Limitations on citizens' ability to conduct transactions requiring the use of gold or foreign currencies. Exchange controls are usually imposed when a country's official reserves are deemed inadequate to meet all possible calls on them and the authorities wish to give some users priority over others.

Exchange Equalization Account. An account controlled by the Treasury and administered by the BANK OF ENGLAND, which buys and sells sterling for gold and foreign currencies in order to prevent undesirable fluctuations in the sterling EXCHANGE RATE.

exchange of shares. (1) A company may take over or merge with another company by offering shares in exchange for the issued share capital of that company. (2) Two companies may exchange shares so that each holds part of the share capital of the other. Although the two companies retain their separate identities, mutual or cross-shareholdings, especially if accompanied by INTERLOCKING DIRECTORATES, imply a willingness to take the partners' interests into account.

exchange rate. The exchange rate is the rate at which a currency is exchanged for another currency, for a basket of currencies, for special drawing rights, or for the European Currency Unit. A floating exchange rate is not subject to any form of government intervention, the rate being determined by the balance of the demand for and supply of that currency on the foreign exchange market. Demand and supply are affected by any transaction that involves a flow of money into or out of the country, as recorded in the BALANCE OF PAYMENTS. Many of these transactions involve the movement of goods and services, but some may result from SPECULATION, and some from non-speculative capital flows, as emphasized in the PORTFOLIO BALANCE APPROACH. If a country wishes the exchange rate to respond to changes in the balance of supply and demand but wishes to discourage undue fluctuations in the rate, it may engage in managed or dirty floating. The central bank intervenes in the foreign exchange market to smooth out fluctuations which it believes do not reflect changes in the country's fundamental economic position. Sometimes managed floating involves the co-operation of several countries. For example in 1985 leading trading nations agreed that the dollar's exchange rate was too high, and these countries co-ordinated their actions to ensure that the decline in the dollar's value took place in an orderly fashion.

A greater measure of intervention by the monetary authorities is required under a fixed exchange rate system. The authorities take whatever action is needed to maintain the agreed target rate or parity. (Fixed rates are usually allowed to fluctuate within narrow margins.) Intervention in the foreign exchange market may be sufficient to deal with mild or temporary pressure on the interest rate, but prolonged, heavy pressure may lead to changes in FISCAL and MONETARY POLICIES designed to modify the level of economic activity and thus the pattern of overseas trade and payments. If the government decides that the cost of defending a fixed rate is too great, e.g. if the required fiscal and monetary policies would lead to a rise in unemployment, it may change the parity of the currency. DEVALUATIONS of a currency tend to be substantial, e.g. in 1967 sterling was devalued against the dollar by 14 per cent. Upvaluations (revaluations) tend to be more modest, e.g. the parity of the Deutschmark has been increased several times by 5 per cent. Other exchange rate systems come between fixed and floating rates. Under a crawling peg or sliding parity system a devaluation would be spread in small percentages over a number of months or perhaps years. Future rates would be known, an advantage for importers and exporters, while the monthly adjustments would be too small to invite large speculative movements. In a moving parity system, the par rate would be automatically adjusted according to a moving average of rates over the previous months.

Exchange Rate Mechanism. *See* EUROPEAN MONETARY SYSTEM.

exchange rate regime. A description of the conditions under which governments allow the exchange rate to be determined.

exchange rate target. An exchange rate target may play an important role in MONETARY POLICY. In the late 1980s UK government policy was designed to keep the sterling-Deutschmark exchange rate stable.

Exchequer. The account of the central government with the BANK OF ENGLAND.

excise duties. A form of tax on a limited range of goods, the most important of which are oil products, tobacco goods and alcoholic drinks. Excise duties may be imposed to raise revenue, and they contribute more than a tenth of government revenue from TAXATION. They may also be imposed to discourage consumption for health or environmental reasons. The tax element (excise duties plus VAT), accounts for more than half of the typical price of a litre of petrol or a bottle of spirits and three quarters of the price of a packet of cigarettes. Since a differential rate of tax in favour of unleaded petrol was introduced in 1987, unleaded's share of the market has risen from nil to nearly 50 per cent.

exclusive dealing. There are several forms of exclusive dealing between a manufacturer and a distributor (wholesaler or retailer). A seller may sell to only a single distributor in a given area (exclusive supply). This prevents competition from other distributors, but the favoured distributor may be required by the seller (or may decide on his own initiative) to invest in better facilities for consumers. With exclusive purchase a distributor agrees to stock the products of only a single manufacturer. Finally, exclusive supply and exclusive purchase may be combined in a single agreement.

exclusive purchase. *See* EXCLUSIVE DEALING.

exclusive supply. *See* EXCLUSIVE DEALING.

ex-dividend. When shares are sold ex-dividend, the purchaser does not have the right to the next dividend distributed.

ex-factory. When the price of a product is quoted ex-factory, it does not include the cost of delivery to the customer's premises.

existence values. *See* TOTAL ECONOMIC VALUE.

exogenous variable. A variable whose value is not determined within a set of equations or an ECONOMIC MODEL.

expansion investment. *See* GROSS INVESTMENT.

expansionary gap. Another terms for INFLATIONARY GAP.

expansionary policy. Another term for REFLATION.

expectations. The views of economic agents about the future behaviour of relevant economic variables. Economics tends to be ambivalent about expectations. On the one hand expectations are not considered in the model of PERFECT COMPETITION. If, as the model assumes, there is perfect information, each firm should expect any innovation to be so quickly diffused throughout the industry that there is no opportunity to earn additional profit, and hence no incentive to innovate. And yet innovation is assumed to occur. On the other hand expectations are prominent in OLIGOPOLY models. For example the KINKED DEMAND CURVE is based on the assumption that each producer expects its rivals to react to price changes in a particular way. Expectations have played a bigger role in MACROECONOMICS than in MICROECONOMICS. Many years ago J.M. Keynes noted the likely effect on investment of businessmen's ANIMAL SPIRITS. In more recent years considerable attention has been given to the implications of the expectations of future price changes held by workers and employers. Some theories have been developed assuming ADAPTIVE EXPECTATIONS and others assuming RATIONAL EXPECTATIONS.

expectations-augmented Phillips curve. *See* PHILLIPS CURVE, EXPECTATIONS-AUGMENTED.

expenditure. Total or aggregate expenditure is another term for AGGREGATE DEMAND.

expenditure approach. *See* NATIONAL INCOME ACCOUNTING.

expenditure switching. Policies that maintain the level of planned AGGREGATE DEMAND but influence its distribution between DOMESTIC ABSORPTION and net EXPORTS are known as expenditure switching policies, as opposed to expenditure changing policies that modify aggregate demand.

expenditure tax. A number of economists have proposed that a tax should be levied on expenditure, defined as receipts in cash and kind (including the proceeds of sales of financial assets) minus saving (net acquisition of financial assets) and business expenses. The advantages claimed for the tax are that it would avoid anomalies due to differences in taxation of different forms of income, and would encourage saving. Note that the taxes on expenditure that are in force at present, e.g. value added tax, have a different rationale and method of administration.

expense preference. Refers to the fact that managers benefit from expanding their staff, through increased personal prestige and possibly a higher salary. If a firm is not subject to competition, its costs may be higher because of expense preference.

experience effect. *See* LEARNING EFFECT.

exploitation. Paying a resource less than its MARGINAL REVENUE PRODUCT.

Export Credits Guarantee Department. A government agency which provides insurance for exporters against loss due to the inability or refusal of debtors to pay, refusal to accept goods on delivery, and the imposition of EXCHANGE CONTROLS by importing countries. The ECGD may also subsidize bank loans to exporters, subject to limits on both the rate of interest and period of repayment for loans, agreed by members of the Organization for Economic Co-operation and Development.

export incentives. Incentives available to exporters but not to producers of goods for home consumption. Incentives might include subsidies to production, preferential access to credit, tax concessions, insurance at preferential rates. However the GENERAL AGREEMENT ON TARIFFS AND TRADE is concerned to limit export incentives.

export-led growth. The growth of the economy in which exports are a 'leading sector'. Export-led growth is most likely to be sustained when (a) the EXPORT MULTIPLIER has a high value, and (b) a substantial proportion of revenue from exports is spent on investment goods leading to an increase in the country's economic CAPACITY.

export multiplier. The ratio of the final increase in national income resulting from an increase in exports, to that increase in exports.

exports. Goods and services produced in one country for purchase by the residents of other countries. Exports are normally sold within the boundary of the importing country and paid for in the currency of that country.

ex-post. The situation after something occurs. The term refers to the actual outcome, e.g. the saving that occurred, as opposed to the saving that was expected or planned.

ex-rights. When the price of a share is quoted ex-rights, purchasers do not qualify for any rights issue recently made or about to be made.

external balance. A country is said to be in external balance when the current account of the BALANCE OF PAYMENTS balances.

external benefits. *See* EXTERNALITY.

external costs. *See* EXTERNALITY.

external debt. The amount owed by one country to another.

external deficit. A deficit on the current account of the BALANCE OF PAYMENTS.

external diseconomies. *See* DISECONOMIES OF SCALE.

external economies. *See* ECONOMIES OF SCALE.

external finance. *See* BUSINESS FINANCE.

external financing limit. A limit imposed on the amount of a nationalized industry's investment that can be financed by borrowing. The limit varies in accordance with the government's perception of the needs of the industry.

external surplus. A surplus on the current account of the BALANCE OF PAYMENTS.

externality. An externality arises whenever a production or consumption decision of an individual or group of individuals (such as a firm) affects the production or consumption of others, except through market transactions. Some externalities are positive (external benefits), e.g. the building of the Victoria Line on the London underground reduced congestion on other routes and so benefitted people who continued to use those routes. Other externalities are negative (external costs), e.g. the emissions of power stations in the UK have contributed to the formation of acid rain which has damaged property in the UK and other countries. Many negative externalities arise because PROPERTY RIGHTS are not established or exercised. The reduction of these externalities is the province of ENVIRONMENTAL POLICY.

externality, optimal. A level of externality that does not require policy correction, e.g. if the cost of policies to reduce environmental damage would exceed the benefit arising from that reduction.

extrapolation. Estimating future values on the basis of past values in a time series of data.

extrapolative expectations. *See* ADAPTIVE EXPECTATIONS.

F

face value. A security's nominal value. A redeemable security is redeemed at its face value. A share's face value is its par value or, if it has no par value, its issue price. The value of the metal in a coin is normally less than its face value.

factor cost. *See* NATIONAL INCOME ACCOUNTING.

factor endowments. The amounts and quality of the FACTORS OF PRODUCTION in a country. The fact that factor endowments differ between countries is a major reason for international specialization and trade.

factor incomes. The incomes of the owners of the factors of production. The UK NATIONAL ACCOUNTS classify income as: income from employment and self-employment, profits and trading surpluses, rent.

factor markets. The markets for the FACTORS OF PRODUCTION. In simple economic models the sellers are usually individuals or households and the buyers firms or governmental bodies.

factoring. Debts, money owed to a company, are part of that company's assets. Factoring is the purchase of these assets by another company, the factor. The price paid for the debts will be less than the nominal value, because the factor incurs the cost of collecting the debts and assumes the risk that some debtors may be unable or unwilling to pay. (Because the factor is dealing in many debts it enjoys ECONOMIES OF SCALE.) Moreover the factor pays as soon as it acquires the assets, thus improving the seller's cash flow, but does not itself receive payment until the expiry of the period of trade credit granted by the seller.

factors of production. The inputs or resources used in production. The THEORY OF DISTRIBUTION usually distinguishes three factors, labour, land and capital, whose rewards are wages, rent and interest. This leaves one source of income, profits, unexplained, so some economists have distinguished a fourth factor, entrepreneurship. This is, however, not very satisfactory since entrepreneurship is often exercised within the firm, i.e. by labour, whereas profits are distributed to shareholders. Another problem with the simple three-fold classification is that it is often impossible to separate the factors. Even the productivity (fertility) of a farmer's field is likely to have been affected by past applications of labour and capital. In recent years some economists have added a fourth factor of production, energy, on the ground that it is combined with the other three factors in the production process. Again, however, this does not fit well with the usual classification of rewards to factors.

factory gate prices. *See* INFLATION.

Fair Trading Act. *See* COMPETITION POLICY.

Family Expenditure Survey. An annual survey of the purchasing behaviour of about 6500 households. The information provided is used in determining the weights attached to products in calculating the RETAIL PRICE INDEX.

Federal Reserve System. The central banking system of the USA. The system comprises twelve regional reserve banks (which act as CENTRAL BANKS for their members), twenty-five branches and eleven offices, under the control of the Federal Reserve Board.

fertility rate. The number of births per thousand women between the ages of fifteen and forty-five. It is a very useful measure in assessing future population trends.

fiat currency. Another term for FIDUCIARY ISSUE.

fiduciary issue. Paper money not backed by gold. At one time the fiduciary issue was limited, but today the monetary authorities can alter the note issue as they wish, meaning that the note issue is effectively entirely fiduciary.

fiduciary monetary system. A system in which the monetary authorities have control of the issue of a currency which is accepted because of the belief that it represents command over goods and services.

final expenditure. In national income accounting final expenditure on goods and services comprises consumers' expenditure, general government final consumption, gross domestic fixed capital formation, the value of the physical increase in stocks and work in progress, and exports of goods and services.

final goods and services. Goods (and services) bought to be used by the purchaser in their existing form. Consumer goods are invariably final goods. Capital goods may be either final goods, e.g. machines, or intermediate goods, e.g. materials that are transformed during production.

final income. *See* INCOME.

final-offer arbitration. *See* ARBITRATION.

final output. Another term for FINAL GOODS AND SERVICES.

finance. The provision of money for a purpose, and especially for CONSUMPTION and INVESTMENT. Expenditure may be partly funded by an individual's savings and a firm's retained earnings, but the term finance is usually applied to other sources of funding, especially borrowing and raising permanent capital by the issue of shares.

finance company. *See* FINANCE HOUSE.

Finance Corporation for Industry. *See* INVESTORS IN INDUSTRY.

finance house. An insititution that provides various forms of credit, in particular for HIRE-PURCHASE, and also for FACTORING, LEASING, bridging finance and second mortgages. A hire-purchase agreement may be taken out directly with a finance house, the retailer acting as its agent. Finance houses also purchase agreements made with retailers under 'block discounts'. Some finance houses are subsidiaries of manufacturers and provide finance only for the purchase of those manufacturers' products. Other finance houses are independent of such ties (although they may be a subsidiary of a bank) and are free to finance the purchase of any manufacturer's goods. The finance houses obtain funds from the general public (usually paying a higher rate of interest on deposits than offered by banks), from industrial and commercial companies, and from banks and other financial insititutions.

Finance Houses Association. An association of FINANCE HOUSES, the FHA represents its members in discussions with the government, has formulated a code of practice for members, and maintains a credit worthiness register of clients.

financial assets. The most important financial assets are cash, deposits with banks, building societies, etc., bills, bonds, shares, pension entitlements and endowment assurance. These assets vary in liquidity, likely yield, and the degree of uncertainty attaching to that yield.

financial economies. *See* ECONOMIES OF SCALE.

financial intermediaries. Institutions which channel funds from lenders to borrowers, e.g. banks, building societies, discount houses, finance houses, insurance companies and pension funds. Financial intermediaries provide maturity transformation, e.g. depositors in building societies wish to lend short-term, but the funds are transmitted to house purchasers who wish to borrow long-term. They also enable risks to be shared, e.g. by contributions to endowment assurance policies and pension schemes.

Financial Intermediaries, Managers and Brokers Regulatory Association. A self-regulatory organization which supervises companies working as investment managers, brokers etc. FIMBRA has the power to suspend offending members, and to order them to cease conducting and soliciting business.

financial policy. Encompasses monetary, credit, interest rate and exchange rate policies. (Monetary policy is sometimes equated with financial policy.)

financial ratios. The main types of financial ratios (sometimes expressed as percentages) are: (1) tests of profitability, e.g. net profit as a percentage of capital employed; (2) tests of liquidity, e.g. the current or acid-test ratio, defined as CURRENT ASSETS divided by CURRENT LIABILITIES; (3) tests of solvency, e.g. the interest cover, defined as earnings divided by fixed interest payments on long-term loans; (4) overall measures, e.g. the price-earnings ratio, defined as the share's market price divided by current earnings per share.

financial sector. *See* SECTORS OF THE ECONOMY.

Financial Statement and Budget Report. A document which contains a report on recent developments and the outlook for the economy, together with the government's budget proposals. With effect from 1993 this was combined with the Autumn Statement.

financial system. Comprises financial institutions (banks, insurance companies, etc.), the markets in which they trade (money market, stock exchange, etc.) and the instruments they trade (bank deposits, shares, life assurance policies, etc.).

Financial Times share information service. A series of indices published by the *Financial Times* which constitutes the most complete, readily available, record of UK stock market statistics. (Less comprehensive information is also given on overseas markets.) Data is provided on prices, dividends, price-earnings ratios, volume of transactions, etc. The F.T. Industrial Ordinary Share Index is sometimes known as the 30-share index in recognition of the number of shares that make up the index. The small number of shares makes the index easy to calculate but means that it does not always give the most accurate picture of changes in the stock market. A better picture is given by the F.T.-Actuaries all-share index which has 750 constituents, accounting for over 80 per cent of the aggregate value of all the shares quoted on the stock exchange. Other indices published in the paper include the F.T.-Actuaries 500 share index, the F.T.-Stock Exchange 100 index (the largest 100 companies), and the three F.T.-Actuaries fixed interest indices covering British government securities, debentures and loans, and preference shares.

financial year. The year for which the financial accounts of an organization are calculated. It may not coincide with the calendar year.

fine tuning. Government intervention, involving fiscal and monetary policy, designed to correct small movements of macroeconomic variables that are not in accordance with government aims. On the basis of past experience, few economists now believe that the government can, or should attempt to, fine tune the economy.

firm. A firm is a collection of assets, human and non-human, that are managed together. R.H. Coase defined a profitable firm as a collection of assets that yield higher profits when managed together than they would if managed separately. Coase pointed out that there are costs in using the price mechanism, notably information and contract or transactions costs. Some of these costs can be saved by forming a firm and giving the ENTREPRENEUR power to co-ordinate production. The limit to the firm is the efficiency of the entrepreneur.

firm, theory of. *See* THEORY OF THE FIRM.

firm-specific labour market. A situation in which COLLECTIVE BARGAINING occurs within a single firm.

first-best. *See* PARETO EFFICIENCY.

first in first out. A method of valuing stocks. Materials are assumed to be drawn from stock in the order in which they were put in, and the cost of these materials is deemed to be the cost of the earliest batch of materials in stock (historic cost).

first world. The industrialized countries of Western Europe, North America, Japan and Australia.

fiscal drag. With a system of PROGRESSIVE TAXATION an increase in prices can cause an increase in the proportion of income paid in tax, a process known as fiscal drag. If income rises at the same rate as prices, the effect of fiscal drag is a fall in REAL (after-tax) INCOME. The reverse situation can arise when prices fall.

fiscal neutrality. A tax system which causes as few distortions to economic behaviour as possible, e.g. if an INDIRECT TAX had to be imposed to finance government expenditure, and the tax was applied to all products at the same rate, switching of purchases between products would be limited.

fiscal policy. Policy relating to government expenditure and taxation. The government may attempt to achieve several objectives (not necessarily concurrently) by the use of fiscal policy. It may influence AGGREGATE DEMAND, which in turn can influence the rate of inflation, employment (and unemployment), output and the balance of payments. Aggregate demand can be affected by changes in both government expenditure and taxation. The government may influence the pattern of expenditure by imposing INDIRECT TAXES at different rates on different products, and by granting subsidies on MERIT GOODS. (The subsidies may be given to private-sector producers or may take the form of public sector production at low or even zero prices.) It may redistribute real income by a system of PROGRESSIVE TAXATION and by means-tested benefits. Finally, it may increase incentives to effort and risk-taking by reducing tax rates.

fiscal stance. The fiscal stance may be expansionary, when policy aims to increase AGGREGATE DEMAND and NATIONAL INCOME, contractionary, when policy aims to reduce aggregate demand, or neutral, when policy aims to have no effect on aggregate demand.

Fisher equation. *See* EQUATION OF EXCHANGE.

Fisher hypothesis. Irving Fisher advanced the hypothesis that a 1 per cent increase in inflation will give rise to a 1 per cent increase in interest rates.

fixed assets. Fixed assets are defined by accountants as those assets which are retained for the benefit and permanent use of the business, such as premises, plant and machinery, vehicles, fixtures and fittings (and also goodwill). In economic theory the SHORT RUN is defined as that period in which some of the firm's assets are fixed; in other words the quantity of these assets determines the firm's CAPACITY.

fixed capital. *See* CAPITAL.

fixed capital formation. Additions to physical productive assets that yield a continuous service beyond the period in which they are purchased, e.g. plant, machinery, hospitals, roads and vehicles. More than 70 per cent of gross domestic fixed capital formation is undertaken by businesses (including public corporations) and the rest is accounted for by government investment and personal sector investment in dwellings.

Table 14   Gross domestic fixed capital formation, 1991

	Percentages
Vehicles	8.9
Plant and machinery	35.4
Dwellings	17.4
Other new buildings	33.9
Land and existing buildings	4.4
	100

Source: *United Kingdom National Accounts*

Subtracting CAPITAL CONSUMPTION gives net capital formation or, more simply, capital formation. If capital formation is positive, there is an increase in the CAPITAL STOCK and in productive CAPACITY.

fixed charge. The assignment of particular assets of a company as COLLATERAL SECURITY for a debt.

fixed costs. *See* COSTS.

fixed debenture. *See* DEBENTURES.

fixed exchange rate. *See* EXCHANGE RATE.

fixed investment. Another term for FIXED CAPITAL FORMATION.

fixed throttle. Policies, especially relating to the growth of the money supply, designed to ensure that AGGREGATE DEMAND grows at a constant rate, equal to the long-run growth of productive CAPACITY.

fixed trust. *See* UNIT TRUST.

flat yield. *See* YIELD.

flexible exchange rate. *See* EXCHANGE RATE.

flexible trust. *See* UNIT TRUST.

flight from money. A substantial increase in the demand for real assets when high inflation and high interest rates make holding money very expensive.

flight of capital. The large-scale transfer of capital out of a country, usually because of unstable political conditions or because of a fear that the currency will depreciate or that the transfer of capital will be restricted.

floating capital. *See* CAPITAL.

D

floating charge. An assignment of the total assets of a company or individual as COLLATERAL SECURITY for a debt.

floating debenture. *See* DEBENTURES.

floating debt. (1) Any short-term debt. (2) That part of the NATIONAL DEBT that consists of short-term borrowing, i.e. TREASURY BILLS and WAYS AND MEANS ADVANCES.

floating exchange rate. *See* EXCHANGE RATE.

floor prices. Minimum prices imposed by the government or as part of a COMMODITY AGREEMENT.

flotation. Raising capital by issuing shares to the public.

flow of funds. The transfer of money between sectors of the economy. Official statistics identify the flow of funds between four sectors: personal, enterprises, financial companies and government.

Food and Agriculture Organization. A United Nations organization which conducts research, produces forecasts of future production, recommends minimum nutritional standards, and offers technical assistance with the aim of improving the standard of living in agricultural areas.

forced saving. (1) Saving in excess of planned saving because of the unavailability of goods and services which consumers and organizations had planned to purchase. (2) From the point of view of the private sector, forced saving occurs when revenue from taxation exceeds government expenditure.

foreign aid. Assistance provided by one country or group of countries to another, usually from a developed to a LESS DEVELOPED COUNTRY. Official aid, provided by governments and international organizations, might take the form of grants, loans at low rates of interest, assistance in kind, e.g. foodstuffs, or technical assistance. Official aid accounts for around one third of total funds transferred, but for over 80 per cent of the funds received by the LEAST DEVELOPED COUNTRIES. Most of the remainder is accounted for by loans from commercial banks and foreign investment by companies. These funds are provided in the expectation that they will yield a commercial return, and they may not seem to constitute aid in the everyday sense of the word. They do, however, help the development of the countries to which they go.

foreign currency bank deposits. UK bank deposits in currencies other than sterling.

foreign direct investment. When a company opens a unit, e.g. a factory, in an overseas country it is known as foreign direct investment. Direct investment is often undertaken only after a company has established relationships overseas in other ways, e.g. selling through foreign agents while continuing to manufacture at home. Foreign direct investment, which has increased in importance as part of the process of GLOBALIZATION, is of two broad types. (1) Investment in production facilities whose output is initially destined for the home market, but which may subsequently be sold in international markets, is known as factor-based FDI. The motive for factor-based FDI is to enable the firm to locate where it is cheapest or most efficient to produce. Factor-based FDI is especially likely to occur where goods are standardized, wages are a relatively high proportion of total costs, and firms compete mainly on price. (2) Where output is destined entirely or mainly for the host country, the main motive is to be closer to individual markets. Market-based FDI is most likely when competition is by service, requiring producers to monitor the needs of individual customers, to provide training for customers, to give advice on the installation and operation of machinery and so forth.

foreign exchange. Claims on another country in the form of the currency of that country and interest-bearing bonds. (Some economists and most bankers use the term foreign exchange to refer to currency only.)

foreign-exchange market. The market in which trading occurs in currencies of other countries. This market is international, comprising markets in all the main financial centres of the world. Information passes freely between the markets and transactions are conducted electronically. Foreign exchange dealers can make profits either by ARBITRAGE or by successful SPECULATION.

foreign exchange rate. *See* EXCHANGE RATE.

foreign exchange reserves. The stock of foreign currencies held by a country's CENTRAL BANK.

foreign investment. The acquisition by residents (individuals or organizations) of one country of assets in another country. The assets may be financial, e.g. shares in other companies (PORTFOLIO INVESTMENT), or physical (FOREIGN DIRECT INVESTMENT).

foreign sector. *See* SECTORS OF THE ECONOMY.

foreign trade multiplier. A version of the MULTIPLIER that emphasizes foreign trade, rather than investment or government expenditure, as a stimulus to growth. Empirical research suggests that the foreign trade multiplier is a good predictor of economic performance in many countries, and that differences in export growth relative to the income elasticity of demand for imports are a major source of differences in international growth rates.

forward exchange market. *See* FORWARD MARKET.

forward integration. *See* VERTICAL INTEGRATION.

forward market. A market in which assets are traded at a price fixed at the time of the trade but for future delivery and payment (the forward price). The asset may be physical, e.g. wheat, copper, or financial, e.g. foreign currency. The forward price may be either above or below the current (SPOT) price, depending upon traders' views about possible changes in price before delivery. If it is expected that the spot price at the time of delivery will be the same as the spot price today, the forward price will be less than this. The difference between the expected spot price and the forward price is the risk premium; it is the amount that sellers are willing to forego in order to be certain about the price they will receive.

forward price. *See* FORWARD MARKET.

fractional reserve banking system. A banking system in which the banks' reserves of cash are only a fraction of their total assets, thus making CREDIT CREATION possible.

franchising. An arrangement under which an independent firm or individual (the franchisee) sells a product under the brand name of the franchisor. Franchisees provide their own capital and pay the franchisor a royalty on sales. They may also agree to purchase supplies from the franchisor. In return the franchisor, in addition to granting permission to use its brand name, often provides training and advice on e.g. site selection and operating the business.

free depreciation. *See* CAPITAL ALLOWANCES.

free-enterprise economy. *See* FREE-MARKET ECONOMY.

free entry. The absence of any impediment to new firms wishing to enter a market; a characteristic of perfect competition.

free goods. Goods which have no price, because PROPERTY RIGHTS have not been established or exercised, and which do not require the use of FACTORS OF PRODUCTION, e.g. fresh air, sunshine. The term does not refer to goods such as education which are provided without charge, and in fact the term free resources might be less misleading.

free market. A market in which price and output are determined by the actions of buyers and sellers not subject to any outside restriction or regulation.

free-market economy. An economy comprising a set of free markets. In practice in all economies at least some markets are subject to regulation.

free on board. The valuation of goods up to the point of embarkation on ship or plane. The valuation includes transport and insurance costs only up to that point. UK exports are officially valued fob. Since imports are valued COST, INSURANCE and FREIGHT (cif), they are adjusted so that they too are entered fob in the balance of payments accounts.

free port. A port which cargo can enter without the imposition of TARIFFS and some other taxes. These concessions, and the absence of other restrictions, encourage the establishment of manufacturing firms using imported materials. There are six free ports in the UK in which imports are free of TARIFFS, EXCISE DUTIES and VALUE-ADDED TAX. These taxes have to be paid when goods pass from the free port to other parts of the domestic market.

free reserves. Reserves held in excess of legal requirements.

free-rider problem. If a firm tried to finance a project by contributions from all those who would benefit, some people might refuse to contribute because they believed that the project would still go ahead, and they would therefore still benefit. They would be free riders. But if a sufficiently large number of people acted in this way, insufficient funds would be subscribed, and the project would not proceed, even though the total benefits would have exceeded the total costs.

free trade. No restrictions are imposed on the flow of goods and services between countries, i.e. no TARIFFS, QUOTAS, SUBSIDIES, VOLUNTARY EXPORT RESTRAINTS, or preferential government purchasing policies. Free trade is required for the fullest development of international specialization in accordance with the principle of COMPARATIVE ADVANTAGE. But in practice trade barriers are widespread.

free-trade area. A grouping of countries which have removed all restrictions on trade between members, but which remain free to impose whatever restrictions they wish on trade with non-members. (This freedom is the basic distinction between a free-trade area and a common market.)

free-trade zone. An area in which goods may be processed without attracting taxes or duties or being subject to certain government regulations. A FREE PORT is a free-trade zone with respect to imports.

frictional unemployment. *See* UNEMPLOYMENT.

fringe benefits. Benefits to employees over and above wages or salaries, e.g. free medical insurance, the use of a company car. Economists argue that in principle fringe benefits are a less efficient form of reward than money which can be spent as the

94

recipients please. However some fringe benefits are taxed less than the equivalent monetary reward would be.

full-cost pricing. A pricing procedure which takes as its starting point estimated cost at the expected output, to which is added a margin to arrive at the price. The cost base may be average total (variable plus fixed) costs, to which a profit margin is added, or average variable (or prime) costs, to which a margin to cover fixed (or overhead or supplementary) costs and profit is added. In either instance the margin may vary as demand conditions vary.

full employment. *See* EMPLOYMENT, FULL.

full employment budget. An estimate of what the government's budget would be if the economy were fully employed. This will differ from the actual budget, because unemployment reduces tax revenue and increases public expenditure. The full employment budget is a useful indicator of the government's FISCAL STANCE.

full employment output. The output that would be produced if all resources, including labour, were fully employed.

full-funding rule. *See* FUNDING.

full-line forcing. The refusal by a manufacturer to supply some articles from its product range unless the distributor buys the entire range. This device inhibits competition, especially when the manufacturer has a clear advantage over rivals in some of its products.

functionings. A word coined by A. Sen to refer to such social factors as freedom from hunger and avoidable morbidity, and freedom of movement. These are important aspects of welfare which are affected by policies towards LESS DEVELOPED COUNTRIES.

fundamental equilibrium exchange rates. The exchange rates which it is suggested, on the basis of past experience, are required to produce equilibrium on the current and capital accounts of the BALANCE OF PAYMENTS.

funded debt. Short-term debt that has been converted to long-term debt. The term is sometimes applied to all government securities quoted on the stock exchange.

funding. The sale of long-term securities and the use of the money raised to repay short-term debt. Companies may undertake funding when their CASH FLOW is insufficient to repay short-term debt or to take advantage of low rates of interest on long-term debt. The government tries to manage its debt in such a way as to minimize the cost of borrowing. But it also seeks to avoid adding to the volume of LIQUID and NEAR MONEY assets in a way that would add to inflationary pressures. This means that if the government adds to the money in the economy by spending more than it receives in taxation, it should take the same amount of money out of the economy by funding. In technical terms this full funding rule implies that the authorities seek to fund, by sales of debt outside the banking and building society sectors, the net total of: maturing debt, plus the PUBLIC SECTOR BORROWING REQUIREMENT, plus any underlying change in foreign exchange reserves. If the government is in financial surplus, the same principle applies in reverse; the funding rule now becomes an unfunding rule. On some occasions the government departs from the full funding rule. Overfunding occurs when the total of funding is more (or the total of unfunding less) than required by the rule. Underfunding occurs when the total of funding is less than required by the rule.

future goods. Goods that may be produced in the future. In a free-market economy the PRICE MECHANISM generates signals leading to the re-allocation of resources and changes in the pattern of output. But doubts have been expressed by some economists about the ability of the price system to generate signals early enough to allow adequate adaptation to the impending depletion of resources. They argue that there is not a satisfactory market in future goods.

futures. Contracts made in a future market or FORWARD MARKET for the purchase and sale of a physical or financial asset on a specified future date.

G

gains from trade. The additional production and consumption that arise when countries engage in international trade rather than being self-sufficient. These gains are said to be maximized when trade takes place in accordance with the principle of COMPARATIVE ADVANTAGE.

galloping inflation. Another term for HYPERINFLATION.

game. A situation in which intelligent decisions by two or more economic agents are necessarily interdependent.

game theory. A mathematical theory which can be applied to situations in which the actions of one economic agent lead to a reaction by another agent. The first agent will take this likely reaction into account in deciding its policy. Game theory is most readily applied where there are only two agents, e.g. wage bargaining between a union and an employer, or a market shared between two suppliers (DUOPOLY). Games may be classified as zero-sum games, in which one agent's gain is another agent's loss; non-zero-sum games, in which one agent's decision may benefit all agents; co-operative games, in which COLLUSION is possible; and non-co-operative games, in which it is not.

gateways. Grounds on which parties to an agreement registered under the Restrictive Trade Practices Act 1956 can seek to justify the agreement.

gearing. The relative importance of loan capital in the overall capital structure of a firm. There are several measures of gearing. Equity gearing is the ratio of borrowing to equity finance. Capital gearing is borrowing as a percentage of net tangible assets. The gearing ratio most commonly used is the ratio of debt finance to the total of debt plus equity finance. When liability to taxation has been taken into account, borrowing is usually a cheaper form of business finance than equity finance or retained earnings, and this provides an incentive for a high gearing ratio. On the other hand a high ratio carries the danger that in times of low profitability the firm may be unable to meet the interest payments due on its borrowing and may be forced into liquidation, as happened with a number of large property companies in the early 1990s. Moreover the possibility of this happening will reduce the attractiveness of the company as a vehicle for equity investment.

gearing ratio. *See* GEARING.

General Agreement on Tariffs and Trade. An agreement signed in 1947 by twenty-three contracting parties (CPs), a number that has since increased to over a hundred. The agreement set up an international organization based in Geneva and it is this organization, rather than the agreement itself, that is usually referred to. The members of GATT are pledged to the expansion of multilateral trade, and to the removal, or at least a reduction, of measures which distort the pattern of trade. A key provision in the GATT charter is the most favoured nation or non-discrimination clause, which forbids CPs from discriminating between trading partners. An agreement reached with one CP must be extended to all others. This principle encourages multilateral rather than bilateral negotiation. (As an exception to this principle, countries can operate discriminatory trading arrangements as members of a COMMON MARKET or FREE TRADE AREA.) Another important principle applied by GATT is reciprocity, meaning that if one CP makes a concession to another, e.g. reducing TARIFFS, the CP that benefits must make an equivalent concession. (An exception to this principle is that less developed countries are allowed to benefit unilaterally from tariff reductions.) Despite these exceptions, non-discrimination and reciprocity have marked the eight rounds of multilateral negotiations sponsored by GATT. By the end of the seventh (Tokyo) round, tariffs on industrial goods had been reduced to an average of 5 per cent, as compared to the average of 40 per cent when the first round started. On the other hand NON-TARIFF barriers had increased and were used in a discriminatory manner, e.g. quotas restricted the exports of textiles and clothing from less developed and newly industrialized countries. Moreover agriculture had remained outside GATT. Consequently when the eighth (Uruguay) round began in 1986 these two issues formed an important part of the agenda. In fact differences of view over agriculture were the main reason why the negotiations were continued until 1993.

general arrangements to borrow. *See* INTERNATIONAL MONETARY FUND.

general equilibrium. When there is no excess of demand or supply in any of a set of interrelated markets.

general equilibrium analysis. Economic analysis that takes account of the inter-relationships among markets. For example the consequences of an improvement in the quality of a product would be studied with respect to that market (e.g. more demanded, higher output and employment), the market for COMPLEMENTARY PRODUCTS (similar consequences) and the market for SUBSTITUTE PRODUCTS (less demanded, lower output and employment).

general government final consumption. Spending by central and local government on goods and services.

geometric progression. A series of values having the form: a, $a + (ar)$, $a + (ar^2)$, etc. This form would apply to a loan at compound interest where a is the principal and r the rate of interest.

Gibrat effect. Using mathematics R. Gibrat showed that in principle increasing CONCENTRATION could be explained solely by dispersion in the growth rates of firms, i.e. even in the absence of mergers.

Giffen good. A product with a backward sloping DEMAND CURVE. In theoretical terms this can be explained by assuming that the product is an INFERIOR GOOD and that the income effect of a price change outweighs the substitution effect. Giffen goods are named after Sir Robert Giffen who was said to have observed in the nineteenth century that when the price of a product rose, its consumption by certain groups in society increased. The product is said by some writers to have been bread, and by others to have been potatoes. In fact it seems unlikely that the alleged observation actually occurred.

gilt-edged securities. Fixed interest securities issued by the British government. The securities are traded on the stock exchange where a number of firms operate as gilt-edged market makers. Some gilts are dated, some undated. Most have a fixed rate of interest, but some are INDEX-LINKED, the rate of interest being tied to, but greater than, the change in the retail price index.

Gini coefficient. A coefficient, based on the LORENZ CURVE, which shows the degree of inequality in a frequency distribution.

globalization. The tendency for firms to establish units world wide, wherever the market is big enough to allow ECONOMIES OF SCALE to be enjoyed. This leads to an increase in the number and size of MULTINATIONAL ENTERPRISES. A feature of globalization is that goods, services, capital, labour and ideas are transferred internationally within firms rather than through external markets.

gold standard. When in the past a country adopted the gold standard, the government fixed the value of the domestic currency in terms of gold, maintained the CONVERTIBILITY of the currency into gold, and ensured that the MONEY SUPPLY increased only in line with increases in official holdings of gold. When all countries were on the gold standard, a BALANCE OF PAYMENTS surplus resulted in an inflow of gold and therefore an increase in the money supply. In theory this would lead to higher prices, higher imports and lower exports, thus correcting the balance of payments imbalance. However, market imperfections meant that the adjustment process might operate very slowly.

golden handshake. A large severance payment made to a director or employee who is dismissed before the expiry of his or her contract.

golden hello. A large lump-sum payment made to a person to persuade him or her to join an organization.

golden parachute. *See* TAKEOVER.

golden share. The government retained a golden share in several PRIVATIZED companies, enabling it to prevent unwelcome, and especially foreign, takeovers.

Goodhart's law. Charles Goodhart, formerly economic advisor to the Bank of England, formulated the law that whenever the monetary authorities try to control the money supply by acting on one variable, that variable ceases to function as a reliable indicator of the money supply.

goodness of fit. *See* REGRESSION ANALYSIS.

goods characteristics theory. A theory of demand in which the characteristics of products are treated as goods. The theory can help to define the boundaries of markets and throws light on the conditions under which a firm has an independent demand curve.

goodwill. Intangible assets of a company, e.g. consumer loyalty, reputation. It is included within FIXED ASSETS in a firm's balance sheet.

government expenditure. In the UK NATIONAL ACCOUNTS two broad types of government expenditure are distinguished, expenditure on goods and services, and transfers (grants, subsidies and debt interest). Expenditure on goods and services forms part of AGGREGATE DEMAND, but transfers do so only indirectly, if and when they are spent by the recipients. Consequently in the THEORY OF INCOME DETERMINATION, government expenditure refers only to spending on goods and services.

Table 15 General government expenditure, 1991

	Percentages
Expenditure on goods and services	55
Subsidies	3
Grants	33
Debt interest	7
Non-trading capital consumption	2
	100

Source: *United Kingdom National Accounts*

The main areas of expenditure are social security (32 per cent of total spending), health (14 per cent), and defence (12 per cent).

government failure. Government intervention may be required in order to correct MAR-KET FAILURE, e.g. by levying taxes on firms that cause pollution. But intervention may it-self cause a reduction in net welfare, e.g. it is known that government subsidies to irrigation, pesticides, energy and fertilizers have contributed to environmental damage.

government securities. All government debt, including bonds and Treasury bills.

government stocks. *See* GILT-EDGED SECURITES.

government subsidies. Negative TAXES, given to encourage particular forms of econ-omic activity. Subsidies can be given either to producers or consumers, but in practice they go mainly to producers. Subsidies to producers can take the form of grants, loans at preferential rates of interest, insurance cover at preferential rates, the provision of facilities below cost, and exemption from the payment of taxes. They may be given to encourage: industrial activity in certain areas as part of REGIONAL POLICY; the production of certain goods as part of INDUSTRIAL POLICY; the provision of MERIT GOODS; exports; or to correct for EXTERNALITIES. The government should, of course, weigh the benefits to the recipients of subsidies against the disbenefits of the taxation required to finance subsidies.

green economics. Green economics is concerned with similar issues to ENVIRONMENTAL ECONOMICS. It advocates that less attention be paid to ECONOMIC GROWTH per se and more to SUSTAINABLE DEVELOPMENT.

greenmail. *See* TAKEOVER.

gross dividend yield. *See* YIELD.

gross domestic product. One of several measures of economic activity derived in NATIONAL INCOME ACCOUNTING. GDP can be measured at market prices, but by subtract-ing taxes on expenditure (net of subsidies) we arrive at GDP at factor cost, the best measure of the utilization of domestic resources.

gross fixed capital formation. *See* FIXED CAPITAL FORMATION.

gross income. *See* INCOME.

gross investment. Total investment, comprising investment required to compensate for depreciation (replacement investment), and investment which leads to an expan-sion of economic capacity (net or expansion investment).

gross margin. The difference between the price at which a retailer sells a product and the price the retailer pays to the manufacturer or wholesaler.

gross national disposable income. GROSS NATIONAL PRODUCT adjusted to take account of changes in the TERMS OF TRADE. An improvement in the terms of trade would cause the GNDI to increase.

gross national product. GROSS DOMESTIC PRODUCT plus net PROPERTY INCOME FROM ABROAD. GNP at factor cost is the best measure of income received by UK residents.

gross national product deflator. An index of prices which, when applied to values of the gross national product at CURRENT PRICES, gives GNP at CONSTANT PRICES, a better indicator of REAL values.

gross profit. *See* PROFIT.

gross redemption yield. *See* YIELD.

Group of Seven. An informal grouping of industrialized nations, USA, Canada, France, Germany, Italy, UK and Japan, who meet regularly to consider ways in which their countries' policies might be made mutually reinforcing. The Group of Seven may also act as a pressure group, e.g. in trying to persuade the European Economic Community to reduce agricultural subsidies.

Group of Ten. The GROUP OF SEVEN countries plus Belgium, the Netherlands and Sweden. The group was formed in 1967 to contribute additional funds to the International Monetary Fund under the General Arrangements to Borrow.

growth of the firm. Firms may grow internally, i.e. by acquiring more resources and producing more goods and services, or by joining their activities with those of another firm. (A merger denotes that the firms join by mutual consent; a takeover that one firm takes the initiative.) Growth, whether internal or by merger/takeover, can be in several directions. With horizontal growth the firm continues at the same stage of operations, e.g. manufacturing or retailing, with a largely unchanged range of products. Vertical growth (or integration) can be either forward, taking the firm nearer to the customer, e.g. a food manufacturer might begin acting as a wholesaler, selling direct to retailers; or backward, taking the firm near to the sources of raw materials, e.g. the food manufacturer might move into farming. With lateral growth the firm stays at the same stage of operations but makes a significant change to its product range, e.g. a car manufacturer might begin to assemble buses. Finally conglomerate growth involves undertaking a range of very diverse activities. Horizontal, and to a lesser degree lateral, growth is most likely to lead to ECONOMIES OF SCALE, especially technical. The motives for vertical growth are more often strategic, i.e. to secure markets (forward) or supplies of raw materials (backward). Conglomerate growth should give rise to risk-bearing economies.

growth theory. Growth theory is concerned with the determinants of the growth of the economy as a whole: the contributions of capital and labour, the role of saving and investment, the significance of technical progress, etc. The conditions under which an economy would achieve balanced growth (all variables growing at the same rate) have been analysed, and complicated mathematics have been brought to bear in the attempt to discover the conditions for optimal growth, i.e. the rate of growth which maximizes social welfare.

guaranteed price. In an attempt to protect the incomes of producers, and especially of farmers, arrangements have been made whereby producers are paid a guaranteed price for their output. If the balance of supply and demand is such that price would be below the guaranteed or target price, the authorities enter the market as purchasers at the guaranteed price.

Gutman effect. This arises when reductions in tax rates lead to the declaration of tax liabilities arising from transactions that were not previously declared. These transactions are now declared because the balance of penalties for declaration and non-declaration has altered. This effect, named after P. Gutman, can be seen as contributing to the LAFFER CURVE, or as operating in conjunction with it.

H

hammered. When a member of the STOCK EXCHANGE cannot meet his obligations he is said to be hammered.

hard currency. A currency for which there is a high demand in the FOREIGN-EXCHANGE MARKET.

Harrod-Domar model. A GROWTH THEORY model which suggests that there is no reason why economic growth should be BALANCED. The model assumes that there is a natural rate of growth, and an actual rate. The natural rate is determined by the increase in the labour force. The actual rate is determined by the saving rate and the capital-output ratio. There is, therefore, no reason why these two rates should correspond, i.e. no reason why full employment should be maintained. (This conclusion depends upon the assumptions that the relative price of capital and labour is fixed, and that they are always employed in equal proportions. These assumptions rule out the possibility that an increase in the labour supply might drive down the relative price of labour and thus lead to a more LABOUR INTENSIVE form of production.) The model also assumes that there is a warranted rate of growth, determined by firms' expectations of changes in demand. If the actual rate exceeds the warranted rate, firms respond by increasing investment to the level warranted by the actual growth, but this investment causes a further rise in actual growth. (The reverse applies if the actual rate is initially below the warranted rate.) This causes an unstable growth path. (This conclusion follows from the assumption that investment is determined solely by the operation of the ACCELERATION PRINCIPLE.)

headline inflation. *See* INFLATION.

headline unemployment. Another term for REGISTERED UNEMPLOYMENT.

Heckscher-Ohlin principle. International specialization and trade occurs because of COMPARATIVE ADVANTAGE which, the Heckscher-Ohlin principle states, arises from differences in FACTOR ENDOWMENTS between countries.

hedging. Actions taken by buyers or sellers to protect themselves against the consequences of possible future price changes, especially by dealing in FORWARD MARKETS. The SPOT prices in many primary goods markets, e.g. foodstuffs, minerals, are extremely volatile, and this adds considerably to the risks borne by businesses, especially small businesses with little by way of capital reserves. For example assume that a tin mine requires a price of £8000 a tonne to operate profitably and that the current spot price is £8200. Although the owners of the mine expect price to continue at this level, they recognize from past experience that it could turn out to be so far below this that they would have to close the mine. To hedge against this risk they might enter into a contract to deliver tin in a year's time at a price of £8000 a tonne. The purchase of ORDINARY SHARES is sometimes said to be a hedge against inflation. This is because past experience has shown that over a long period higher prices for goods and services have been accompanied by higher share prices.

hedonic analysis. Analysis which seeks to explain the prices of DIFFERENTIATED PRO-DUCTS by identifying the values attached to the characteristics of these products.

Herfindahl index. A measure of market or industry concentration. The value of the index is given by the sum of the squares of the market share of each firm in the industry. In a pure monopoly the index would take the value 1 and in an industry with n firms with equal market shares it would take the value $1 \div n$.

heterogeneity. *See* PRODUCT DIFFERENTIATION.

hidden economy. *See* BLACK ECONOMY.

hidden reserves. The valuation of assets in a firm's balance sheet at a level below the market valuation. This may occur because the assets have not been revalued in a period of inflation.

hidden unemployment. *See* DISGUISED UNEMPLOYMENT.

hierarchy. A firm or other organization can be seen as a collection of people assigned to different layers in a hierarchy, the basis of the assignment being authority, supervision or remuneration. The idea of hierarchy is very important in the approach to the THEORY OF THE FIRM developed by O. Williamson.

high-powered money. *See* MONETARY BASE.

hire-purchase. A form of instalment credit used for the purchase of durable goods, e.g. furniture, plant and equipment. The usual arrangement is that the purchaser pays an initial deposit and then repays the balance in equal instalments. (The initial balance and repayment period have sometimes been subject to government control.) The item becomes the property of the owner when the final instalment has been paid.

historic-cost accounting. In financial accounting the costs of assets, e.g. machinery, materials, are entered at their acquisition or historic cost. This may give a misleading picture of the firm's profitability when these assets are used to produce outputs whose prices change over time.

hit and run entry. Denotes that a firm enters a market with the intention of making a quick profit before leaving the market. The term is associated particularly with the theory of CONTESTABLE MARKETS.

hoarding. The accumulation of idle assets, financial (especially money) or physical. Physical assets may be hoarded because their price is expected to rise.

holding company. A company that controls one or more other companies, usually by holding a majority of the shares in these subsidiaries. This can be a cheaper method of obtaining control than by buying all the assets of the subsidiary.

homogeneous products. Products that are seen by purchasers as perfect substitutes.

horizontal equity. *See* EQUITY.

horizontal integration. *See* GROWTH OF THE FIRM.

hot money. Funds which flow into a country in response to high interest rates. The inflow may improve the BALANCE OF PAYMENTS, but the improvement may only be temporary since these funds are highly volatile and can quickly flow out again in response to a change in interest rate differentials.

household. An economic unit defined as a single person living alone, or a family or group of people living together and benefiting from housekeeping shared in common.

Details of household expenditure are given annually in the Family Expenditure Survey. Although it is conventional to use such terms as the individual's demand or the individual's preferences, it is recognized that in many instances the individual is actually representing a larger household. Similarly, producers of many consumer goods are most interested in the household, e.g. in the proportion of households possessing a car or a television set. Once a very high proportion of households possess the article in question, replacement sales form a high proportion of total sales.

human capital. The stock of expertise accumulated by a worker. A worker's expertise may be due partly to natural ability, but the development of that ability requires investment in education and training. (Admittedly for some outstanding ENTREPRENEURS this education has been obtained in the 'university of life'.) As with investment in machinery, the purpose is to increase the worker's productivity and income-earning potential. (It is not suggested that this is the sole purpose of education; it is recognized that education may be both an investment and a consumption good.) Human capital is sometimes firm-SPECIFIC, i.e. the skills acquired would be worth virtually nothing to any other employer. There is a strong incentive for the employer to invest in this type of human capital. In other instances the skills may be more widely applicable, and this can be a disincentive to an employer to invest, lest the trained workers are then hired by other employers willing to pay higher wages and salaries. (The employer will be more willing to train if trainees are prepared to accept a lower wage.) If this disincentive is strong, the amount of education and training provided nationally might be deemed to be too little. (There is some evidence of a link between the amount of education and training and the rate of economic growth.) This could then be seen to justify the subsidizing of education and training.

human development index. A ranking system devised by the UN Development Programme that combines income, literacy and life expectancy in an attempt to measure the quality of life in its 160 member states. In 1992 Canada was ranked first, followed by Japan, Norway, Switzerland and Sweden. The UK was ranked tenth.

human suffering index. An index devised by the Washington based Population Crisis Committee in an attempt to measure human suffering. The index takes account of ten factors such as access to clean water, adequate food and education. In 1992 Mozambique had the highest level of suffering, followed by Somalia, Afghanistan, Haiti and the Sudan. The countries with the least suffering were Denmark, Holland, Belgium, Switzerland and Canada. The UK also had a low ranking, twenty-second.

hyperinflation. A very rapid rate of INFLATION causing money to lose its value to the point where BARTER becomes the preferred means of exchange.

hypothesis. A theoretical explanation that can in principle be tested against the facts, e.g. that an increase in the price of a product will cause the quantity demanded to fall. The usual scientific method is to set up an experiment in an attempt to refute a hypothesis, but economists normally adopt a much weaker test, seeing conformity of observed facts with their prediction as confirming a hypothesis.

hypothetical compensation test. *See* COST BENEFIT ANALYSIS.

hysteresis. An economy experiences hysteresis when its long-run equilibrium depends on the path followed in the short-run, e.g. if the long-run equilibrium in the labour market was affected by a short-run fall in the demand for labour. This could happen if the fall in demand caused a permanent fall in supply, (a leftward shift in the JOB ACCEPTANCE SCHEDULE). This shift could occur for several reasons: (1) Some INSIDERS become OUTSIDERS, and when the demand for labour subsequently increases the smaller number of insiders, having a greater scarcity value, are able to obtain higher wages than before the initial fall in demand. (2) The increased unemployment causes an increase in the number of DISCOURAGED WORKERS. (3) The reduced labour demand leads to a lower level of search activity in the labour market. This continues after demand revives, causing a greater degree of mismatch between the offers of employers and workers. (4) During a recession, firms reduce investment expenditure, resulting in a fall in the capital stock. This has the effect of leaving the marginal productivity of, and hence the demand for, labour permanently lower than it would otherwise have been.

I

identification problem. A problem that arises in REGRESSION ANALYSIS when it is difficult to identify the relationships between variables because they change simultaneously, e.g. when a change occurs in both supply and demand conditions, each of which could result in a change in price.

identity. *See* ACCOUNTING IDENTITY.

idle balances. Idle balances or idle money is money that is not on DEPOSIT, invested in other FINANCIAL ASSETS, or held for TRANSACTIONS purposes. J.M. Keynes identified the SPECULATIVE motive as one reason for holding idle money.

idle money. *See* IDLE BALANCES.

illiquidity. A situation in which assets cannot be quickly turned into money.

immobility of factors. Land is almost entirely immobile by nature. Labour may be occupationally or industrially immobile because of a lack of the skills and abilities required by those firms with job vacancies, or because workers do not have the qualifications or experience demanded by the government, employers, professional associations or trade unions. Labour may be geographically immobile because of a lack of suitable housing in areas of labour shortage, or because of family ties or responsibilities. Other factors contributing to labour immobility are the existence of unemployment benefit and other social security benefits, and ignorance about job vacancies. Capital is the most mobile factor of production, but its mobility may be reduced by ignorance about profitable opportunities for investment, or by government restrictions on the flow of investment funds.

impact effect. The immediate effect of a change in a variable. The term occurs most often in analysing the consequences of an increase in demand. It is assumed that supply will not respond immediately, i.e. the very short run SUPPLY CURVE is vertical. The increase in price is therefore greater than it is in the longer term when supply is more ELASTIC.

imperfect adaptation. It is sometimes said that borrowers benefit, and lenders lose, from inflation. But if this is so, it is due to the fact that the price of credit adapts imperfectly to inflation. If for every 1 per cent rise in inflation, the interest rate rose by 1 per cent, as suggested by the Fisher hypothesis, the impact of inflation on lenders and borrowers would be neutral.

imperfect competition. When there is imperfect competition the firm's demand curve is downward sloping, i.e. in order to sell more the firm must reduce its price. There are three broad types of imperfectly competitive market: MONOPOLY, in which there is a single supplier, OLIGOPOLY, in which a few firms account for a large share of the market, and MONOPOLISTIC COMPETITION, in which there are a large number of suppliers of differentiated products.

imperfect information. *See* INFORMATION.

imperfect substitutes. Products are imperfect substitutes when they are perceived as different by purchasers. Different products are usually highly imperfect substitutes (if they are substitutes at all), e.g. air and rail travel. Different brands of the same product, e.g. two branded washing powders, will usually be seen as closer but still imperfect substitutes. The same would apply to two identical products sold under different conditions, e.g. with different levels of before- and after-sales service. When all the substitutes for a firm's product are imperfect, the DEMAND CURVE for that product slopes down from left to right.

implicit contract theory. This theory, developed in particular by M.N. Bailey and C. Azariadis, attempts to explain why wages are not more responsive to fluctuations in demand. Workers are assumed to be RISK-AVERSE and therefore to dislike the substantial variations in income that would occur if their pay was linked to their marginal revenue productivity at every stage of the business cycle. They prefer to be paid less than the value of their marginal product in periods of high labour demand (the income foregone acting as an 'insurance premium'), in return for being paid more than the value of their marginal product (an insurance payment) at other times. Employers are assumed to be happy to provide this insurance and smooth workers' incomes over the business cycle, provided that they receive an adequate return, i.e. provided that their wage bill is below what it would be if wages fluctuated freely over the cycle.

implicit cost. Another term for IMPUTED COST.

import compression. A country may attempt to remedy a current deficit on the BALANCE OF PAYMENTS by adopting either export expansion or import compression policies, the latter usually entailing a reduction in AGGREGATE DEMAND.

import deposits. In order to discourage imports a government may require importers to deposit a percentage of the value of their imports with the government. This is in effect a tax on imports for the period of the deposit at the rate of the percentage deposit required multiplied by the rate of interest. The scheme also reduces the LIQUIDITY of importers.

import duties. *See* TARIFFS.

import licence. A document giving an importer the right to import the products to which the licence refers. Import licences can be used to restrict imports, e.g. by limiting the number of licenses issued or by imposing bureaucratic procedures to slow their issue.

import penetration. The percentage of consumption accounted for by imports.

import quota. *See* QUOTA.

import restrictions. A wide variety of measures may be adopted in order to restrict imports, including TARIFFS, QUOTAS, IMPORT LICENCES and IMPORT DEPOSITS. These restrictions might be imposed to protect domestic industries and so maintain employment, or to correct a BALANCE OF PAYMENTS deficit.

import substitution. The domestic production of goods to replace imports. Import substitution has been undertaken by many developing countries as they have begun to industrialize.

import surcharge. A temporary increase in TARIFFS to correct a short-term BALANCE OF PAYMENTS deficit.

import tariffs. *See* TARIFFS.

imports. Goods and services purchased by the residents of one country which have been produced in other countries.

impossibility theorem. *See* SOCIAL-WELFARE FUNCTION.

imputed cost. The cost of using an asset owned by the user. The asset might be the owner's time, and the imputed cost would be the income that the owner could earn by using his time in another way, i.e. the opportunity cost. The same principle would apply to the use of other assets such as profits ploughed back into the business and premises owned by the business.

imputed income. *See* INCOME.

in the Bank. When the DISCOUNT HOUSES borrow money from the BANK OF ENGLAND, acting as LENDER OF LAST RESORT, they are said to be 'in the Bank'.

inactive money. *See* IDLE BALANCES.

incentive contracts. Contracts between principal and agent, e.g. employer and employee, which are an incentive to the agent to perform satisfactorily. The contract may be fully specified, e.g. piecework at an agreed rate, or implicit, e.g. that satisfactory performance in one grade will lead to promotion to a higher grade within a given number of years.

incidence of taxation. The incidence of taxation indicates where the burden of taxation is ultimately borne. For example if a tax is placed on a product, the price of the product may rise by the full extent of the tax, by less than the tax, or not at all. In the first instance the purchaser bears the full burden of the tax, in the last instance the producer bears the full burden, in the remaining instance the burden is shared.

income. A flow of money (or benefits in kind) to an economic agent. Income is usually a reward for the use of assets: wages and salaries for the use of workers' time and abilities, interest for the provision of temporary capital (lending), profits for the provision of permanent capital (dividends paid to shareholders), rent for the renting of land and premises. But there are several exceptions to this rule; TRANSFER PAYMENTS, e.g. unemployment benefit, are paid without any service being given by the recipient. The same applies to gifts. Finally, economists may impute income to the use of assets even when there is no flow of money. The item rent in the UK NATIONAL ACCOUNTS includes income imputed to people who occupy their own houses. Government statisticians provide several definitions and measures of income. Original income comprises earnings from employment and self-employment, plus occupational pensions and annuities, plus investment income (including income from property), plus other income, e.g. alimony, imputed income from rent-free accommodation. Adding cash benefits, e.g. state retirement pensions, to original income gives gross income. Subtracting income tax and employees' national insurance contributions from gross income gives disposable income. Subtracting all indirect taxes, e.g. value added tax, gives income after cash benefits and all taxes. Finally, adding benefits in kind, e.g. education, health, gives final income.

income, distribution of. *See* DISTRIBUTION OF INCOME.

income approach. *See* NATIONAL INCOME ACCOUNTING.

income consumption line. In INDIFFERENCE CURVE ANALYSIS the income consumption line or curve joins points of tangency of indifference curves to budget lines. The path traced by the income consumption line shows the effect of changes of income on consumption.

income effect. A change in the price of a product causes a change in consumers' REAL INCOME and therefore in their demand for goods and services. The size of the income effect depends upon the percentage of expenditure accounted for by the product whose price changes, and the size of the price change.

income elasticity of demand. The proportionate (or percentage) change in the quantity of a product demanded, divided by the proportionate (percentage) change in income. Products for which IED is positive are called normal goods. Within this category, if IED exceeds one demand is said to be income elastic; if IED is between zero and one demand is said to be income inelastic. Products for which IED is negative are called inferior goods.

income expansion path. In INDIFFERENCE-CURVE ANALYSIS the income expansion path shows how the chosen combination of goods varies as the consumer's income changes.

income tax. A tax levied on income. In the UK income tax is levied on income from employment, pensions, investment income and the profits of the self-employed (including partnerships), and accounts for over a quarter of total receipts from TAXATION. Taxable income is calculated after deducting personal and dependent's allowances (usually index-linked), certain life assurance contributions, and interest payments on mortgages up to £30 000. The personal allowance is currently £3445, and a married couple, or a lone parent, can claim an additional allowance of £1720. The tax is progressive, since the personal allowance means that no tax is paid on the first slice of income, and also because the rate of tax increases as taxable income increases (at present there are three bands, taxed at 20, 25 and 40 per cent). In recent years the top rate of income tax has been reduced in a number of countries, partly on the grounds that high tax rates are a disincentive to effort and risk-taking, and also lead to more tax avoidance and evasion. There seems to be some evidence to support this view, although in principle higher tax rates could lead to more effort, as workers have to work harder in order to maintain their living standards.

income terms of trade. *See* TERMS OF TRADE.

incomes policy. *See* PRICES AND INCOMES POLICIES.

incorporation. Formation of a company.

increasing-cost industry. *See* DECREASING RETURNS TO SCALE.

increasing returns to scale. Increasing returns to scale exist if, when the SCALE OF ORGANIZATION is increased by increasing all INPUTS in the same proportion, OUTPUT increases by a bigger proportion. An implication of increasing returns to scale is that the long-run SUPPLY CURVE is downward sloping. If all firms in an industry experience increasing returns, we speak of a decreasing cost industry.

independent variable. When two variables are linked or associated, a change in the independent variable leads to a change in the dependent variable. For example in a consumption function income would be the independent variable and consumption the dependent variable.

index fund. A fund – often a mutual fund such as a unit trust – which invests in the shares which make up a particular stock exchange index.

index-linked. *See* INDEXATION.

index number. An index number expresses data relative to the base year. It is conventional to give the index the value 100 in the base year; a value in a subsequent year of, say, 110 would mean that the variable had increased in value by 10 per cent. In principle the data may refer to a single item, but in practice it often refers to an average of many items, and these are usually weighted in accordance with their relative importance. For example, in constructing the RETAIL PRICE INDEX the weights used are the share of expenditure accounted for by each item. A Paasche or current-weighted index would use expenditure in the current period as weights. A Laspeyre or base-weighted index would use expenditure in the base period. These may, of course, give different answers, especially when a considerable number of years separates the base from the current period.

Table 16   Paasche and Laspeyre price index

	Share of expenditure in		Price in	
	base year	current year	base year	current year
Durables	10	15	100	150
Non-durables	60	45	100	130
Services	30	40	100	180

Paasche index	$15 \times 150 = 2\,250$
	$45 \times 130 = 5\,850$
	$40 \times 180 = \underline{7\,200}$
	$15\,300 \div 100 = 153$

Laspeyre index	$10 \times 150 = 1\,500$
	$60 \times 130 = 7\,800$
	$30 \times 180 = \underline{5\,400}$
	$14\,700 \div 100 = 147$

indexation. Tying the value of a variable to changes in an index of prices so as to maintain the real value of the VARIABLE (*See also* REAL VARIABLE). Variables whose values change in line with the retail price index include state retirement pensions, the occupational pensions of civil servants and local authority employees, and the interest paid on government index-linked stock. The threshold above which inheritance tax is payable is also index-linked unless in any particular year Parliament decides otherwise.

indicative planning. The formulation by the government of plans, for output, investment, etc., for the guidance of the private sector. Given that the plans of the various sectors of the economy are compatible, each sector should achieve the targets, provided that all other sectors do so. The first attempt at indicative planning in the UK was undertaken by the NATIONAL ECONOMIC DEVELOPMENT COUNCIL which published a number of reports discussing the implications, for the economy as a whole and for seventeen industries, of a 4 per cent growth rate. However the economy grew at a much slower rate, invalidating the whole exercise. The publication in 1965 of the National Plan represented a more extensive, but no more successful, planning exercise. Only ten months after its publication, an economic 'freeze' ensured that the projected growth rate would not be achieved.

indifference curve. An indifference curve joins points representing bundles of goods – one measured on the x axis and the other on the y axis – which would yield the consumer equal satisfaction, (the consumer is indifferent between these alternative combinations). Provided that the consumer prefers more of a product to less, i.e. that the marginal utility derived from the product is positive, a number of conclusions can be drawn about indifference curves. Two curves cannot intersect. If they did it would mean that the combination of goods represented by the point of intersection would give equal satisfaction to combinations on two indifference curves, one of which would represent more goods than the other, e.g. five apples plus three oranges and four apples plus three oranges. Indifference curves slope downwards, indicating that as the consumer gives up units of one product (measured, say, on the y axis), she will require more of the other product (measured on the x axis) to maintain the same level of satisfaction.

Moreover a DIMINISHING MARGINAL RATE OF SUBSTITUTION implies that indifference curves will be convex to the origin. (There are two exceptions to this rule. If two products are seen by the consumer as perfect substitutes the indifference curve is a downward sloping straight line. If the products are perfect complements the curve is L shaped, since an increase in the quantity of one product will not yield additional satisfaction unless the quantity of the other product is also increased.)

indifference-curve analysis. A method of analysing choice between two variables, subject to a constraint. The variables might be income and leisure, present and future consumption, etc. But the method is most commonly applied to the consumer's choice between two products. It leads to the (perhaps obvious) conclusion that price and quantity demanded are inversely related. Indifference-curve analysis is said to have an advantage over analysis based on MARGINAL UTILITY in that consumers, instead of having to place absolute values on the utility derived from a product (cardinal utility), need only perform the 'easier' task of ranking combinations of products in terms of more or less satisfaction (ordinal utility). (It is possible to be sceptical about this alleged advantage on the grounds that a cardinal measure of utility is required in order to carry out the ranking.) The basic tools of indifference-curve analysis are the indifference map, consisting of a large number of INDIFFERENCE CURVES, and the consumer's BUDGET LINE. The quantity of one product is measured on the x axis and the quantity of another product (or money income) is measured on the y axis. A change in the price of one product, the price of the other product (or money income) remaining unchanged, causes the budget line to cut the axis at a different point, and to become tangential to a different indifference curve. Successive points of tangency are joined to form a price consumption curve, an indicator of the shape of the consumer's demand curve.

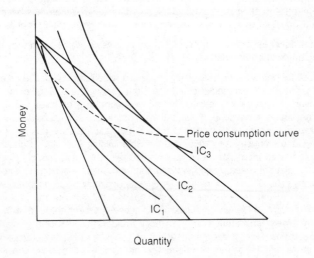

Figure 6   Indifference curves and the price consumption curve

indifference map. *See* INDIFFERENCE-CURVE ANALYSIS.

indirect costs. *See* COSTS.

indirect taxation. Taxation imposed on various forms of expenditure, e.g. VALUE-ADDED TAX, EXCISE DUTIES, stamp duty on the purchase of houses, vehicle-license duties. Indirect taxation accounts for almost half of the government's revenue from taxation, but it has two disadvantages. First, it is frequently REGRESSIVE. Second, the application of taxation at different rates to different products (one aim of which may be to make taxation less regressive) distorts RESOURCE ALLOCATION. Indirect taxes may be either SPECIFIC or AD VALOREM.

indivisibilities. If it is not possible to employ sufficiently small quantities of inputs to minimize AVERAGE COST whatever the level of output, indivisibilities are said to exist. Indivisibilities may apply to any input, but are very common in plant and equipment. An implication of indivisibilities is that an increase in output may well lead to a fall in short-run average cost.

induced expenditure. Expenditure which results from a change in autonomous expenditure. For example, an increase in government spending on road-building (autonomous expenditure) would lead to an increase in consumption (induced consumption) through the MULTIPLIER process. An increase in the propensity to consume, and hence in the level of consumption, would lead to an increase in investment (induced investment) through the operation of the ACCELERATION PRINCIPLE.

inductive method. The collection and consideration of data in order to arrive at generalizations or formulate HYPOTHESES.

Industrial and Commercial Finance Corporation. *See* INVESTORS IN INDUSTRY.

industrial democracy. The participation of employees in decision-making. This is most fully developed in producer CO-OPERATIVES. In West Germany employees elect members to the supervisory boards of large companies and there has been pressure to extend industrial democracy, in this and other forms, within the European Community.

industrial economics. The branch of economics concerned with the behaviour of firms and market performance.

industrial policy. Industrial policy includes a wide range of measures explicitly directed either at a particular sector of industry or at altering the sectoral composition of output. Government subsidies, especially for investment, may be given to industries in danger of decline, e.g. because of international competition. The subsidies may be tied to the scrapping of excess capacity and the reorganization of the industry, as was done under the Cotton Industry Act, 1959, and the Shipbuilding Act, 1967. Subsidies may also be given to new industries, especially where their success is thought to depend upon the exploitation of research and development, e.g. micro-electronics, fibre-optics, biotechnology. The British Technology Group was originally given government funds in order to help inventors and researchers to market their inventions and innovations. The government also assists research and development through work undertaken in government laboratories, and indirectly through the financing of work undertaken in universities. One of the purposes of INDICATIVE PLANNING as practised in the UK has been to remove or reduce information deficiencies, especially concerning plans and targets in other sectors. The government maintained until 1992 a structure for the gathering and dissemination of information under the auspices of the NATIONAL ECONOMIC DEVELOPMENT COUNCIL. NATIONALIZATION and PRIVATIZATION, and the regulation of nationalized and newly privatized industries, are also sometimes classified under the heading of industrial policy.

industrial property rights. Patents, brand names and copyright, which give protection and legal redress against theft.

industrial sector. *See* SECTORS OF THE ECONOMY.

industrial union. A trade union whose members all work within one industry, e.g. the National Union of Mineworkers.

industrialization. A substantial increase in the proportion of resources devoted to manufacturing. Industrialization has been the key to rapid industrial growth in some less developed countries, e.g. South Korea.

industry. The Standard Industrial Classification classifies industries on the basis of the products made, but with particular reference to the materials used rather than the markets supplied. For example plastic buckets are classified under plastics, metal buckets under metal working, and wooden buckets under wood products, although all three products are sold in the same market. Economic theorists have sought definitions that could be more readily used in the analysis of markets. In E.H. Chamberlin's theory of MONOPOLISTIC COMPETITION, a market or industry was a group of closely substitutable products. More recently K.J. Lancaster has focussed attention on the characteristics possessed by goods as a possible basis for delineating markets or industries.

inelastic. *See* ELASTICITY.

infant industry argument. If differences in efficiency in an industry are due solely to the fact that the industry is more mature in some countries than others, protection from international competition is justified for the less mature, or infant, industry. Being protected, the industry will be able to increase its efficiency to the point where it can compete on level terms. There are two weaknesses in this argument. First, competition can be a spur to increased efficiency, and this may be blunted by protection. Second, if an infant industry does become capable of competing on level terms, the protection may not be removed.

inferior good. *See* INCOME ELASTICITY OF DEMAND.

inflation. A sustained rise in the average price of goods and services. This simple definition conceals a considerable debate as to the most appropriate measure of the price rise. The most commonly quoted measure of price changes is the RETAIL PRICE INDEX, changes in which are known as the 'headline' rate or simply the rate of inflation. It has been suggested that a better measure of the underlying rate would be obtained by excluding mortgage interest payments from the RPI. The justification for this step would be threefold. First, when the government adopts a restrictive MONETARY POLICY in order to counter inflation and this leads to higher interest rates, inflation as measured by the RPI will, perversely, increase. Moreover the effect may be prolonged if the higher inflation leads to higher wage demands and so to still higher prices. Second, there is little evidence that mortgage interest rates have continued to rise over time, thus contributing to a sustained rise in prices. Third, inflation relates to a general rise in prices, and there is no evidence that mortgage interest rates rise in line with prices in general. So far the Retail Prices Index Advisory Committee, which advises the government, has not been persuaded by these arguments, although the debate continues. (Ironically the Committee has stated that the RPI is not a cost of living index, an index that would properly include mortgage interest payments.) In the meantime the Central Statistical Office publishes the 'underlying' inflation rate (the RPI stripped of mortgage interest payments and seasonal food prices). Another measure of inflation is the price of manufacturing output ('factory gate prices'). This can be a good indicator of future changes in the RPI, when the goods currently leaving the factory reach the consumer. Yet another measure, known as core inflation, is obtained by excluding from the price index of manufacturing output food (because of seasonal variability), drink and tobacco (because of their sensitivity to changes in excise duties). Finally, inflation can be defined as an excess of demand over supply at existing prices. This would usually lead to a rise in prices, but sometimes governments impose controls in order to try to prevent price rises. This situation is known as suppressed or repressed inflation.

inflation, theories of. Although several possible causes of inflation can be identified, economists differ as to their relative importance, especially in respect of the initial impetus to inflation. The simplest theories of inflation are that inflation is due to either (a) an excess of demand over supply at current prices (demand-pull inflation) or (b) a rise in costs, e.g. higher wages or imported raw materials, which leads to higher prices (cost-push inflation). Since there can be feedback between the prices of goods and of labour, the initial impetus can give rise to an inflationary spiral, the lead coming from either the price of goods (price-wage spiral) or of labour (wage-price spiral). Different theories of the causes of inflation lead to different conclusions as to what policies should be adopted in order to prevent or counter inflation. Some economists favour FIS-CAL and MONETARY POLICIES aimed at preventing excess demand. Within this group, monetarists, believing that inflation is a monetary phenomenon, emphasize the need to ensure a more steady and modest growth in the money supply. Other economists would put more more emphasis on PRICES AND INCOMES POLICIES.

inflation accounting. Accounting procedures which allow for changes in prices in an attempt to give a more accurate picture of changes in the firm's real profitability. These procedures include revaluing assets at current or replacement cost, and the LAST IN FIRST OUT method of valuing stocks. Official recognition of the validity of inflation accounting is given in a small way by allowing tax relief on profits arising from STOCK APPRECIATION.

inflation illusion. *See* MONEY ILLUSION.

inflationary gap. When AGGREGATE DEMAND exceeds AGGREGATE SUPPLY at the full employment level of output, an inflationary gap is said to ∍xist.

informal economy. *See* BLACK ECONOMY.

information. NEO-CLASSICAL economics assumes that economic agents have perfect information, e.g. that firms are fully aware of future demand and cost conditions when making price and output decisions. Having this information they are able to use marginal analysis in order to make decisions that maximize profits (or minimize losses). G. Stigler suggested that marginal analysis could be applied to situations in which agents do not have full information. He argued that they would search for information up to the point where the benefit received from the next piece of information was equal to the cost of finding it. More recently other economists, especially those of the AUSTRIAN school, have criticized this approach to information. Since by definition it is impossible to value information that has not yet been acquired, the marginalist approach advocated by Stigler cannot be used. However these economists are well aware of the benefits of acquiring new information. Indeed I. Kirzner sees the ENTREPRENEUR as a decision maker whose entire role arises out of his alertness to hitherto unnoticed opportunities. Information is often asymmetric, i.e. one agent has more information than another. Models have been developed which explore the implications of this situation, e.g. the likely outcome of wage bargaining when the employer has more information about the firm's profitability and liquidity than the trade union.

information agreements. Agreements between firms to exchange information on aspects of their business, e.g. costs, investment and output plans, and pricing decisions. Pre-notification agreements involve giving details of price (or other) changes before they occur, while in post-notification agreements details are given after the changes have been made. Information agreements might have socially beneficial effects, e.g. in enabling investment plans to be co-ordinated so as to avoid a shortage or excess of capacity, but some agreements, especially pre-notification agreements relating to price, are potentially anti-competitive. Indeed such agreements have sometimes been introduced when price-fixing agreements have been declared illegal. Since 1968 information agreements have been registrable in the same way as price-fixing agreements.

infrastructure. Infrastructure includes roads, railways, water, and telecommunications systems. Infrastructure aids economic development, and in less developed countries a shortage of private capital means that infrastructure projects are often publicly financed.

inheritance tax. Introduced instead of capital transfer tax in 1986, inheritance tax is levied on money left by people at death and on gifts made up to seven years before death. The term inheritance tax is misleading since it suggests that tax is levied on the amount inherited by one person, whereas it is levied on the total amount left by the donor. The tax is levied at a rate of 40 per cent on transfers above a minimum threshold, currently £150 000, which is INDEX-LINKED.

initial allowances. *See* CAPITAL ALLOWANCES.

injections. A highly simplified model of the CIRCULAR FLOW OF INCOME has two sectors, households and firms. Households supply inputs to firms who convert them into outputs, which are bought by the households out of the incomes received from the firms. A more comprehensive model includes other forms of spending, government spending, investment and exports, which act as injections to the circular flow.

innocent entry barrier. A BARRIER TO ENTRY into a market, not deliberately erected by existing suppliers, e.g. an absolute cost advantage over potential entrants.

innovation. The introduction by firms of new processes and products. Innovation is the application of inventions, and is the intended outcome of most expenditure on research and development.

input. A FACTOR OF PRODUCTION.

input-output analysis. An analysis of the flows of goods and services between sectors of the economy (including final consumption). This analysis makes it possible to trace throughout the economy the effects of a change, e.g. in costs, originating in one sector. It is used extensively in development planning.

insider trading. Some people obtain information, before the general public, that will affect the price of a company's shares, e.g. the board of directors becomes aware of changes in company profitability. If this advance price-sensitive information influences a decision to buy or sell shares, this is known as insider trading.

insiders. People who are in employment and therefore influence wage negotiations. A distinction is made between insiders and OUTSIDERS in some models of the labour market.

insolvency. A firm is insolvent when its total LIABILITIES, including EQUITY CAPITAL, exceed its ASSETS.

institutional economics. Economics which draws on observation of economic and social institutions, and analyses the role of these institutions in moulding preferences and guiding action. Institutional economists draw on the insights of a wide range of previous writers in the fields of economics and sociology including K. Marx, T.B. Veblen, G. Myrdal, J.M. Keynes and H. Simon.

institutional investors. The majority of shares, in many companies, are held by institutional investors: PENSION FUNDS, INSURANCE COMPANIES, INVESTMENT TRUSTS and UNIT TRUSTS. It is estimated that institutional investors account for over 80 per cent of the total value of shares listed on the London stock exchange, as compared to 30 per cent thirty years ago.

insurance. A contract whereby, in return for a premium or series of premiums, the insurer undertakes to pay a specified sum if a certain event occurs. The sum may be an absolute amount, e.g. some forms of medical insurance pay a given amount for each day spent in hospital, or it may vary in accordance with the disbenefit suffered, e.g. the value of house contents damaged by fire.

insurance broker. An individual (or firm) who sells insurance on behalf of insurance companies and who subsequently deals, again on behalf of the company, with any claims that arise.

insurance company. There are in the UK several hundred insurance companies which sell policies relating to both INSURANCE and ASSURANCE. They invest the premiums paid on these policies in various forms of income-yielding assets, e.g. government securities, shares, property, in order to ensure that they have a sufficient proportion of liquid assets to meet their liabilities, the sums promised in their contracts, when they become due. The UK is an international centre for insurance, and nearly half of the premium income of British insurance companies comes from overseas countries. This income constitutes an important part of the UK's invisible earnings on the BALANCE OF PAYMENTS.

intangible assets. Assets such as goodwill and reputation, included within a company's FIXED ASSETS.

integration. *See* GROWTH OF THE FIRM.

intellectual property. Intellectual property consists of ideas which have commercial value. These ideas may be expressed in designs, computer programs, textbooks, etc. The protection of intellectual property rights was one of the issues discussed in the Uruguay round of talks sponsored by the GENERAL AGREEMENT ON TARIFFS AND TRADE.

Inter-American Development Bank. Established to give financial assistance to the developing countries of Latin America and the Caribbean, the Bank now has twenty-five members in those areas plus others in North America, Europe and the Far East. It provides finance on commercial terms and as SOFT LOANS. About a quarter of its funds have been used to finance energy projects.

inter-bank market. The market in which banks lend to each other on a wholesale, unsecured basis.

inter-company market. Loans that are made between companies without going through a financial intermediary.

intercept. The point at which a line cuts an axis.

interdependence. When a large proportion of a market is shared among a few large firms, i.e. in OLIGOPOLY, the firms are interdependent. Each firm, recognizing that other firms will be affected by, and respond to, its actions, takes these reactions into account in making decisions.

interest. The payment made by a borrower for the use of capital. The rate of interest is expressed as a percentage of the sum borrowed or outstanding.

interest, theories of. Several theories to explain the rate of interest have been formulated. In theories originating in CLASSICAL ECONOMICS the rate is determined by the interaction of the demand for, and supply of, funds. (The loanable funds theory was developed most fully by K. Wicksell, a Swedish economist, in the early twentieth century.) The strength of demand is related to businessmen's expectations regarding profits, which in turn are influenced by the MARGINAL EFFICIENCY OF INVESTMENT. Supply is dependent on decisions to save, which are in turn influenced by people's TIME PREFERENCE. For other economists time preference is the major determinant of the rate of interest. Putting this the other way round, the abstinence theory sees interest as a payment for abstaining from current consumption. The higher is people's valuation of consumption now as compared to future consumption, the higher will be the rate of interest. Productivity theories of interest emphasize the yield from investment. Present goods (including CAPITAL GOODS) are worth more than FUTURE GOODS, and there must therefore be a positive rate of interest by which the two are equated.

interest cover. The number of times the interest on a firm's LOAN CAPITAL could be paid out of its EARNINGS.

interest rate. *See* INTEREST.

interest swaps. Interest swaps involve an exchange of (a) the income streams yielded by two different assets or, more frequently, (b) obligations to service loans, especially as between fixed and floating cost borrowing. A small company might wish to borrow at a fixed rate but finds that the cost of a small issue of bonds would be prohibitive. It can arrange an equivalent amount of floating rate borrowing, e.g. from a bank, and 'swap' this obligation with a larger company which is able to issue bonds at a lower cost. For being enabled in effect to enter the fixed-rate market the smaller company will pay the larger company a fee. Swaps can also be used for HEDGING and for SPECULATION.

interim dividend. *See* DIVIDEND.

interlocking directorates. An exchange of directors between companies, a possible means of enabling the companies to co-ordinate their activities.

intermediate areas. *See* REGIONAL POLICY.

intermediate goods. Intermediate goods or products are used in the process of producing final goods, e.g. flour which is used by a bakery to make bread.

intermediate targets. Government policy can be seen as comprising instruments which have an impact on intermediate targets which help to achieve policy objectives. For example, the Bank of England might raise the price at which it makes money available to the banking system (instrument) in an attempt to restrict the money supply or to cause a general rise in interest rates (intermediate targets) in the belief that this would cause a fall in the rate of inflation (policy objective).

intermediate technology. In many instances LESS DEVELOPED COUNTRIES benefit most from the introduction of new methods of production which are more advanced technologically than existing methods but less advanced than methods used in mature economies. The advantage of this intermediate technology over the most advanced technology is that it is often less CAPITAL and more LABOUR INTENSIVE, and requires a less highly trained labour force. In these ways it fits better with the FACTOR ENDOWMENTS of less developed countries.

internal balance. A country is in internal balance when AGGREGATE DEMAND is just sufficient to absorb FULL EMPLOYMENT OUTPUT.

internal capital market. The allocation of a firm's funds among competing projects. Those submitting the projects act as ENTREPRENEURS, and if the internal capital market is to function efficiently, the firm should institute a system that rewards entrepreneurial success, e.g. by promotion, bonus payments, etc.

internal costs. *See* PRIVATE COSTS.

internal economies of scale. *See* ECONOMIES OF SCALE.

internal-external balance model. A model which demonstrates the inter-relationships between macroeconomic policy objectives relating to full employment and price stability (internal balance), and balance of payments equilibrium (external balance).

internal finance. *See* BUSINESS FINANCE.

internal labour market. An internal labour market indicates that a firm has largely insulated itself from the external labour market by recruiting only at certain (usually low) job levels and filling senior posts by internal promotion. When appointed, workers are allocated to a certain level in the hierarchy and paid the appropriate wage. The co-operation of workers is encouraged by establishing clear promotion routes.

internal market. The Single European Act 1987 provided for the completion of the internal market within the European Community by the end of 1992. For this to be achieved a large number of measures were required including: the removal of physical barriers, e.g. customs formalities, immigration control procedures; the removal of technical barriers, e.g. differences in legal frameworks concerning the selling of financial services, nationality requirements for public sector jobs; the removal of fiscal barriers, e.g. differences in the coverage and rates of value added tax.

internal rate of return. The internal or DCF rate of return of a project is the rate of discount at which the present value of future net cash inflows would equal the initial cash outflow (the amount invested). This can be expressed as:

$$CO = \sum \frac{NCI}{(1+r)^n}$$

where CO is the cash outflow,
          NCI is the net cash inflow
          n is the number of years that elapses, after the cash
             outflow, before a given cash inflow is received
          r is the internal rate of return.

If the rate of return exceeds the company's COST OF FINANCE, the project would lead to an increase in the company's NET WORTH. Consider the following example, the purchase of wine to be stored (at zero cost) for one year and then to be re-sold. This gives us the simplest possible form of the expression:

$$CO = \frac{NCI}{(1+r)}$$

If the cost of the wine was £100 000 and the estimated re-sale price was £120 000 we would have:

$$£100\,000 = \frac{£120\,000}{(1.2)}$$

i.e. the internal rate of return would be 20 per cent. If the firm's cost of capital was less than 20 per cent, the investment would leave it better off. (If the pattern of cash flows is so erratic that a net cash outflow occurs in more than one period, there is more than one rate of return, and this may make the above rule less easy to apply.) The internal rate of return is also known as the marginal efficiency of capital (marginal referring to the project in question), the marginal productivity of capital, and the marginal efficiency of investment.

internalization. Conducting transactions within a firm rather than through the market. VERTICAL INTEGRATION is a prime means of internalization.

International Bank for Reconstruction and Development. The IBRD which, like the International Monetary Fund, was established at the 1944 Bretton Woods conference, began operations in 1946. The membership of the Bank is similar to that of the IMF. The IBRD is popularly known as the World Bank and this title is used by the IBRD itself to describe collectively the IBRD and its affiliates, the International Development Association, the International Finance Corporation, and the Multilateral Investment Guarantee Agency. Members subscribe to the Bank roughly in accordance with the size of their economies, but its major source of funds is borrowing on world markets. The interest charged on IBRD loans is therefore market-related, although it is able to borrow on the best commercial terms. IBRD loans are made either to governments or under government guarantee for a wide range of development and welfare purposes, mainly to the better-off (income per head up to $4300) LESS DEVELOPED COUNTRIES. New loans totalled $16 000 millions in 1991. When the Bank lends money to assist a country's development it tries to ensure that the country concerned has a programme designed to reduce poverty. Such a programme would involve policies to make use of the country's most abundant asset, labour, together with the provision of social services, especially primary education, basic health care, family planning facilities and advice on nutrition. There was initially a clear distinction between the work of the Bank and the IMF. The Bank was concerned with microeconomic development by means of specific projects in agriculture or manufacturing. The IMF was concerned with macroeconomic issues and especially balance of payments problems. However this distinction is now less clear. In recent years the IBRD's lending policies have evolved in a way which has brought them closer to those of the IMF. It has introduced programme lending, not tied to specific projects, to support development programmes in countries with short-term foreign exchange difficulties. It has also begun to participate in joint operations with the commercial banks. The aim of this co-operation is to provide loans with longer maturities than would normally be available directly from private sources and, by strengthening investors' confidence, to promote an increase in capital flows.

international commodity agreements. These agreements are designed either to raise or to stabilize the price of primary commodities, e.g. cocoa, tin. The agreements have attempted to achieve these aims by means of either export QUOTAS, which reduce supply, and/or BUFFER STOCKS, which try to maintain a balance between demand and supply at around the target price. Most agreements have been short-lived, either because of the difficulty of gaining the co-operation of all the producer countries, or because consumer countries were unwilling to bear the increasing cost of operating the agreement.

International Development Association. An affiliate of the International Bank for Reconstruction and Development, the IDA provides loans at low or zero interest for projects in the poorer LESS DEVELOPED COUNTRIES (income per head up to $750), that would not be feasible if finance had to be obtained at normal commercial rates. These projects often have a long life and are capital intensive, e.g. roads, power supplies. New loans totalled $6000 millions in 1991.

International Energy Agency. The aims of the IEA, founded in 1974, are to reduce member countries' dependence on oil supplies, protect them against the disruption of oil supplies, and develop a stable international energy market. Member countries agree to hold certain stocks of oil, and during the Gulf war the IEA authorized the release of stocks and the introduction of demand-cutting measures in order to put pressure on prices which had risen sharply after the invasion of Kuwait.

International Finance Corporation. This affiliate of the International Bank for Reconstruction and Development was established mainly to stimulate the provision of private-sector assistance to the LESS DEVELOPED COUNTRIES. In addition to making loans, the IFC can hold shares in companies.

International Labour Organization. Set up in 1919, the ILO became affiliated to the United Nations in 1946. Among its aims is the improvement of working conditions, and to this end it has drawn up a labour code. The ILO provides technical assistance to LESS DEVELOPED COUNTRIES with regard to training.

international liquidity. International liquidity can be narrowly defined as the quantity of gold, RESERVE CURRENCIES and SPECIAL DRAWING RIGHTS available to finance international trade. It can also be broadly defined as these items plus measures agreed by various countries which serve to increase the liquidity of particular countries at particular times, e.g. the GENERAL ARRANGEMENTS TO BORROW, Eurocurrency swaps.

international monetarist position. *See* MONETARISM.

International Monetary Fund. The IMF was established at the 1944 Bretton Woods conference to oversee the new system of fixed but adjustable exchange rates, to develop the system by encouraging the elimination of exchange restrictions and to ensure that the system remained stable by providing temporary loans to countries suffering balance of payments difficulties. The Fund now has 168 members, and when all the countries of the former Soviet Union have joined, virtually every country of any size will be a member. Members' quotas are related to the size of their economies, trade and foreign currency reserves. A member's quota determines its contribution to the Fund, the amount it can borrow, and its voting rights. Seventy-five per cent of a member's contribution is paid in the member's own currency and twenty-five per cent in RESERVE CURRENCIES. (In addition the Group of Ten provide further resources under the GENERAL ARRANGEMENT TO BORROW.) The IMF has also from time to time provided an increase in international liquidity through the issue of SPECIAL DRAWING RIGHTS. These are in effect entries in members' bank balances and can be used for settlements between central banks and with the IMF. The main use of IMF funds was initially to help countries to deal with temporary BALANCE OF PAYMENTS difficulties without resorting to excessive deflation, protection or competitive devaluations. It provides short-term financial assistance, usually at market rates, to such countries, normally on condition that they adopt policies to improve their balance of payments. In some instances these policies require government action, e.g. monetary or fiscal measures to reduce demand. But in other instances, and especially in its structural adjustment programmes, the IMF has required a reduced state involvement in the economic life of the nation. This type of assistance has become less important for two reasons. On the one hand, some countries have increasingly met their need for temporary assistance by borrowing from commercial banks without needing to submit to the policy conditions imposed by the IMF. On the other hand some members were unable to pay market rates of interest or repay loans within the usual timescale. To meet the needs of this second group of countries, most of which are in Sub-Saharan Africa, the Fund developed a number of facilities to provide loans on highly concessional terms with long repayment periods: the Trust

Fund, the Structural Adjustment Facility and the Extended Structural Adjustment Facility. The IMF has also acted as mediator in negotiations between less developed countries which have difficulty in repaying loans and the banks from which they have borrowed. The banks have re-scheduled their lending and the IMF has provided additional funds, both on condition that the borrowers implemented an austerity programme. IMF lending programmes are now in place in fifty countries. However, repayments to the Fund exceeded new lending for the first time in 1987, leading to renewed criticism of the IMF's operations by some Third World countries. These countries want a further lengthening of maturities and easing of lending conditions, subsidies to reduce the interest cost to poor countries borrowing from the Fund, and an increased allocation of SDRs, made according to need rather than quota, thus using the SDR as a form of aid.

International Standard Industrial Classification. *See* STANDARD INDUSTRIAL CLASSIFICATION.

international trade. Trade in goods and services between two countries (bilateral trade) or more than two (multilateral trade). Neo-classical economics suggests that total welfare will be maximized when international specialization and trade take place in accordance with the principle of COMPARATIVE ADVANTAGE. But the operation of this principle is hindered by various forms of protection, e.g. tariffs, quotas, voluntary export restraints. The reduction of these trade barriers is a major objective of the GENERAL AGREEMENT ON TARIFFS AND TRADE. International trade may also be inhibited by a shortage of INTERNATIONAL LIQUIDITY, a matter which has engaged the attention of the INTERNATIONAL MONETARY FUND. Post-Keynesian and Marxian economists suggest that the pattern of international trade reflects the outcome of institutional factors, and especially the impact of colonization on the economic structures of countries. They would see little advantage for poor countries in maintaining the present international division of labour.

intervention. Any measure adopted by the government which affects the operation of market forces. Intervention may either interfere with the operation of market forces, e.g. the imposition of a TARIFF which causes the price of imports to rise, or improve the operation, e.g. when a takeover that would reduce competition is prevented.

intra-industry trade. International specialization and trade within a given industry, e.g. British cars are sold in Germany and German cars in Britain. This trade exists because different brands of a given product are seen as incorporating different bundles of characteristics which meet the wants of different consumers. As incomes have grown, consumers have become able to pay to have their wants satisfied more exactly, and intra-industry trade has increased as a proportion of the total. On the supply side, a desire to obtain economies of scale provides an incentive for intra-industry trade.

inventories. Another term for stocks of raw materials, components, semi-finished and finished goods. Increases in inventories are a form of INVESTMENT.

inventory investment cycle. When fluctuations in the level of inventories have a regular pattern there is said to be an inventory investment cycle. Since there is an OPPORTUNITY COST of holding inventories, firms seek to reduce their level by such methods as just-in-time delivery. But having done so, they try to maintain a constant inventory-output ratio. This means that planned inventories would change in line with output, and that the inventory investment cycle would coincide with the BUSINESS CYCLE. However inventories may not change as planned. Because of imperfect information, lags in ordering, etc. the first effect of an increase in output may be a fall in inventories. Conversely a fall in output may lead to a rise in inventories.

inverse relationship. If a relaticnship is inverse, or negative, an increase (decrease) in one variable is associated with a decrease (increase) in another variable.

investment. Investment is expenditure on investment goods, i.e. physical assets that produce a stream of services, e.g. machinery, buildings, roads, raw materials. If NET INVESTMENT is positive it results in an expansion of economic CAPACITY, i.e. it enables more goods and services to be produced in future periods. Expenditure on the purchase of shares etc. (financial or portfolio investment) is often referred to as investment, but would not be classified as such by the economist because it does not add to economic capacity.

investment allowances. *See* CAPITAL ALLOWANCES.

investment appraisal. The examination of the expected revenues and costs of investment projects in order to decide which projects (if any) should be undertaken. The main methods of investment appraisal are the INTERNAL (DCF) RATE OF RETURN, NET PRESENT VALUE, and PAYBACK METHODS.

investment demand schedule. A firm's demand for investment funds depends upon the cost of those funds and the potential rates of return of projects for which those funds might be used. The investment demand schedule is a table or line on a graph showing the volume of investment opportunities with differing potential rates of return. For any firm there are a few projects that appear likely to yield very high returns and far more projects with potentially lower returns. The potential yield from any project can be influenced by a large number of factors. For example, an increase in national income is likely to increase the yield from many projects, thus causing the investment demand schedule to change; when expressed in graphical form, an increase in national income would cause the schedule to shift to the right.

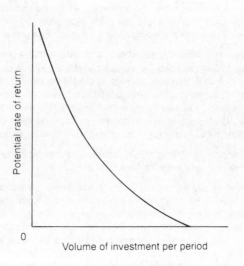

Figure 7 An investment demand schedule

investment expenditure. *See* INVESTMENT.

investment goods. *See* INVESTMENT.

investment incentives. *See* CAPITAL ALLOWANCES.

Investment Management Regulatory Organization. One of the self-regulatory organizations set up under the Financial Services Act 1986, IMRO oversees the operations of the managers of investment funds, e.g. the funds of pension schemes. Its failure to detect or prevent the theft of around £450 millions from the pension funds of the companies headed by Robert Maxwell led to the resignation of IMRO's chairman and some senior executives in 1992 and to calls for a review of the self-regulatory mechanism established under the 1986 Act.

investment schedule. A schedule showing the relationship between national income and the level of investment. It should not be confused with the INVESTMENT DEMAND SCHEDULE.

investment trust. A company which issues shares and fixed-interest securities and uses the money raised to buy shares in other companies. People buying shares in an investment trust are in effect buying into a much larger number of companies, thus spreading risk. Investment trusts are one of the largest forms of institutional investor, managing about twice the funds managed by unit trusts. Their management expenses are paid out of income received from investments. Some investment trusts UNDERWRITE new issues.

investments. An item in the balance sheets of many companies. The investments held by the commercial banks are mainly securities issued, or guaranteed, by the government, all of them having a fixed redemption date. The banks like to hold stocks with less than five years to run to maturity, although a few stocks with longer maturities might be held. Investments usually yield a higher rate of interest than more liquid assets, and involve less risk than advances. In other companies investments (sometimes called trade investments) can cover a wider range of securities, including fixed interest securities and shares held in other companies. The shares may be held purely for income or they might indicate that the company could in the future make a TAKEOVER bid.

Investors in Industry. Investors in Industry (3i) is the name taken in 1983 by Finance for Industry, a holding company formed ten years earlier. At present 3i is owned 85 per cent by the English and Scottish commercial banks and 15 per cent by the Bank of England, but a stock exchange flotation is planned for 1994. 3i provides investment funds through a number of subsidiaries, the most important being the Industrial and Commercial Finance Corporation which currently has investments (shares and loans) in about 4000 (mainly small and medium sized) companies. Many of these investments were made at a very early stage of a company's growth, when it was unable to raise sufficient finance from the banks or by the public issue of securities. Another 3i subsidiary, the Finance Corporation for Industry, performs a similar function for larger companies. In the year 1991–1992 3i made over 800 investments, totalling over £400 millions, bringing its total investments up to £2.6 billions.

invisibles. In the BALANCE OF PAYMENTS accounts, invisibles comprise: trade in services, e.g. insurance, travel; transfers, e.g. military and economic assistance provided by the government to other countries; interest, profits and dividends remitted from abroad. Subtracting payments made under these headings from payments received gives the invisible balance. This has invariably been positive in the UK.

invisible foot. The American economist Charles Tiebout has argued that local government should be organized in a large number of small areas, since this enables the

E

widest choice of combinations of taxation and spending. By moving between locations people find the combination which suits them best (the invisible foot), thus helping the efficient allocation of resources.

invisible hand. Adam Smith believed that the greatest benefit to society as a whole would result from allowing individuals freedom to pursue their own interests (the invisible hand). However, Smith recognized that the government would sometimes need to curtail this freedom, e.g. if it was used to restrict trade.

involuntary exchanges. Exchanges which one person would have preferred not to make. It is assumed that most EXCHANGE is voluntary, but it is difficult to determine which exchanges involving taxation and government expenditure are voluntary and which are involuntary.

involuntary saving. *See* FORCED SAVING.

involuntary unemployment. *See* UNEMPLOYMENT.

inward investment. Investment in one country financed by the residents of another country. It includes both PORTFOLIO and DIRECT INVESTMENT.

IOU money. A medium of exchange based on the debt of an individual or institution, e.g. a bank.

irredeemable securities. Securities which have no date for the repayment of the sum borrowed, e.g. CONSOLS. The stock is bought only for the interest received.

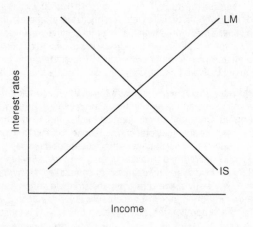

Figure 8   The IS-LM model

IS-LM model. A macroeconomic model showing the conditions under which the economy will reach equilibrium. The IS curve or schedule shows the different combinations of income and interest rates at which the goods market would be in equilibrium, and the LM curve (schedule) the combinations of income and interest rates compatible with equilibrium in the money market. The point at which these two curves intersect indicates the point of equilibrium. The model can also be used to show the effects of a change in any of the factors influencing either curve. For example, an increase in the real supply of money would, on certain assumptions, cause the LM curve to shift to the right, leading to a fall in the equilibrium rate of interest and a rise in the equilibrium level of income.

isocost line. A line showing alternative combinations of resources or inputs that could be acquired by a given outlay, the slope of the line reflecting the relative prices of the resources. Isocost lines can be used together with ISOQUANTS to identify the OPTIMUM combination of inputs.

isoproduct curve. *See* ISOQUANT.

isoquant. A line showing alternative combinations of inputs that could be used to produce a given output. Isoquants slope down from left to right because if less of one input is used, more of another input must be used in order to maintain output. They are also convex to the origin because the marginal product of each input diminishes as more of that input is used. The optimum combination of inputs that should be used for a given outlay is indicated by the point of tangency of the relevant ISOCOST LINE to an isoquant.

issued capital. That part of a company's capital that investors have subscribed to in exchange for the issue of shares. It may be the same as or less than the AUTHORIZED CAPITAL, and the same as or more than the PAID-UP CAPITAL.

issuing house. A merchant bank or other institution which organizes the raising of money by the issue of securities by clients. The issuing house advises on the terms and timing of the issue, and arranges the UNDERWRITING.

Issuing Houses Association. Represents the interests of issuing houses in discussions with the stock exchange, the Bank of England, etc.

J

J-curve. A curve, roughly J shaped, which depicts the changes in the BALANCE OF PAYMENTS current account following a devaluation of the currency. At first the current balance deteriorates. But with more time to adjust to higher import and lower export prices, the elasticities of demand increase, their sum becoming greater than one, leading to an improvement in the current balance.

job acceptance schedule. The number of workers who would choose to accept jobs at various real wage levels. This is less than the number in the labour force, the difference representing VOLUNTARY UNEMPLOYMENT.

job rationing hypothesis. The hypothesis that some firms attempt to cream the market by offering more than the going rate of pay and creating a job queue within particular occupations.

job search. Simple job search models suggest that a searcher's behaviour will be a function of the cost of the search and the dispersion of wages in the market in which search is undertaken. Some models assume that the worker chooses at random a certain number of firms, searches these firms and then takes the highest offer observed. But it can be shown that this fixed-sample rule is inferior to the sequential optimal-stopping rule when the searcher knows the distribution of job offers. Models incorporating the sequential rule assume that the individual searches one firm per period, and decides whether to take its job offer (if made) before searching any more firms.

jobcentres. Jobcentres, sponsored by the government, bring together employers with vacancies and people seeking work.

joint costs. Costs which are incurred in the production of two or more products, and which can be allocated among those products only on an arbitrary basis.

joint demand. Another term for COMPLEMENTARY DEMAND.

joint products. Products which are necessarily produced together, e.g. wool and lamb or mutton. It is impossible, except on an arbitrary basis, to allocate costs between products which are jointly supplied.

joint-stock banks. A term used occasionally to refer to COMMERCIAL BANKS.

joint-stock companies. *See* LIMITED COMPANIES.

joint supply. *See* JOINT PRODUCTS.

joint venture. A business formed by two or more companies (or other institutions).

junk bonds. Bonds issued by companies without any underlying assets as COLLATERAL SECURITY. Junk bonds have often been issued to raise money to finance a TAKEOVER bid.

just-in-time manufacture. In order to reduce INVENTORY levels, deliveries of components, etc. are received only shortly before being used in assembly operations.

K

Kaldor-Hicks test. *See* COST BENEFIT ANALYSIS.

Keynesian economics. A set of economic doctrines whose origins can be found in the work of J.M. Keynes. One of the major achievements of Keynes himself was to demonstrate the conditions under which the economy might reach EQUILIBRIUM at less than full employment. An implication of Keynes's analysis was that in this situation the government should increase public spending in order to increase AGGREGATE DEMAND. This policy has been advocated by many economists who have been influenced by Keynes. However it has been recognized that increased aggregate demand can lead to inflation, and in order to counteract this, some Keynesian economists have advocated the use of PRICES AND INCOMES POLICIES. Keynesian economics can be contrasted with CLASSICAL ECONOMICS the assumptions of which, especially the flexibility of prices, lead to the conclusion that the economy tends towards full employment equilibrium. These contrasting views were brought together in the neo-classical synthesis which, while maintaining that the economy does have a tendency to move towards full employment, at least in theory, accepts that in practice unemployment can persist on account of price rigidities and institutional inflexibility. Economists who would all accept the labels Keynesian or neo-Keynesian, hold different views of the importance of these rigidities and this inflexibility. Some see them as being likely to persist for very long periods, implying that vigorous and sustained DEMAND MANAGEMENT POLICIES are required if full employment output is to be achieved. (Since boosting demand may lead to balance of payments problems, these policies may have to be supplemented by temporary import controls.) Other Keynesians, assuming a greater degree of flexibility and being more concerned about the inflationary impact, advocate policies to boost demand for only much shorter periods. Keynes's emphasis on economics out of equilibrium has led into a brand of disequilibrium economics developed by R. Clower, A. Leijonhufvud and E. Malinvaud. These writers have argued that it is possible for disequilibrium to persist because of interactions between different sectors of the economy. If this is so, price flexibility is not guaranteed to bring about full employment. Another fairly recent development has been the search for convincing microeconomic explanations of price inflexibility, explanations based on the assumptions of utility maximization by individuals and profit-maximization by firms. (Economists working in this area have been variously labelled as neo-Keynesians and New Keynesians.) The explanations advanced include the IMPLICIT CONTRACT THEORY and the EFFICIENCY WAGE hypothesis, both relating to wages, and the shopping model, applied to PRICE STICKINESS in product markets.

Keynesian unemployment. *See* UNEMPLOYMENT.

kinked demand curve. A proposition of OLIGOPOLY theory that the demand curve for each firm's products is elastic in respect of price increases but inelastic in respect of price reductions. (This is explained by the hypothesis that each firm believes that rivals would match a price reduction but not a price increase.) This means that any price change would lead to a fall in revenue and that to maintain price is likely to be the most profitable policy. Moreover, because with a kinked demand curve the MARGINAL REVENUE curve has a discontinuous segment, an increase in MARGINAL COST would not necessarily lead to a change in the profit-maximizing price. For these reasons the kinked demand curve has been seen as explaining the alleged stickiness of prices in CONCENTRATED markets. However, empirical research suggests that when transaction, rather than list, prices are considered, it is doubtful whether prices are especially sticky in such markets.

Kondratieff cycle. N. Kondratieff, a Russian economist, claimed to have identified a BUSINESS CYCLE with a duration of fifty years. Extrapolating from Kondratieff's findings, we arrive at the conclusion that the last part of the twentieth century will be a period of low economic activity!

L

labour. A factor of production. Like the other factors, labour is not homogenous; different workers have different skills and abilities, either innate or acquired.

labour, demand for. Labour is demanded for its contribution to production, i.e. it is a derived demand. If the quantity of labour employed could be changed while the quantities of other factors remained constant, the contribution of labour, its MARGINAL REVENUE PRODUCT, could then be identified. Labour would be recruited up to the point where its MARGINAL COST equalled its marginal revenue product. This analysis assumes that the firm's aim is short-run profit maximization. Even if it is not possible to identify its marginal revenue product, and even if the firm takes a longer-term perspective, the demand for labour will still be influenced by its contribution to output in relation to the contribution and prices of other factors. So if, for example, the price of capital, e.g. machinery, increased, labour would be substituted for capital, i.e. production would become more labour intensive.

labour force. The number of people in employment plus the number available for work.

labour force schedule. The number of people who would be in the labour force at various real wage levels.

labour intensive. A process that uses a large amount of LABOUR in relation to other FACTORS OF PRODUCTION is said to be labour intensive.

labour-managed firm. A firm in which the workers appoint members of the workforce to manage the firm.

labour market. The set of arrangements whereby those demanding and those supplying labour are brought together, and agreements are made concerning the terms and conditions of employment. We can analyse the labour market for the economy as a whole, for an industrial or geographical sector, or for an individual firm.

labour market policies. Government policies to influence the operation of labour markets. These include a large number of measures, many of which could also be considered under other policy headings. One of the major aims of policy has been to increase the level of training, especially of young people (through the Youth Training Scheme) and other unemployed workers who do not have marketable skills. A variety of training schemes for the long-term unemployed have been launched, several of which were incorporated in Employment Training, launched in 1988. Over 200 000 people a year receive a combination of practical and classroom training for up to a year. (In November 1992 it was announced that Employment Training and the much smaller Employment Action programmes were to be combined in a new scheme, Training for Work.) In 1990 the first of a chain of eighty-two Training and Enterprise Councils began operation. The TECS (and the corresponding Local Enterprise Companies in Scotland), government funded and headed by local employers, cover an area with an average working population of around a quarter of a million, and their brief is to support the training and enterprise activities that are required to meet the demands of the local labour market. Local labour markets are also affected by the various forms of assistance provided as part of the government's REGIONAL POLICY. The Enterprise Allowance Scheme, under which unemployed workers starting up in business are paid an allowance during the first year, is most likely to have an impact in the area where the assistance is given. The efficiency of labour markets in general should be improved by the operation of JOBCENTRES. Labour markets are subject to the influence of trade unions, and governments have sought in recent years to reduce this influence and strengthen the rights of individual workers. The Trade Union Act 1984, and a series of Employment Acts passed in the 1980s: removed the legal protection for CLOSED SHOPS; required mandatory secret postal ballots for elections to union executives; required that proposed strike action should proceed only if supported by members in a ballot; restricted 'lawful trade disputes' to those between workers and their own employers, making 'political' strikes and inter-union disputes unlawful; declared secondary action, i.e. action against an employer not party to the dispute, to be unlawful. A number of Acts have sought to improve the position of women in the labour market, including the Employment Protection Act which made it easier for them to return to work after childbearing, the Equal Pay Act and the Sex Discrimination Act.

labour mobility. The ease with which workers can move from one occupation, industry or region to another. For the economy as a whole mobility is aided by the fact that there are constant flows of people entering the workforce, e.g. after completing their education, and leaving the workforce, e.g. on retirement. Governments have adopted a number of measures to increase labour mobility including subsidized training, the provision of assistance to workers moving to another part of the country in search of work, and encouraging employers and unions to reduce barriers to occupational mobility. Increased labour mobility is an important aim of SUPPLY-SIDE POLICIES.

labour supply. The supply of labour can be measured in several ways. The JOB ACCEPTANCE SCHEDULE and the LABOUR FORCE SCHEDULE both relate the number of workers to the real wage rate. More complex measures would take account of the quality of labour and the amount of effort supplied per worker.

labour theory of value. *See* MARXIAN ECONOMICS.

labour turnover. The number of employees leaving a firm in a year, as a percentage of total employees.

Laffer curve. A curve which implies that tax revenue will be maximized at moderate rather than very high or very low rates of tax. The curve is named after Arthur Laffer, an American economist who argued that the economy could be expanded without a BUDGET DEFICIT. Lower taxes would lead to lower prices, higher output (because lower direct taxes would reduce disincentives), and higher government revenue (partly because of the higher output, partly because of less tax avoidance). Although the evidence concerning Laffer's hypothesis is mixed, it provided theoretical support for the reductions in the top rates of tax that occurred in the USA and the UK in the 1980s.

lagged relationship. When the value of a variable in one period is associated with the value of another variable in another period. For example farmers' decisions about which crops to grow this year might be influenced by the relative prices of crops last year.

lagging indicators. *See* ECONOMIC INDICATORS.

lags. In analysis employing the COMPARATIVE STATICS approach, lags are not considered. But lags occur in many areas of economic activity and can sometimes have important consequences. For example in some models the level of INVESTMENT undertaken in a given period is assumed to be that required to bring the actual capital stock up to the desired level. But investment is usually an extended process, with substantial lags between recognition of the need and opportunity to invest and the decision to invest, between the decision and the start of investment expenditure, and between the start of expenditure and completion. Models which take account of such lags seem to predict investment expenditure better than simple stock-adjustment models. The conclusions drawn from models of OLIGOPOLY, especially those using GAME THEORY, depend heavily upon what a firm believes about lags in its rivals' reactions. On the one hand it may believe that rivals will match a price cut so quickly that purchasers are not aware of any change in price differentials (the assumption underlying the KINKED DEMAND CURVE). On the other hand it may believe that price cuts can be kept secret from rivals, especially if no list prices are published, or discounts from list prices are known only by its customers. If each firm holds this belief, a 'sticky prices' model becomes less appropriate.

laissez-faire. The limitation of government intervention in economic activity to the minimum required to ensure the efficient functioning of a FREE-MARKET ECONOMY. This view dominated CLASSICAL ECONOMICS, and has been prominent in the writings of F.A. Hayek (recently deceased) and the public choice school of economists, e.g. G. Tullock, J.M. Buchanan.

land. A factor of production, land includes (geographical) land, the oceans and outer space, together with the natural resources contained therein. In terms of surface area the supply of land is fixed. On the other hand the supply of natural resources, included within land, changes over time. The application of capital and labour can affect the quality of land, either for better (improved fertility through irrigation), or for worse (soil erosion, dust bowls).

land bank. Land that is taken out of production as farmers receive government compensation for output foregone.

Laspeyres index. *See* INDEX NUMBER.

last in first out. A method of valuing stocks. It is assumed that materials currently used are those last received into stock. This method ensures that changes in the prices of materials are quickly reflected in recorded costs.

lateral growth. *See* GROWTH OF THE FIRM.

launch aid. A government grant or subsidized loan given towards the cost of developing a new product.

law, economic. *See* ECONOMIC LAW.

law of one price. If there were no obstacles to trade, and transport costs were zero, the real price of a given product would be the same in all countries.

lay-off. A firm lays-off workers when it temporarily discontinues their employment.

leading indicator. *See* ECONOMIC INDICATORS.

leads and lags. Payments of debts incurred in international trade may be advanced (leads) or delayed (lags), in particular because the exchange rate is expected to change. For example, if American importers of British goods have agreed to pay in sterling they will pay early if the dollar is expected to fall in value, and late if it is expected to rise.

leakage between markets. Leakage between markets implies that customers are able to buy a product in one market and re-sell it in another, or that customers are able to

131

move from one market to another market in which the same product is sold. Where leakage is significant, PRICE DISCRIMINATION is less likely to be profitable.

leakages. Leakages or withdrawals from the CIRCULAR FLOW OF INCOME comprise SAVING, IMPORTS and TAXES.

learning curve. *See* LEARNING EFFECT.

learning effect. The first systematic observations of the learning or experience effect were made in the production of aircraft in the 1930s, and during the Second World War similar effects were observed in the production of the Liberty ships, the first of which took several months to build and the last only three days. Subsequent studies by the Boston Consulting Group of a wide range of manufacturing and non-manufacturing industries led them to conclude that average cost declined by 20 to 30 per cent each time accumulated production was doubled. (This relationship can be plotted as a learning curve.) The learning effect means that in each successive period a firm's average COST CURVE will be below its previous position and, other things being equal, below the average cost curve of potential entrants to the market. This cost differential can act as a BARRIER TO ENTRY.

lease. An agreement by the owner of an asset to allow another party (the lessee) to use it for a given period at a specified rent. Leases are commonly granted on premises (offices, shops etc.), vehicles and, to an increasing degree although still less frequently, machinery. Leases on premises are frequently subject to review, on terms specified in the original contract. In some instances, and especially in leases on equipment and machinery, the asset becomes the property of the lessee, perhaps for a nominal payment, when the lease expires. This is in effect a form of HIRE-PURCHASE.

leaseback. In a sale and leaseback agreement the owner sells an asset on condition that it is leased back for a specified period. The owners of property frequently make such agreements in order to release capital to be used for the repayment of debts, the expansion of the business, etc.

leasing. Renting assets, e.g. property, machinery. Leasing agreements may also provide for maintenance and servicing, enabling the lessee to concentrate on other aspects of the business. Leasing allows assets to be acquired when the leasee is not able to afford to purchase outright, or prefers to use CAPITAL in other ways.

least developed countries. Following a United Nations' definition, countries are classified as least developed on the basis of three indicators: low GROSS DOMESTIC PRODUCT, a small manufacturing base (relative to GDP) and a low literacy rate. The average income per head of the thirty-one countries so classified in 1980 (20 of which were in Africa) was only a quarter of that in other LESS DEVELOPED COUNTRIES.

least squares regression. *See* REGRESSION ANALYSIS.

legal tender. Legal tender comprises those means of payment which the courts will accept without question as discharge of a debt. In England and Wales these are Bank of England £5, £10, £20 and £50 notes plus £1 coins. Smaller value coins are legal tender only up to certain limits, e.g. 50p coins up to £10. In Scotland, only coins are legal tender, although banknotes are much used, often in preference to coins.

lender of last resort. An essential function of a CENTRAL BANK is the willingness to lend to the BANKING SYSTEM whenever required, (but on the Bank's terms). In countries other than the UK the central bank lends direct to the commercial banks, but in the UK the BANK OF ENGLAND provides money to the DISCOUNT HOUSES, either by lending on the security of bonds, or by rediscounting eligible paper (bills and short-term bonds). If the authorities wish to encourage a rise in interest rates they will provide this money at above MONEY MARKET rates. (Conversely, if rates of interest are high and the discount houses are experiencing difficulty, the government broker may buy bills from them at the market rate to ease the pressure on their LIQUIDITY, an operation known as 'the back door'.)

Lerner index. A.P. Lerner suggested that the degree of MONOPOLY in a market could be measured by: (price minus cost) divided by price.

less developed countries. No definition of less developed countries is entirely satis-factory. If we start from the economic characteristics of developed countries, in particu-lar a process of industrialization and a level of national income high enough to generate sufficient saving to finance the investment required for future economic growth, less developed countries can be defined as those which do not possess these characteristics. However this might include New Zealand which, until recently, had one of the highest living standards in the world. As an alternative to looking at the nature of the country's economy, one can classify countries on the basis of income. For example in 1985 the World Bank defined less developed countries as those with a GROSS NATIONAL PRODUCT per head of less than $400 in 1983. Not surprisingly, non-monetary indicators tend to move in line with income. For example countries with a low GNP tend to have a high infant mortality and a low level of literacy.

leverage. Another term for GEARING.

leveraged buyouts. Buyouts or TAKEOVERS in which a high proportion of the funds are borrowed. The funds might be borrowed short-term from the banks, the security for the loans being in effect the assets of the company bid for, or in exchange for the issue of JUNK BONDS (mezzanine finance).

liabilities. Amounts owing to others. Liabilities may be classified as fixed, e.g. mort-gages, long-term loans, and current, e.g. outstanding invoices, tax due.

licensed deposit-takers. LDTs, e.g. FINANCE HOUSES, are authorized by the Bank of England to take deposits from the public, but not to operate as banks.

licensing. The government may adopt a system of licensing in order to restrict entry into a market, e.g. the franchises granted to independent television companies. Since the licencees often have to meet certain conditions with regard to quality, safety, conti-nuity of supply, etc., a licensing system can also act as a means of control.

Life Assurance and Unit Trust Regulatory Organization. One of the self-regulatory organizations set up under the Financial Services Act 1986. LAUTRO, as its name suggests, oversees the operations of companies providing life assurance and running unit trusts.

life-cycle hypothesis. Developed by F. Modigliani and A. Ando, this theory implies that the main determinant of CONSUMPTION is average long-run income. The consumption of each household, including any gifts to children, is assumed to depend upon expected lifetime earnings. Individual households will spend more than their expected average income in some years, e.g. when raising a family in the early years of their career, and less in other years, e.g. when their children have left home. But in the population as a whole these deficits and surpluses tend to cancel out.

limit price. The highest price that an existing supplier can charge that would not be profitable for new suppliers.

limit pricing. When existing suppliers set the highest price that they can without attract-ing new suppliers into the market, they are practising limit pricing.

limited companies. A company is an organization that is legally allowed to produce and trade, and which has a legal existence apart from its owners. Most companies are limited (sometimes being known as joint-stock companies), denoting that the liability of the owners is limited to the money subscribed in buying shares, (including any still to be subscribed if the shares are not PAID UP). The worst that can happen is that the shares become worthless.

limited liability. *See* LIMITED COMPANIES.

linear programming. A mathematical technique for the solution of problems in which a maximum or minimum of a function is to be determined, subject to a set of constraints. For example in the refining of crude oil, where variations in the source of oil and in the refining process can alter the mix of outputs, linear programming can be used to identify the most profitable output mix from a given expenditure on materials and operating expenses.

linear relationships. A relationship between an independent and a dependent variable that would be best represented on a graph by a straight line.

linkages. Technical relationships between firms, e.g. the supply of components by one firm to another. Strong linkages encourage the geographical concentration of the industries in question.

liquid assets. Assets which can be converted quickly into money, with no or negligble consequential loss. These include MONEY MARKET loans, Treasury bills, bank and building society deposits on normal notice. (Cash is of course also a liquid asset.)

liquidation. The process by which a company ceases to exist, its assets being distributed among its creditors.

liquidity. Formally, liquidity refers to a firm's ability to meet its current obligations. A common measure of liquidity is the ratio of CURRENT ASSETS to CURRENT LIABILITIES. More generally, liquidity refers to the proportion of a firm's assets that are in the form of LIQUID ASSETS.

liquidity preference. As originally formulated by J.M. Keynes this referred to the holding of money in preference to bonds, but the concept was subsequently widened to include other assets in addition to bonds. Keynes assumed that the lower the rate of interest the more money (and the fewer bonds) people would wish to hold. This was partly because the opportunity cost of holding money would be low, and partly because a low rate of interest corresponds to a high price of bonds, increasing the probability that bond holders would suffer a capital loss due to a future fall in bond prices.

liquidity ratio. As part of the attempt to control the money supply the authorities have sometimes required the banks to keep a certain proportion of their assets in a liquid form. Both the proportion and the definition of liquid have varied.

liquidity trap. J.M. Keynes advanced the hypothesis that when the rate of interest had fallen to a certain level, further increases in the MONEY SUPPLY would be held by the public, i.e. would not be used to buy bonds, meaning that the interest rate would not fall further. There is little evidence of a liquidity trap, at least in the post-war period.

list price. The published price of a product, no allowance being made for discounts of any kinds.

listed company. A company that has obtained permission for its shares to be admitted to the STOCK EXCHANGE's official lists. For its shares to be listed and tradeable on the exchange, the company must be registered as a PUBLIC LIMITED COMPANY and at least a quarter of its shares must be made available for trading.

listed securities. Securities issued by LISTED COMPANIES.

Lloyd's. An incorporated society whose members offer insurance against a wide range of risks. The members or 'names' are organized into syndicates (a member may join one or more syndicates). Each syndicate is led by an underwriter who writes policies on behalf of the members, the policies being sold to clients by brokers. Members bear unlimited liability and in the early 1990s a considerable number of members suffered very heavy losses as substantial claims had to be met. This led to the setting up of a committee, under Sir David Walker, to enquire into the market's working practices. The committee found that the judgement of some underwriters had been seriously flawed and suggested improved forms of control that would limit the consequences should similar flaws occur in the future. A second committee, under Sir Jeremy Morse, also reported in 1992. It recommended sweeping changes in the governance of Lloyds, including the establishment of two supervisory bodies, a market board and a regulatory board.

loan. Money borrowed by an institution or individual. Loans can be secured or unsecured, short-term, long-term, or with no maturity date. The rate of interest on a loan depends upon the length of the loan, the credit-worthiness of the borrower and on general market conditions at the time that the loan is arranged.

loan capital. Another term for DEBENTURES.

loanable funds. *See* INTEREST, THEORIES OF.

local monopoly. *See* MONOPOLY.

local multiplier. *See* MULTIPLIER.

localized industry. An industry a large proportion of whose capacity is located in a few areas. A localized industry can take full advantage of LINKAGES and EXTERNAL ECONOMIES OF SCALE, but a decline in the industry can have serious economic and social consequences in the areas concerned.

location theory. Location theory is concerned with the factors which influence firms' location decisions. There are advantages in locating near to raw materials and to markets, but firms often have to choose one or the other (or a compromise). The greater the weight lost in the manufacturing process, the greater the incentive to locate near to the sources of raw materials. Conversely, the higher the ratio of weight or bulk to value, the greater the incentive to locate near to markets. LINKAGES provide an incentive to locate in existing centres of the industry. On the other hand market rigidities, especially with respect to labour, may be an incentive to locate away from existing centres. Improvements in communications can loosen ties both to sources of materials and labour and to the market. Empirical studies of location decisions suggest that firms carry out only a limited search in trying to identify a satisfactory, rather than the optimum, location. Moreover one factor may assume overwhelming importance in the choice of location, e.g. the need to offer a good quality of life to senior employees.

lockout. The exclusion of workers from the workplace by their employer.

Lombard rate. A lending rate of the Bundesbank which sets a ceiling for German money market rates.

Lomé conventions. A series of agreements signed at Lomé by the members of the European Community and the less developed countries in Africa, the Caribbean and the Pacific (the ACP states). Under these conventions all ACP industrial exports and most agricultural exports enter the Community duty free. These countries have also received assistance from two Community institutions, the European Development Fund and the European Investment Bank.

London derivatives market. This market actually comprises four markets: the LONDON INTERNATIONAL FINANCIAL FUTURES AND OPTIONS EXCHANGE, which accounts for about 66 per cent of transactions, the London Metal Exchange (21 per cent), the International Petroleum Exchange (9 per cent), and the London Futures and Options Exchange (4 per cent).

London inter-bank offer rate. The key rate at which banks lend to each other in the EUROCURRENCY and other INTER-BANK MARKETS. LIBOR is often used as a guide for interest rates on other loans.

London International Financial Futures and Options Exchange. A market in which a wide range of FUTURES and OPTIONS is traded, e.g. bonds in sterling, other currencies and the ECU, equity options. The trading floor's 1000 screens and 440 dealer board consoles are thought to form the world's biggest digital board system, with some 3000 lines.

long-dated securities. Securities with a maturity date many years ahead (many usually being interpreted as fifteen or more.)

long run. The long run is defined by economists not in terms of a particular number of years, but as the period in which all FACTORS OF PRODUCTION are variable, i.e. there is nothing to prevent the firm from changing the SCALE OF ORGANIZATION. Since all factors are variable, so too are all costs. Because firms can experience both ECONOMIES and DISECONOMIES OF SCALE, in principle the long-run average cost curve could be any shape. But it is usually assumed that average cost declines, as economies outweigh diseconomies, up the MINIMUM EFFICIENT SCALE of output. As output increases beyond that point average cost is constant at first, but eventually begins to increase as diseconomies outweigh any further economies.

long-run Phillips curve. *See* PHILLIPS CURVE, EXPECTATIONS AUGMENTED.

long-term unemployed. People who have been seeking work for at least twelve months.

Lorenz curve. A curve showing the degree of inequality of a frequency distribution, in which the cumulative percentage of a population, e.g. number of firms, is plotted against the cumulative percentage of the variable being studied, e.g. market share. A straight line, rising at 45° from the origin, indicates perfect equality, e.g. that 20 per cent of the firms account for 20 per cent of the market, 50 per cent of the firms account for 50 per cent of the market and so forth. The more the Lorenz curve departs from the 45° line, i.e. the greater its curvature, the greater the degree of inequality. In a single-firm monopoly the curve would be the shape of a reverse L. The Gini coefficient gives a summary measure of inequality. It is calculated as the area between the Lorenz curve and the 45° line, divided by the area above the 45° line. The coefficient would have a value of 1 in a single firm monopoly and 0 where all firms have equal market shares.

loss leader. A product sold at a price below cost in order to attract customers who will also buy profitable products.

Lucas critique. Robert Lucas argued in the 1970s that it was wrong to assume that economic relationships that held in the past would continue to hold even when conditions changed. The implication of Lucas's argument is that the effects of government policy cannot be predicted on the basis of macroeconomic models, even if the changes are announced beforehand. Such models incorporate the estimated responses of individuals at times when different policies were in force, and these responses are likely to be contingent upon, rather than invariant to, future policies. Further implications are that macroeconomic policy should be limited to ensuring a stable currency and predictable environment, and that it should be essentially NON-DISCRETIONARY.

lump-sum tax. A lump-sum, or poll, tax, must be paid irrespective of status or behaviour with regard to income, expenditure, etc. The advantage of the tax is that it does not DISTORT behaviour in any way. The disadvantage is that it is REGRESSIVE.

luxury goods. A term sometimes applied to products with an INCOME ELASTICITY OF DEMAND greater than one.

M

M-form enterprise. A term applied by Oliver Williamson to the multidivisional enterprise. This form of organization is designed to overcome the problems caused by large size, especially the pressure of work on senior executives, the increased complexity of decision-taking, and the growing separation of different functions. In the M-form enterprise each division acts like a quasi-firm, but is responsible to the top board of directors, which is able to concentrate on broad strategic issues. Closer auditing of performance is possible, and Williamson has argued that M-form enterprises are better able to enforce the objectives of top management which are likely to focus on profits, as against the individualist goals of lower management such as growth, increased sales and increased expenditure on their own perquisites.

Maastricht Treaty. A treaty signed in December 1991 by the heads of government of the member states of the EUROPEAN COMMUNITY, under which it was agreed that the second stage of EUROPEAN MONETARY UNION would begin in 1994. (The rejection of the Treaty by Denmark, following a referendum, required the reconsideration of some of the original provisions of the Treaty.)

macroeconomics. The study of national and international economic systems. Macroeconomics is concerned with the behaviour of very large groupings of economic agents, e.g. the SECTORS OF THE ECONOMY, and with aggregate stocks and flows, e.g. the money supply, consumption, investment.

mail order. *See* RETAIL TRADE.

managed bonds. Bonds, usually purchased by a single payment, which run for up to twenty years. The investor's money is generally put into a mixture of shares, property and fixed interest securities.

managed currency. A currency is said to be managed when the government fixes or influences its value in the FOREIGN EXCHANGE MARKETS.

managed floating. *See* EXCHANGE RATE.

managed fund. A fund where the underlying investments are usually a mix of shares, property and fixed interest securities. Managed funds are usually issued and managed by life assurance companies.

managed rate. An increasing proportion of bank OVERDRAFTS are being offered at a managed rate of interest rather than at a rate linked to the BASE RATE. Managed rates are more stable, but seem on the whole to be higher than the alternative.

management buy-in. The purchase of part or all of the assets of a firm by outside investors who subsequently manage those assets.

management buy-out. The purchase of part or all of a firm's assets by some of its managers who thereafter exercise management control of those assets. Successful management buy-outs are often followed by the LISTING of the new firm on the stock exchange, e.g. Unipart, MFI. When large firms go into receivership, they may be sold by multiple buy-outs. Coloroll, Reponse and British and Commonwealth produced seven buy-outs each. In the early 1990s the joint management buy-in and buy-out (Bimbo) increased in popularity.

managerial diseconomies. *See* DISECONOMIES OF SCALE.

managerial economies. *See* ECONOMIES OF SCALE.

managerial theories of the firm. The best known managerial theories of the firm are those developed by W.J. Baumol, R. Marris and O. Williamson. These theories all adhere to neoclassical traditions of constrained MAXIMIZATION and produce qualitative COMPARATIVE STATIC predictions. But they differ with regard to the assumed objectives of managers. Baumol suggested that managers attempt to maximize revenue from sales, Marris that they maximize asset growth, and Williamson that they maximize a utility function including 'staff or emoluments'. All theories recognize that the firms' performances are monitored externally and that this limits the exercise of managerial discretion. Baumol included a minimum profit constraint in his model, and Marris a valuation ratio constraint to reflect pressure from shareholders.

manpower planning. Forecasting future needs for workers with various skills and abilities. Manpower planning can be undertaken at the national level, but is most usually undertaken by individual firms as a basis for future recruitment and training programmes.

manpower policy. *See* LABOUR MARKET POLICIES.

marginal analysis. Analysis of the consequences of very small changes in economic variables. In microeconomics, EQUILIBRIUM is often assumed to involve maximization of a variable, e.g. profits, requiring marginal adjustments, e.g. in output.

marginal benefit. Another term for MARGINAL UTILITY.

marginal cost. The change in cost resulting from a change in output of one unit. This change in cost arises from the change in the quantity of variable factors used. Since all factors are variable in the long-run whereas at least one is fixed (not variable) in the short run, it follows that short-run and long-run marginal cost will differ. If AVERAGE COST falls as output increases, marginal cost is less than average cost; if average cost rises as output increases, marginal cost is greater than average cost.

marginal-cost pricing. Setting a price for a product equal to the cost of producing the last unit of that product. Consumers are assumed to allocate their spending so that they obtain at least as much benefit from the last unit of a product bought as they would have obtained from any other product(s) that could have been bought with the same outlay. Only if the price equals marginal cost can we be sure that there is a net benefit to society of using resources to produce this last unit of the product. In other words marginal-cost pricing enables decisions to be made which lead to the efficient allocation of resources. However, severe practical difficulties may arise in administering this pricing rule. First, it is not clear whether price should be set equal to short-run or long-run marginal cost. Consumers' decisions on spending are basically short-run, suggesting short-run marginal cost as the basis. On the other hand the efficient allocation of resources is heavily influenced by INVESTMENT decisions, which are essentially long run in nature. Second, if AVERAGE COST falls as output increases (perhaps because of ECONOMIES OF SCALE), marginal cost is less than average cost, meaning that a price equal to marginal cost will cause the firm to operate at a loss. Conversely, if average cost is rising, marginal cost will exceed average cost. Since average cost is assumed to include normal profit, a price equal to marginal cost will give rise to SUPERNORMAL PROFIT.

marginal efficiency of capital. *See* INTERNAL RATE OF RETURN.

marginal efficiency of investment. *See* INTERNAL RATE OF RETURN.

marginal firm. If an industry comprising firms of differing levels of efficiency is in EQUILI-BRIUM, the marginal firm is the highest cost firm, only just able to survive at the equilibrium price.

marginal physical product. The additional output produced when one more unit of a FACTOR OF PRODUCTION is employed, the quantities of other factors remaining unchanged. It is usually assumed that as more labour is employed the marginal physical product increases at first because, for example, some tasks can be performed by two but not by one worker, but then declines and might eventually become negative.

marginal product. *See* MARGINAL PHYSICAL PRODUCT.

marginal productivity of capital. *See* INTERNAL RATE OF RETURN.

marginal productivity theory of wages. A theory which suggests that the wage rate level is determined partly by the marginal revenue product of labour. Consider first an industry comprising a large number of firms, none of which employs enough labour to affect its price (wage rate). The wage rate is determined by the interaction of aggregate demand and supply. Aggregate demand for labour depends upon the marginal revenue product of all the firms in the industry. As each firm employs more workers the marginal revenue product diminishes, i.e. the demand curve slopes down from left to right. The supply of labour to the industry depends upon the number of qualified workers and the wage rates in other industries. The supply curve of labour slopes up from left to right. indicating that the higher the wage rate the more workers seek employment in this industry. The market or going wage rate is that at which quantity supplied and demanded are equal. Each firm in the industry can employ as many workers as it wishes at the going wage rate, meaning that the average and marginal cost of labour are identical. The firm will engage additional workers up to the point where the marginal revenue product falls to equal the wage rate. For the firm that can attract more workers only by offering a higher wage rate, the marginal cost of labour will exceed the average cost (the wage rate). Employment will again be at the point where marginal cost equals marginal revenue product, but this will now exceed the wage rate (the average cost of labour). Since marginal revenue product can be identified only if all other factors are fixed, this is essentially a short-run explanation. However, broader changes in productivity will affect the demand for labour, and hence the wage rate, in the long run.

marginal propensity to consume. The change in consumption that occurs as a result of a change in income, divided by that change in income.

marginal propensity to import. The change in imports that occurs as a result of a change in income, divided by that change in income.

marginal propensity to save. The change in saving that occurs as a result of a change in income, divided by that change in income.

marginal propensity to spend. The change in expenditure that occurs as a result of a change in income, divided by that change in income.

marginal propensity to taxation. The marginal propensity to taxation, or the marginal rate of taxation, is the change in tax paid that occurs as a result of a change in income, divided by that change in income.

marginal propensity to withdraw. The sum of the marginal propensity to save, the marginal propensity to import and the marginal propensity to taxation. When a change in income refers to national income the marginal propensity to withdraw plus the marginal propensity to spend must equal one.

marginal rate of leakage. Another term for the marginal propensity to withdraw.

marginal rate of substitution. The marginal rate of substitution is the rate at which a consumer needs to substitute one product for another in order for the utility or satisfaction derived from the two products to remain constant. The marginal rate of substitution between A and B diminishes the more of A that is consumed in a given period. For example assume that a consumer obtains a certain amount of satisfaction from 12 oranges plus 10 apples, and that this satisfaction would also be obtained from 14 oranges plus 9 apples, i.e. by substituting 2 oranges for 1 apple. To continue to obtain the same level of satisfaction the consumer might then need to substitute 3 oranges for the next apple given up, i.e. a combination of 17 oranges plus 8 apples.

marginal rate of taxation. (1) Another term for MARGINAL PROPENSITY TO TAXATION. (2) The highest rate of tax paid by an individual. In a PROGRESSIVE system of taxation, the marginal rate of taxation normally exceeds the average rate.

marginal rate of transformation. The output of a good that has to be foregone in order to increase the output of another good by one unit. The marginal rate of transformation measures the slope of the PRODUCTION POSSIBILITY FRONTIER.

marginal revenue. The change in revenue as a result of a change in sales of one unit. If the firm is a PRICE TAKER, e.g. in PERFECT COMPETITION, marginal revenue equals average revenue (price). But if the firm is a PRICE MAKER, e.g. a MONOPOLIST, marginal revenue is less than average revenue. For example, a monopolist might be able to sell 10 units at a price of 100 pence (revenue £10.00), 11 units at 99 pence (revenue £10.89), and 12 units at 98 pence (revenue £11.76). As price (average revenue) falls to 99 pence, marginal revenue is 89 pence; as price falls to 98 pence marginal revenue is 87 pence.

marginal revenue product. The additional revenue obtained by employing one additional unit of a FACTOR OF PRODUCTION. If the firm is a price taker, e.g. in perfect competition, marginal revenue product is calculated by multiplying the MARGINAL PHYSICAL PRODUCT by the price of the product. (In this situation some economists use the term MARGINAL VALUE PRODUCT.) If the firm is a price maker, e.g. a monopolist, it is necessary to subtract from the revenue received for the extra output, the reduction in revenue from the previous output that would have been sold at a higher price had output remained at a lower level. For such firms marginal revenue product diminishes more rapidly than marginal physical product.

marginal social product. The change in social welfare that results from employing one additional unit of a FACTOR OF PRODUCTION. This comprises the factor's MARGINAL REVENUE PRODUCT, any CONSUMER SURPLUS enjoyed by purchasers of the product, and any EXTERNALITY accruing to those not concerned with the production or consumption of the product.

marginal utility. The utility or satisfaction derived from the consumption of an additional unit of a product. The law of DIMINISHING MARGINAL UTILITY is used in an explanation of the shape of the demand curve.

marginal utility of money. *See* DIMINISHING MARGINAL UTILITY.

marginal value product. This is defined in the same way as marginal revenue product, i.e. the additional revenue obtained by employing one additional unit of a FACTOR OF PRODUCTION. Indeed many economists use only the latter term. Those economists who make a distinction use marginal value product when the firm is a price taker, e.g. in perfect competition, and marginal revenue product when it is a price maker, e.g. a monopolist.

mark-up. The margin added to cost in setting a price.

market. A set of arrangements whereby potential sellers and potential buyers of goods, services or resources can meet.

market, efficient. A market is said to be efficient when all available information is taken into account in forming expectations.

market capture. See REGULATORY CAPTURE.

market-clearing price. See EQUILIBRIUM.

market conduct. It has been suggested that the structure of a market affects the conduct or behaviour of the firms in that market, which in turn affects their performance. Two aspects of conduct felt to be especially important are whether or not existing firms seek to prevent new firms from entering the market, and how sensitive prices are to changes in the balance between demand and supply.

market demand curve. See DEMAND CURVE.

market economy. See FREE-MARKET ECONOMY.

market failure. Market failure is said to occur when imperfections in the market mechanism result in a pattern of resource allocation incompatible with maximum ECONOMIC EFFICIENCY. Government intervention is frequently justified on the ground that it is required to correct market failure (although critics of intervention point out that it can give rise to GOVERNMENT FAILURE). Aspects of market failure include the under-supply of MERIT and PUBLIC GOODS, a failure to take account of EXTERNALITIES, the existence of MONOPOLIES, an inability to provide sufficient information to allow informed decisions to be taken about the supply of FUTURE GOODS, and excessive price fluctuations.

market forces. Market forces include anything that affects demand and supply, the determinants of prices and outputs, and hence RESOURCE ALLOCATION.

market makers. Firms which buy and sell SHARES on their own behalf on the stock exchange, aiming to make a profit out of the difference between buying and selling prices. They may make a market in as many shares as they choose. There are also market makers in the FOREIGN-EXCHANGE and GILT-EDGED markets, where they quote prices for currencies and gilts respectively.

market performance. This refers to certain aspects of the performance of the firms, and especially the major firms, in a market or industry. Aspects of performance considered to be especially important are the level of costs, the profit rate, the rate of process and product innovation, and the ratio of advertising expenditure to sales revenue. (This last is sometimes classified as an aspect of MARKET CONDUCT.)

market power. Denotes that firms have some freedom as to the prices they charge, i.e. the demand for their products is not highly price elastic.

market saturation. A term used particularly with reference to CONSUMER DURABLE goods. A market is saturated when almost all households possess the product in question, so that future sales depend largely on replacement sales and sales to new households.

market segmentation. Policies designed to create and supply SUBDIVISIONS of a MARKET.

market share. The proportion of total sales in a market accounted for by the sales of one producer (or, less commonly, one type of product).

market structure. Economists' interest in market structure is due to the fact that it is believed to affect MARKET CONDUCT and PERFORMANCE. The most important aspects of market structure are the number of suppliers in the market and their relative market shares. It is believed that a highly CONCENTRATED market gives the opportunity for undesirable forms of conduct and performance. It is this belief that has led governments to take action against MERGERS and MONOPOLIZATION.

market supply curve. *See* SUPPLY CURVE.

marketing. Discovering the wants of customers and seeking to generate profits by satisfying those wants.

marketing economies. *See* ECONOMIES OF SCALE.

marketing mix. The various measures adopted by firms in an attempt to sell products at a profit: sales promotion, pricing, the development of new products, the provision of before- and after-sales service, etc. Apart from pricing, all these measures are forms of PRODUCT DIFFERENTIATION.

Marshall-Lerner condition. Devaluation will lead to an improvement in the BALANCE OF PAYMENTS current account if the sum of the price elasticities of demand for imports and exports exceeds one (more accurately, if the sum is more negative than minus one).

Marxian economics. Economics contained in, or inspired by, the writings of Karl Marx. Central to Marxian economics is the labour theory of value, which states that the value of goods is derived from the amount of labour input they embody. This theory was first advanced by Adam Smith and David Ricardo, but its implications were explored most fully by Marx. He made a distinction between value thus determined, which he called exchange value, and use value. He applied this distinction to the market for labour, itself regarded as a commodity. Wages were deemed to be determined by the exchange value of labour, which was in turn determined by the amount of labour time required to 'produce' a worker, i.e. to rear, feed, clothe and shelter him. However, employers (capitalists) force workers to work more hours than this required minimum, retaining the surplus of the use value over the exchange value. (The surplus arose not from selling each article at a price in excess of its exchange value, but from the production of more articles than the required minimum.) The capitalists invested their surpluses in labour-saving machinery, and the resulting competition for jobs helped to ensure that wages were kept down to the exchange value. Capital accumulation, predicted Marx, would have two further consequences. It would give rise to the creation of MONOPOLIES, and would lead to a feeling of alienation among workers, especially as production lines became automated and craft skills declined. This alienation would eventually lead workers to overthrow the capitalist system. Marxian economics is open to criticism on several grounds. It fails to address what is generally seen as the central issue of microeconomics, namely how relative prices are determined. (This failure led to difficulties in running the Soviet economy, whose planners did not want to make any allowance for the use of capital equipment in calculating production costs. This meant that the more capital-intensive the production process, the more underpriced was the resulting output.) Marx's analysis of the consequences of investment are suspect, insofar as investment increases the MARGINAL PRODUCTIVITY OF LABOUR, and so leads to an increase in wage rates. Moreover his prediction of the demise of capitalism has, of course, not been fulfilled. However it should be remembered that capitalism today differs in several respects from that observed by Marx. In most countries there is a MIXED ECONOMY, with considerable government intervention. Moreover the dangers of increasing CONCENTRATION of industry have been recognized, one of the aims of government intervention being to curb the activities of monopolies, and firms have taken steps to try to prevent alienation. Although Marx's predictions have not been fulfilled, this is not, of course, to say that capitalism is entirely healthy. A number of countries, including the UK, are experiencing a longer period of recession than for many decades, and Marxian economists attribute this in part to the fact that an increasing proportion of the employed labour force is becoming unproductive in the sense of not being a source for further accumulation, embodying technical advances and bringing productivity growth.

mass production. The manufacture of large quantities of a product (usually standardized). Industries using mass production methods tend to be highly CONCENTRATED, with high BARRIERS TO ENTRY.

maturity. The date at which a redeemable security becomes payable.

maturity transformation. *See* FINANCIAL INTERMEDIARIES.

maximin strategy. In GAME THEORY each player has to choose among alternative strategies. The pay-offs from these strategies are uncertain, but it is assumed that it is possible to identify the minimum and maximum pay-off from each strategy. A maximin strategy has the highest minimum pay-off. It is the course of action that would maximize profits (or minimize losses), should the worst scenario considered come to pass.

maximization. Microeconomic theories frequently assume maximization as an objective of economic agents: firms, consumers and workers. However, different assumptions are sometimes made about the variable that they seek to maximize. This is particularly true of firms, which have been assumed to maximize short-run profits, long-run profits, sales revenue, growth, etc. Moreover some theories assume objectives other than maximization, e.g. Cyert and March's BEHAVIOURAL THEORY OF THE FIRM assumes 'satisficing' rather than maximizing behaviour. There is more general agreement with the assumption that consumers spend their incomes in such a way as to maximize their expected utility or satisfaction. The advantage of making the assumption of maximization (and of minimization) is that it simplifies analysis and makes it possible to construct models in which equilibrium positions can be clearly identified. But at times this involves a loss of realism that some economists consider unacceptable.

mean. *See* AVERAGE.

means test. Granting state benefits only to people whose income and/or wealth is below a certain level.

median. *See* AVERAGE.

mediation. The use of a third party to settle a dispute, e.g. between employer and employees.

medium of exchange. *See* MONEY.

medium-term financial strategy. A strategy operated by the UK government in the 1980s, in an attempt to reduce inflation. The strategy encompassed both monetary policy (a reduction in the growth rate of the MONEY SUPPLY), and fiscal policy (a reduction in the PUBLIC SECTOR BORROWING REQUIREMENT both in absolute terms and as a percentage of gross domestic product). Both policy objectives, and especially the former, proved difficult to achieve, and the strategy became gradually less prominent as greater emphasis was given to EXCHANGE RATE targets and the UK's obligations as a member of the European EXCHANGE RATE MECHANISM.

memorandum of association. A document which must be submitted to the Registrar of Companies when a company is formed. It contains details of the type of business to be undertaken, the amount of AUTHORIZED CAPITAL, and a statement that liability is limited.

menu costs. The menu costs of inflation comprise the additional resources required by firms in updating information on price tags, containers, etc., as prices change rapidly, and the extra effort required by consumers to absorb the new information.

mercantilism. A doctrine developed in the seventeenth century that a country should try to ensure that it had a surplus of exports over imports so that it could benefit from the consequential inflow of gold. The doctrine is reflected today in government measures to curb imports or subsidize exports.

merchant banks. Thirty-three institutions are currently recognized by the Bank of England as merchant banks. These banks provide a variety of services, including the acceptance of BILLS OF EXCHANGE, arranging the issue and placing of company securities, managing investment portfolios and UNIT TRUSTS, advising on and helping to finance TAKEOVERS, providing risk capital for small firms, and dealing in gold and EUROCURRENCIES.

merger. A merger occurs when two companies combine their assets to form a new company. Both companies are willing participants, whereas in a TAKEOVER one company is enthusiastic and the other reluctant. Mergers, whether horizontal, vertical or conglomerate, contribute to the GROWTH OF THE FIRM and to market or industrial CONCENTRATION.

Mergers Panel. All proposed mergers above a certain size are considered by the Mergers Panel which recommends which should be examined by the MONOPOLIES AND MERGERS COMMISSION.

merit goods. Goods and services which the government believes are socially desirable. This belief leads to government intervention to ensure that consumption of these goods is higher than it would be under the free interplay of market forces. Higher consumption is brought about by GOVERNMENT SUBSIDIES and, in some instances, by compulsion. For example, children are forced to stay at school until reaching a certain age, and the education is provided free.

mezzanine finance. *See* JUNK BONDS.

microeconomics. The focus of microeconomics is the study of markets. This entails the study of the behaviour of participants in these markets: producers, consumers, workers, investors, etc. The determination of prices, the allocation of resources, and the efficiency of markets are areas of especial interest.

minimization. The minimization of certain variables, and especially costs, is one of the key assumptions of traditional economic theory. However this assumption has been challenged by, for example, behavioural theories of the firm. For example traditional theory assumes that firms always operate on the lowest feasible average cost curve, whereas the concepts of ORGANIZATIONAL SLACK and X–INEFFICIENCY imply that they frequently operate on higher cost curves.

minimum efficient scale. The lowest rate of output per period at which average cost would be at a minimum. In order to operate at the MES the firm must choose (a) the SCALE OF ORGANIZATION whose minimum average cost is less than at any other scale, and (b) that output at which this minimum is attained.

minimum lending rate. The minimum rate of interest at which the BANK OF ENGLAND provides money to the DISCOUNT HOUSES and thus to the remainder of the banking system. The pre-announcing of MLR was abandoned as a general policy in 1981, and since then the use of MLR has been made public very infrequently (about once every five years!).

145

minimum price. (1) A price maintained by interference with the free interplay of market forces. A minimum price for labour may be set, e.g. by MINIMUM-WAGE LAWS or through the operations of WAGES COUNCILS. Some COMMODITY AGREEMENTS specify a minimum price that will be sustained by purchasing by the relevant authority. (2) In the THEORY OF THE FIRM, the minimum price equals minimum average variable cost. Unless the firm can obtain this price it will cease operations.

minimum sustainable rate of unemployment. *See* UNEMPLOYMENT, NATURAL RATE OF.

minimum-wage laws. Proponents of legislation to prevent employers paying less than a certain wage advocate this policy as a method of reducing poverty and inequalities of income. However these aims may not be achieved. If other workers are able to obtain corresponding increases so as to restore wage differentials, this is likely to cause prices to rise so that REAL WAGES will rise by less than money wages (and perhaps not at all). If wage differentials are eroded, i.e. if the relative price of more highly paid workers falls, we would expect employers to substitute these workers for lower paid workers, (this would happen only after sufficient time had elapsed to reorganize production). Moreover, insofar as the price of capital equipment, relative to labour, fell we would expect capital to be substituted for labour. There is some evidence from the USA that substitution does occur, with the greatest fall in employment, following an increase in the minimum wage, occurring among black teenagers, many of whom would be directly affected by the legislation.

minority interest. That part of a subsidiary's share capital not held by the HOLDING COMPANY.

missing markets. A complete set of markets does not exist for EXTERNALITIES, FUTURE GOODS or RISK.

mixed economy. All contemporary economies are mixed. Resources are owned part publicly and part privately, and are allocated partly by means of the price mechanism (modified by government intervention) and partly by government decisions.

mobility of labour. *See* LABOUR MOBILITY.

mode. *See* AVERAGE.

model. *See* ECONOMIC MODEL.

monetarism. A term applied to a number of linked economic doctrines which became influential in the 1980s and which emphasized the impact on prices of changes in the money supply. The background to the 'rise of monetarism' was an increasing loss of confidence in the ability of DEMAND MANAGEMENT policies, whose theoretical underpinnings lay in KEYNESIAN ECONOMICS, to prevent an increase in unemployment and, of even more concern to some governments, in inflation. Empirical work undertaken by Milton Friedman and his associates suggested that an increase in the money supply was invariably followed, albeit with a lag, by an increase in prices. This was assumed to happen because, with a given LIQUIDITY PREFERENCE function, people would wish to exchange much of the extra money for other assets, including goods and services, i.e. planned AGGREGATE DEMAND would increase. Although the immediate impact of the increase in aggregate demand might be an increase in output, before long the major (and possibly the only) effect would be a rise in prices. If some of the increased money supply was spent on financial assets the price of those assets would rise, i.e. the interest rate would fall. This would cause a planned increase in INVESTMENT spending, which would also lead to a rise in prices. The influence of monetarism on government policy was seen in a greater emphasis on monetary policy, although fiscal policy could not be neglected, since it affects monetary variables. Monetarists also argued that frequent policy changes, characteristic of the demand management policies as operated by many governments, were often counter-productive. They suggested that rather than trying to fine-tune the economy, the government should make clear and then maintain its policy stance. This was the stated aim of the MEDIUM-TERM FINANCIAL STRATEGY. When introducing the strategy the government announced that it intended to gradually reduce the rate of growth of the money supply until price stability was achieved. (Monetarism suggests that this would require the money supply to expand in line with the growth of economic CAPACITY.) In fact the operation of the MTFS could be described, at best, as a partial success. The measure of money to be targeted was changed on more than one occasion, and the targets were frequently missed. These problems led to a gradual loss of confidence in the MTFS, and towards the end of the decade more attention was given to controlling the EXCHANGE RATE. This accorded with the international monetarist position which sees domestic monetary policy as affecting prices, with a lag, via the exchange rate. According to this view, a relatively high exchange rate is an important counter-inflationary weapon. Another implication of monetarism is that if the government can do little to affect economic capacity and output by policies operating on demand, more attention should be given to SUPPLY-SIDE policies. This happened in the UK in the 1980s.

monetary accommodation. Monetary policy which accommodates a shock, e.g. a rise in wages or import prices, by ensuring that the consequent rise in prices is matched by an equivalent rise in the nominal money supply in order to prevent a fall in the real money supply.

monetary aggregates. Monetary aggregates are measures of the money supply. The number and definitions of these aggregates change from time to time. There are currently four aggregates: $M0$, $M2$, $M4$ and $M5$. $M0$, a narrow measure of money (although known as the wide MONETARY BASE), comprises notes and coin in circulation outside the Bank of England plus bankers' operational balances with the Bank of England. $M4$, a broad measure of money, comprises assets held by the private sector excluding banks and building societies, namely: notes and coin, sterling bank deposits (including sterling certificates of deposits), and building society shares, deposits and sterling certificates of deposit. $M0$ is around 4 per cent of $M4$.

Table 17　Narrow and broad measures of money, June 1992.

Narrow	£ million
Notes and coin in circulation	18 747
Bankers' operational deposits at Bank of England	100
Total:$M0$	18 847
Broad	
$M4$ private sector's holdings of:	
Notes and coin	15 510
Bank retail deposits	145 915
Other interest-bearing bank deposits (incl.CDs.)	153 872
Building society shares and deposits (incl.CDs.)	199 637
	514 934

Source: *Bank of England Quarterly Bulletin*

monetary authorities. *See* BANK OF ENGLAND.

monetary base. The monetary base, also known as high-powered money, is the stock of the economy's most liquid assets. This could be confined to the notes and coin in circulation, but $M0$, the narrowest of the current MONETARY AGGREGATES, also includes bankers' operational balances at the BANK OF ENGLAND. For this reason *M* 0 is known as the wide monetary base.

monetary base control. This involves the banks keeping a known proportion of their deposits in base money, i.e. in items included in the MONETARY BASE, either because they are required to do so by the authorities or for prudential reasons. The authorities then either (a) control the amount of base money in existence and so the total growth of the MONEY SUPPLY, since the banks' balance sheets cannot exceed a specified multiple of the base, or (b) use divergences of the base money figure from the desired trend as the indicator for a change in INTEREST RATES intended to correct the divergence (an indicator system). This form of monetary control has never been employed in the UK, mainly because of the practical difficulties arising from the fact that the banks' holdings of base money fluctuate erratically and unpredictably.

monetary policy. Monetary policy comprises a number of measures (not all of which operate at any one time) designed to influence the MONEY SUPPLY, INTEREST RATES and the EXCHANGE RATE. Measures that might be taken as part of a CONTRACTIONARY POLICY are: (a) Regulations and guidance concerning the amount of BANK LENDING. (b) Regulations relating to BALANCE SHEET ratios, e.g. cash ratio, liquidity ratio. These regulations might be bolstered by measures to sterilize some of the assets that would otherwise have been used by the banks to achieve the required ratio. Alternatively the authorities might engage in open-market operations, selling securities to the public, who pay by drawing on their bank deposits, thus reducing the banks' liquid assets. In order to restore the liquidity ratio to the required level, the banks might have to engineer a multiple contraction of credit. Even if this does not happen, sales of securities tend to depress their price, i.e. to increase the rate of interest. (c) Measures to limit the growth of deposits. (d) Managing the NATIONAL DEBT so as to maximize the proportion held outside the BANKING SYSTEM. (Public expenditure financed by borrowing from the banking system increases the money supply.) This might involve, for example, offering higher rates of interest on National Savings Certificates. (e) Influencing interest rates, e.g. by increasing the Bank of England's base rate, by intervention in the MONEY MARKET or by activating the MINIMUM LENDING RATE. (f) Operating a system of MONETARY BASE CONTROL. At present policy is mainly concerned to influence interest rates, mainly through the Bank of England's dealings with the DISCOUNT HOUSES, rather than the money supply. (The authorities' freedom in this respect was curbed when the UK had an obligation to maintain a stable exchange rate as a member of the European Economic Community's exchange rate mechanism.)

monetary sector. A term used until recently by the Bank of England to encompass the Bank's own banking department, the retail banks, British merchant banks, other British banks, overseas banks and the discount houses.

monetary union. Monetary union can take various forms, involving different degrees of monetary integration. These forms include: (a) a currency union, in which the members adopt a single currency; (b) an exchange-rate union, in which the exchange rates between members' currencies are irrevocably fixed; (c) a free intercirculation union, in which members' currencies are allowed to circulate freely within the union; (d) a parallel currency union, in which a parallel currency circulates side by side with the national currency.

monetary unit. The standard unit of a national or international currency, e.g. the pound sterling.

money. Anything that is generally accepted as a means of payment for goods and services or in the settlement of debts, i.e. anything that acts as a medium of exchange.

Money should also act as a store of value, although it has frequently been deficient in this respect. The value of the pound sterling fell by over three-quarters between 1975 and 1992 and some other currencies have fared very much worse. The value of money may fall so rapidly, as in HYPERINFLATION, that it eventually becomes unacceptable as money. Two other functions of money are as a unit of account, the unit in which prices are quoted, and as a standard of deferred payment or unit of account over time. There are broad and narrow measures of money, or MONETARY AGGREGATES. Deposits in banks and building societies account for the bulk of money, broadly defined.

money, demand for. Several motives for holding money can be distinguished. The transactions demand reflects the fact that the pattern of income, of firms or individuals, seldom coincides with the pattern of expenditure. Consequently both hold a stock of money out of which they can make payments at times when their current income is inadequate. The most important determinant of the transactions demand is the value of transactions the individual or firm expects to make in a given period. Aggregating these transactions gives us GROSS DOMESTIC PRODUCT or NATIONAL INCOME, the main determinant of the total transactions demand. Demand is also influenced by the flexibility of the financial system, including the ease with which money can be transmitted, and the OPPORTUNITY COST of holding money. The precautionary demand is subject to very similar influences to the transactions demand, but it relates to transactions whose value and timing are very uncertain (and which may never occur). The asset demand is similar to Keynes's speculative demand. Wealth may be held in various forms: government stocks, company debentures, shares, property, etc., which offer the prospect of different forms of return: interest, dividends, etc. If money is held in preference to assets which yield positive returns, it indicates that people expect the price of these assets to fall, a change which would cause holders to suffer a capital loss.

money, neutrality of. Money is said to be neutral if changes in its supply affect only the general level of prices. This is assumed to be the case in CLASSICAL ECONOMICS and, in the long run, in MONETARISM. Keynesian economists, on the other hand, would see an increase in the money supply, via its effect on AGGREGATE DEMAND, leading to an increase in output, provided that there was excess capacity initially.

money at call and short notice. Lending by the commercial banks, principally to the DISCOUNT HOUSES, for periods ranging from overnight to fourteen days.

money illusion. People suffer from money or inflation illusion when they confuse nominal and real changes. If a street trader buys a case of toys for £100 and sells them for £120 he may believe that he has made a profit of 20 per cent, whereas if during the same period all prices have risen by 20 per cent, his profit in real terms is zero.

money market. A set of arrangements whereby the sellers and purchasers of short-term securities, and also those wishing to borrow and lend on a short-term basis, are brought together. (Of the total volume of transactions, money-market securities account for about a fifth, and loans and deposits for the remaining four-fifths). The sterling money market had its origin in the nineteenth century, but it has expanded enormously during the last forty years or so, especially with the development of parallel markets, organized mainly by money brokers, alongside the traditional market made by the discount houses. These markets deal in the deposits of local authorities, inter-bank loans, sterling certificates of deposit issued by banks and building societies, and commercial paper issued by industrial companies. The DISCOUNT HOUSES play a crucial role in the money market. The bulk of their assets comprise money market securities, while most of their funding comprises short-term loans and deposits. They thus provide a bridge between the two sections of the market.

money-market instruments. Securities traded on the MONEY MARKET.

money multiplier. *See* CREDIT CREATION.

money stock. *See* MONEY SUPPLY.

money supply. The stock of liquid assets held at a point in time. Several MONETARY AG-GREGATES, alternative measures of the money supply, exist. In simple models of income determination the money supply is often assumed to be EXOGENOUS, being determined by the government. However in practice the demand for money also influences its supply.

Monopolies and Mergers Commission. Originally set up (as the Monopolies Commission) by the Monopolies and Restrictive Practices (Inquiry and Control) Act of 1948, the role of the Commission in the government's COMPETITION POLICY has been extended by subsequent legislation. It can be asked to investigate monopolies (defined as 25 per cent or more of the relevant market) and proposed mergers and to determine whether or not they operate, or are likely to operate, against the public interest. However since most members of the Commission are part-time, they are able to undertake only a few investigations each year.

monopolistic competition. This term was first used by the American economist E.H. Chamberlin to describe a market with a large number of suppliers of products that were slightly differentiated. (In the UK at roughly the same time Joan Robinson constructed a theory relating to this type of market, although she used the phrase imperfect competition.) Because of PRODUCT DIFFERENTIATION each supplier's demand curve slopes down from left to right, as in monopoly. Another feature common to both markets is the earning of supernormal profits in the short run. But in monopolistic competition, unlike monopoly, there are no BARRIERS TO ENTRY. Consequently new firms, attracted by the supernormal profits, are able to enter the market, supplying products which attract some consumers away from existing suppliers. This process continues until all suppliers are earning NORMAL PROFITS (although Chamberlin recognized that as an exception to this general rule some firms might earn supernormal profits even in the long run.) When the market reaches equilibrium, firms produce less than the output at which average cost would be minimized. However against this disadvantage must be placed any increase in consumer welfare that comes from the wider choice given by differentiated products. A problem posed by Chamberlin's model that has never been satisfactorily resolved is how the market, the competing group of firms, is to be defined. The inability to resolve this problem has led some economists to conclude that the model does not allow any questions to be answered that could not be answered by the models of monopoly and perfect competition.

monopolization. The adoption of policies aimed at creating a MONOPOLY, as distinct from a monopoly that is achieved incidentally, and from a NATURAL MONOPOLY.

monopoly. (1) In economic theory a monopoly is a market with a single seller. Since the firm and the industry are identical it follows that the firm's demand curve slopes down from left to right. If the monopolist follows the profit-maximizing rule of producing at the point where marginal cost equals marginal revenue, it will earn SUPERNORMAL or MONOPOLY PROFITS. Since by definition there are BARRIERS preventing the ENTRY of new firms, these profits will be earned both in the short and the long run. Even if profits are higher than in PERFECT COMPETITION, it does not follow that prices will be higher (and output lower) since monopolists enjoy ECONOMIES OF SCALE and so may have much lower costs than the smaller firms in perfect competition. Moreover, large firms can spend more on research and development than small firms and may, therefore, have a higher rate of INNOVATION.

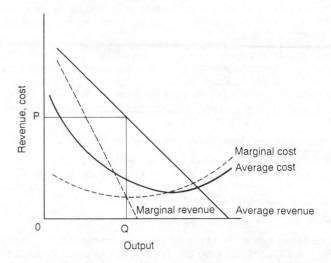

Figure 9   Equilibrium price and output in monopoly

(2) Under legislation passed in connection with the government's COMPETITION POLICY, a monopoly is said to exist when one supplier accounts for at least 25 per cent of the market. A complex monopoly exists when several firms which together have at least 25 per cent of the market so conduct their affairs as to prevent, restrict or distort competition. A local monopoly exists when one supplier accounts for at least 25 per cent of a local (geographical) market. The MONOPOLIES AND MERGERS COMMISSION can be asked to investigate any of these forms of monopoly.

monopoly power. It has been suggested that monopoly power can be measured in terms of the deviation of price from cost as, for example, in the LERNER INDEX. This implies that monopoly power can exist in any market other than perfect competition, i.e. in OLIGOPOLY and MONOPOLISTIC COMPETITION as well as in MONOPOLY.

monopoly profit. The excess of revenue over cost (defined to include NORMAL PROFIT) achieved in MONOPOLY.

monopsony. A market in which there is only one buyer. If there is an upward sloping supply curve for the product or input bought by the monopsonist, an increase in demand will cause a rise in price. This means that the MARGINAL COST exceeds the AVERAGE COST.

Monte Carlo method. A method of estimating probabilities. An activity is simulated a large number of times and probabilities are estimated from the resulting outcomes.

moral hazard. If the act of insurance increases the likelihood of the occurrence insured against, the problem of moral hazard exists. For example, householders insuring against the theft of their possessions may take less care to keep their houses secure and so stand a greater chance of being robbed. Moral hazard may arise in COST-PLUS contracts; since cost increases are paid for by the buyer, the producer has less incentive to keep costs down. If a firm has to bear all the risks associated with spending on research and development, it will monitor this spending very carefully. If the government, in an attempt to encourage R & D activity, shares the risk by taking a shareholding in the firm, the firm will have less incentive to monitor expenditure, and the return to that expenditure may therefore fall.

mortgage. A legal document showing that money has been borrowed with land, property or other assets as COLLATERAL SECURITY. The lender is given conditional ownership of the assets until the loan is repaid. Most houses are purchased with the aid of money borrowed on mortgage from a building society, bank or insurance company. A fall in house prices, as in the early 1990s, can mean that the market value of the house becomes less than the amount of the loan.

most-favoured nation clause. *See* GENERAL AGREEMENT ON TARIFFS AND TRADE.

moving average. An average derived from two or more values of a TIME SERIES. To calculate successive averages, the first value in the time series is dropped and the next value is added. The technique is used in order to eliminate or smooth fluctuations due, for example, to seasonal factors, and to identify long-term trends.

multicollinearity. *See* REGRESSION ANALYSIS.

Multi-fibre Arrangement. An agreement regulating international trade in textiles and clothing. The MFA contains more than 3000 QUOTAS for different countries and products. Although contrary to the principles of the GENERAL AGREEMENT ON TARIFFS AND TRADE, the MFA is exempted from that body's rules.

Multilateral Investment Guarantee Agency. An affiliate of the International Bank for Reconstruction and Development which encourages private direct investment by providing insurance against political risk.

multilateralism. International trade between more than two countries without discrimination.

multinational enterprise. A multinational enterprise or corporation is a company which owns production or service facilities in two or more countries. MNEs are accounting for an increasing share of world output, partly because of an increase in their number and partly because they are growing more rapidly than other companies. The turnover of the largest MNEs, e.g. Exxon, General Motors, Unilever, exceeds the gross domestic product of many countries.

multi-plant operations. Production at more than one plant or location. The main reason for this form of organization is a desire to locate near to the market or to scattered sources of essential inputs.

multiple contraction of deposits. In models of credit creation the amount of credit that can be created by banks is determined by the amount of money deposited with the banks (the MONETARY BASE) and the value of the CASH RATIO desired by, or imposed upon, the banks. If they maintained a 5 per cent cash ratio and their deposits totalled £10 millions they would be able to lend £200 millions. These assets (loans) would be balanced by the £10 millions initial deposits and £190 millions created deposits. If their deposits were to fall to £8 millions, they would have to reduce their lending and deposits by £40 millions to £160 millions, in order to bring the cash ratio back up to 5 per cent. A multiple contraction of deposits would have occurred.

multiple correlation coefficient. A measure of the accuracy by which the value of a dependent variable is estimated by a model or equation containing two or more independent variables. A coefficient value of 1 indicates a perfect correspondence between the predicted and actual values of the variable, a value of 0 indicates no correspondence.

multiple expansion of deposits. *See* CREDIT CREATION.

multiple retailer. *See* RETAIL TRADE.

multiplier. The multiplier is defined as the ratio of the final change in national income (or gross domestic product) resulting from an autonomous change in expenditure, to that autonomous change in expenditure. In simple models the value of the multiplier is given by the formula: one divided by (one minus the MARGINAL PROPENSITY TO CONSUME), or alternatively one divided by the MARGINAL PROPENSITY TO SAVE. In more complex models the value of the multiplier is given by the formula: one divided by (one minus the MARGINAL PROPENSITY TO SPEND) or alternatively one divided by the MARGINAL PROPENSITY TO WITHDRAW. For example with a marginal propensity to spend of 0.5 the value of the multiplier would be 2 and an autonomous increase in investment of £500 millions per period would lead to an increase in gross domestic product of £1000 millions per period. Multipliers are normally estimated for the economy as a whole. But it is possible to estimate local multipliers for particular areas.

multiplier-accelerator model. *See* ACCELERATOR-MULTIPLIER MODEL.

multi-product firm. A firm that makes more than one product. Most firms are multi-product and some of their costs can be allocated between products only on an arbitrary basis, a fact that tends to be ignored in basic theories of the firm.

mutual company. A company owned by those members who transact business with it. The profits of mutual companies are shared out among members, e.g. the bonuses distributed by mutual assurance companies.

N

narrow measures (money). *See* MONETARY AGGREGATES.

Nash equilibrium. Refers to a situation in GAME THEORY when all the participants pursue their best possible strategy in the knowledge of the strategies of all other participants.

National Accounts. *See* UNITED KINGDOM NATIONAL ACCOUNTS.

national debt. The total outstanding debt of the central government. (This definition is usually extended to include the debt of the local authorities and even of the nationalized industries.) In most years the PUBLIC SECTOR BORROWING REQUIREMENT has been positive, leading to an increase in the national debt, and this raises the question as to whether the burden of the national debt is increasing. Although the debt may increase in nominal terms, the increase in real terms is much less because of rising prices. Increases in the gross domestic product further reduce the burden; taking one year with another there has been no tendency, outside periods of major wars, for the debt to increase as a percentage of GROSS DOMESTIC PRODUCT. However an absolute increase in the national debt may have some undesirable consequences. Government borrowing may CROWD OUT private borrowing. If interest rates rise the cost of servicing a given debt increases and this may cause further government borrowing or increases in taxation. Finally, although only a minority of the debt is held overseas, interest on this debt constitutes a debit on the BALANCE OF PAYMENTS account. The debt comprises (a) funded debt, i.e. unredeemable securities, now a very small part of the total; (b) floating debt, i.e. short-term borrowing, e.g. Treasury bills, ways and means advances; (c) other unfunded debt (about three-quarters of the total) some of which is marketable, i.e. government bonds, and some non-marketable, e.g. national savings certificates, premium savings bonds.

National Economic Development Council. A council established in 1962 and abolished in 1992. The Council could be seen as part of the government's experiment in INDICATIVE PLANNING in that it provided a forum where representatives of employers and workers met under the chairmanship of a senior government minister. Surveys of industries and sectors of the economy were undertaken by a number of Economic Development Committees and Sector Working Parties.

National Economic Development Office. The secretariat for the NATIONAL ECONOMIC DEVELOPMENT COUNCIL. Abolished, along with the Council, in 1992.

national income. The sum of incomes received by the residents of a country. In the UK NATIONAL ACCOUNTS national income, or net national product, is calculated by subtracting CAPITAL CONSUMPTION from GROSS NATIONAL PRODUCT at factor cost. Having in this way allowed for the replacement of capacity used in the course of generating income, national income is a good measure of sustainable income. In the THEORY OF INCOME DETERMINATION, the term income is used rather loosely, frequently being used when gross national product or gross domestic product would be more accurate.

national income accounting. The aim of national income accounting is to provide a measure of the value of economic activity in a given period, say a year. In fact in the

154

UNITED KINGDOM NATIONAL ACCOUNTS three alternative sets of measures are presented, utilizing the expenditure, income and output approaches to measurement. With the expenditure approach, consumers' expenditure, general government final consumption, gross domestic fixed capital formation, the value of the physical increase in stocks and work in progress, and exports minus imports, are added together to give GROSS DOMESTIC PRODUCT at market prices. Subtracting taxes on expenditure (net of subsidies) gives GDP at factor cost.

Table 18   National income, 1991

	£ million
Consumers' expenditure	367 853
General government final consumption	121 899
Gross domestic fixed capital formation	95 442
Value of physical increase in stocks	- 5 303
Exports minus imports	- 5 300
Statistical discrepancy	- 445
Gross domestic product at market prices	574 146
Less Taxes (net of subsidies)	-77 145
Gross domestic product at factor cost	497 001
Net property income from abroad	328
Gross national product at factor cost	497 329
Less Capital consumption	-63 968
Net national product = National income	433 361

Source: *United Kingdom National Accounts*

What is expenditure from one point of view is income from another point of view, and GDP at factor cost is also calculated by adding together income from employment, income from self-employment, gross trading profits of companies, gross trading surplus of general government enterprises, rent and interest (actually an imputed charge for the consumption of non-trading capital, e.g. the use of the Houses of Parliament and local town halls), and subtracting any increase in the value of stocks due to inflation (see DISTRIBUTION OF INCOME, Table 10). Since expenditure and income are two sides of the same coin, both approaches should arrive at the same vaue for GDP. However, deficiencies in data collection mean that the two do not match exactly, and they are reconciled by the inclusion of a statistical discrepancy figure. When we add to GDP at factor cost the total of net property income from abroad (rent, interest, profits and dividends received from abroad by UK residents, minus the corresponding payments made abroad) we arrive at GROSS NATIONAL PRODUCT at factor cost. Finally, subtracting capital consumption gives NATIONAL INCOME (net national product).

The output approach also uses measures of income, but by allocating income to the various industrial sectors, e.g. manufacturing, transport, it enables us to see the contribution of these sectors to GDP (the figure for dwellings is imputed output). To avoid DOUBLE COUNTING, only the VALUE ADDED by each sector is recorded. This means that the value of FINAL GOODS is adjusted by subtracting the value of INTERMEDIATE GOODS used in their production. There is also an adjustment for financial services, i.e. for interest payments, again required to avoid double counting. Finally note that the output of the government sector, e.g. education, is valued at the cost incurred in producing that output. All three approaches have two important deficiencies. On the one hand they exclude activities in the non-market sector, e.g. the services of housewives, and so undervalue the total set of activities. On the other hand they include activities which produce ECONOMIC BADS, e.g. pollution, and so overvalue the total set of activities. An unofficial measure which makes these adjustments is NET ECONOMIC WELFARE.

F

national insurance. The payment of contributions giving a right to various benefits as appropriate: unemployment benefit, sickness benefit, industrial injury benefit, child benefit, retirement pensions, etc. (A small part of the contributions goes towards the cost of the National Health Service.) Both employers and employees pay contributions. The employer's contributions are a tax on the use of labour. The employee's contributions are in effect a direct tax, and they are collected, together with income tax, through the pay-as-you-earn system. Married women employees can opt to pay only a small contribution, qualifying them to receive a narrower range of benefits, and a slightly different system applies to the self-employed. National insurance and other social security contributions account for about one-sixth of government revenue from TAXATION.

National Insurance Fund. A government account held at the Bank of England, the National Insurance Fund receives an appropriate transfer from the CONSOLIDATED FUND and pays NATIONAL INSURANCE benefits.

National Loans Fund. A government account held at the Bank of England, the National Loans Fund receives all the money raised by the issue of debt, pays interest on debt, and disburses government loans.

national saving. National saving is the sum of private (PERSONAL and COMPANY) saving and PUBLIC SAVING.

National Savings, Department for. The department that administers government savings schemes. The forms of government borrowing for which it is responsible include national savings certificates, premium bonds, save-as-you-earn, the NATIONAL SAVINGS BANK and the sale of certain GILT-EDGED securities through post offices.

National Savings Bank. The National Savings Bank operates through the post-office network and was formerly known as the Post Office Savings Bank. It offers an ordinary account, from which limited withdrawals can be made on demand, and an investment account, withdrawals from which require one month's notice but which pays a higher rate of interest.

nationalization. The acquisition by the state, usually with the payment of compensation, of the assets of the private sector. Nationalization is claimed to yield several economic benefits, although the widespread PRIVATIZATION programmes of recent years must throw into question the importance of these benefits. The alleged benefits include preventing the earning of SUPERNORMAL PROFITS, especially in NATURAL MONOPOLIES; the redistribution of real income, either towards consumers via price reductions, or workers via wages increases; unified control of the industry enabling more advantage to be taken of ECONOMIES OF SCALE; eliminating the overlapping activities of competing suppliers; ensuring that goods and services are provided in areas that are less profitable to supply because of, for example, additional transport costs to remote locations; ensuring that output is adequate to prevent the emergence of BOTTLENECKS.

nationalized industries. The essential features of nationalized industries are: their assets are in public ownership and vested in a corporation which is primarily engaged in industrial or other trading activities; their revenue is mainly derived from these trading activities, i.e. from the sale of goods and services; their boards are appointed by a government minister, but board members and employees are not civil servants. Publicly owned enterprises which are not nationalized industries include public corporations which do not derive most of their revenue from the sale of goods and services, e.g. the British Broadcasting Corporation, whose main source of revenue is licence fees, and government trading bodies which derive their revenue from sales but do not have independent boards, e.g. HMSO. Industries most commonly nationalized include transport, energy and water supplies, and manufacturing industries such as iron and steel whose products are widely used in other industries.

natural monopoly. A natural monopoly exists when, because of ECONOMIES OF SCALE, the market can be supplied at lowest cost by a single firm. In order to prevent the earning of MONOPOLY PROFIT, natural monopolies may be NATIONALIZED or subject to other forms of REGULATION.

natural rate of growth. *See* HARROD-DOMAR model.

natural rate of increase. The natural rate of population increase is the difference between the BIRTH RATE and the DEATH RATE.

natural rate of unemployment. *See* UNEMPLOYMENT, NATURAL RATE OF.

natural resources. Natural resources are considered as part of the factor of production LAND, but generally have the added characteristic that they must be changed, e.g. by being dug out of the ground, being processed, in order for their value to be released. Natural resources may be renewable, e.g. fish, or non-renewable (depletable) e.g. oil. Resources which are not used up in the process of consumption, e.g. a beautiful landscape which provides enjoyment, are said to be non-expendable.

near money. Near money consists of assets which act as a store of value but which are not accepted as a means of exchange. A good example would be deposits in a building society (although these are included in some official definitions of broad money).

necessities. Necessities are sometimes described as goods that are essential to life, food being an obvious example. However, people differ in their view as to what constitutes a necessity. Cigarettes may be a necessity to a heavy smoker but a nuisance to a non-smoker. This difficulty has led to the adoption of an 'objective' definition, namely a product for which the INCOME ELASTICITY OF DEMAND is less than one.

negative income tax. A government payment to people on very low incomes. Some economists believe that the UK system of SOCIAL SECURITY would be improved by the introduction of a negative income tax.

neo-classical economics. Neo-classical economics adopted the traditions of CLASSICAL ECONOMICS but made distinct advances in the analysis of UTILITY and demand functions, and in laying the foundations of GENERAL EQUILIBRIUM ANALYSIS. In microeconomics a COMPARATIVE STATICS EQUILIBRIUM approach is adopted in the analysis of markets. Macroeconomic statements are frequently derived from the aggregation of microeconomic relationships, a methodology that has been criticized by economists of the Cambridge School, amongst others. These statements have been mainly concerned with equilibrium and growth at full employment, in contrast to the emphasis of Keynesian economists on situations of less than full employment. Another contrast between the two schools concerns the relationship between saving and investment. Neo-classical economists see saving as determining investment, Keynesians the reverse.

neo-classical synthesis. *See* KEYNESIAN ECONOMICS.

neo-Keynesian economics. *See* KEYNESIAN ECONOMICS.

net assets. *See* BALANCE SHEET.

net barter terms of trade. *See* TERMS OF TRADE.

Net Book Agreement. The best known of the very few restrictive agreements approved by the RESTRICTIVE PRACTICES COURT. Under the Agreement, books designated as net are supplied only to booksellers who agree to resell them at the recommended published price.

net capital formation. *See* CAPITAL FORMATION.

net cash flow. Cash inflow minus cash outflow. Sometimes simply called CASH FLOW.

net domestic product. GROSS DOMESTIC PRODUCT minus CAPITAL CONSUMPTION.

net economic welfare. A measure of economic welfare suggested in 1972 by W. Nordhaus and J. Tobin, although the term net economic welfare was actually coined later by P.A. Samuelson. Nordhaus and Tobin adjusted US GROSS NATIONAL PRODUCT by deducting the estimated value of ECONOMIC BADS and adding the estimated value of non-market activities. They found that NEW exceeded GNP but was growing less quickly because of the increasing incidence of bads.

net income. The net income of a business is profit after tax and, where appropriate, minority interest. The net income of an individual is income after tax.

net investment. Gross investment minus DEPRECIATION or capital consumption.

net national product. Another term for NATIONAL INCOME.

net output. In the census of production, net output is defined as sales revenue minus the cost of materials purchased.

net present value. The PRESENT VALUE of a sum to be received in the future is calculated by applying a discount factor to that sum. The net present value of a project is the present value of the income stream arising from that project minus the initial cost of the project. If, when the income stream is discounted at a rate equal to the company's COST OF CAPITAL, net present value is positive, the project would lead to an increase in the company's NET WORTH.

net profit. *See* PROFIT.

net taxes. Taxes minus TRANSFER PAYMENTS.

net transactions in UK assets and liabilities. The official term for the balance on the capital account of the BALANCE OF PAYMENTS. These transactions relate to PORTFOLIO INVESTMENT, FOREIGN DIRECT INVESTMENT, banks' borrowing and lending, public sector borrowing, and the change in the OFFICIAL RESERVES.

net worth. *See* BALANCE SHEET.

neutrality of money. *See* MONEY, NEUTRALITY OF.

new classical economics. A theory of macroeconomic behaviour, developed mainly by R. Lucus, T.A. Sargent and, in the UK, by P. Minford, based on the assumptions of almost instantaneous MARKET-CLEARING and RATIONAL EXPECTATIONS. The analysis is classical in that it assumes that flexible prices and wages restore equilibrium, and new in that it specifies that this occurs very rapidly. In fact adjustment would be instantaneous but for the inconvenience of constantly changing prices, including the price of labour. When firms and workers negotiate a wage rate for the forthcoming period they agree an expected real wage that would clear the market, i.e. any unemployment would be voluntary. Employment and output will only be above the expected level if prices are higher, and therefore real wages are lower, than expected, since the lower real wage will encourage firms to hire more workers. (The additional workers will take the jobs offered only if they do not realize that real wages have fallen.) When wages are next re-negotiated, account will be taken of the unexpected rise in prices; the real wage rate will rise and firms will reduce employment and output. This analysis might seem to lead to the conclusion that by boosting expenditure the government could reduce unemployment in the short term, albeit at the cost of a rise in the rate of inflation.

But this policy would soon fail. Workers would soon start to anticipate the increase in the rate of inflation and wages would be adjusted accordingly. Since, before long, the only effect of higher demand would be higher prices, the policy conclusions are similar to those of monetarism, namely that the government should allow the money supply to expand in line with the growth of economic capacity and should concentrate on SUPPLY-SIDE POLICIES aimed at increasing economic CAPACITY and reducing the NATURAL RATE OF UNEMPLOYMENT.

new growth theory. The main conclusion of this theory, whose major exponent is P. Romer, is that an absence of decreasing returns to capital (broadly defined) means that persistent divergencies in growth rates between countries are possible, and that shocks, e.g. discoveries which boost investment, can have permanent effects on growth.

New International Economic Order. In 1974 the United Nations passed a resolution calling for international co-operation to reduce the gap between the developed and the less developed countries (the North and the South). A vehicle for co-operation would be a new international institution, that would be sponsored by the United Nations, whose aims would be to stabilize the prices of raw materials and increase foreign aid to developing countries.

new-issue market. Transactions on the stock exchange are confined to securities that have already been issued. But the new issue market allows firms to raise additional finance. There are several types of new issues. With a public issue by prospectus, the company offers to the general public a fixed number of shares or debentures at a stated price. An offer for sale is similar to a public issue, but the company sells the securities to an issuing house which subsequently offers them to the general public. With a placing, the securities are again acquired by an issuing house, which then places them with its clients. Rights issues are confined to existing shareholders; shareholders benefit from being able to buy at a price below the current market price, and the company benefits from lower administration costs than for other methods.

new protectionism. As tariffs have been reduced and quota restrictions relaxed, countries have sought other ways of restricting imports, including technical specifications more easily met by domestic than foreign producers, voluntary export restraints and local content requirements.

newly industrializing countries. Countries at a stage of development between less developed and advanced countries, e.g. Mexico, Singapore.

nominal prices. The prices ruling at a given point in time. Nominal or current prices should be distinguished from real or constant prices which take account of changes in the general level of prices.

nominal rate of protection. The protection afforded to domestic producers by a tariff on final products. If a 20 per cent tariff led to an increase in price of 20 per cent in imported products, the nominal rate of protection would be 20 per cent. The nominal rate can be less than the EFFECTIVE RATE OF PROTECTION when domestic producers use imported raw materials or components.

nominal variables. Nominal variables are measured in current prices, which means that changes may be an imperfect indicator of changes in the real values of those variables. For example a rise in nominal income does not necessarily mean that the individual is better off than previously. A rise in the nominal wage rate does not mean that the real cost of labour has risen. A rise in the nominal interest rate does not mean that the real return on capital has risen.

nominee. A token shareholder in whose name shares are registered on behalf of the ultimate owner. Most stockbrokers use nominees rather than registering shares in the name of individual clients, since that would make dealing very cumbersome.

non-discretionary rules. Rules made by policy-makers, perhaps enshrined in legislation, which define the consequences of action. For example some economists have advocated the inclusion of non-discretionary rules in competition policy, e.g. that a firm that was one of the biggest three in a market would be forbidden to merge with another firm, or that any merger between two firms which together would account for at least twenty-five per cent of the market would be forbidden.

non-excludability. If a good is provided for one citizen it is automatically provided for others. Non-excludability is a characteristic of PUBLIC GOODS.

non-expendable resources. *See* NATURAL RESOURCES.

non-market valuation. An estimate of what people would be willing to pay for goods if there was a market in those goods. Non-market valuation is an important issue in ENVIRONMENTAL ECONOMICS.

non-marketable securities. Securities that cannot be sold in second-hand markets, e.g. National Savings Certificates.

non-monetary indicators. Non-monetary measures of the level of a country's development, e.g. literacy, life-expectancy.

non-price competition. The many ways of competing, other than by price, include quality and design, the introduction of new products, advertising, early and reliable delivery, before-sales service and after-sales service. Non-price competition is an important reason for the growth of INTRA-INDUSTRY TRADE.

non-profit enterprises. There are a large number of non-profit making enterprises, ranging from government departments to charities. In recent years economists have given increasing attention to the organization of such enterprises, using some of the concepts developed in MANAGERIAL THEORIES OF THE FIRM.

non-renewable resources. *See* NATURAL RESOURCES.

non-rivalness. The consumption of a good by one person does not impede its consumption by others. Non-rivalness is a characteristic of PUBLIC GOODS.

non-tariff barriers. Barriers, other than tariffs, to the free movement of goods and services in international trade. These barriers include QUOTAS, VOLUNTARY EXPORT RESTRAINTS, EXCHANGE CONTROLS, buying policies, especially in the public sector, which favour domestic producers, technical specifications more easily met by domestic than foreign producers, import deposits, the imposition of high administrative costs on importers due, e.g., to excessive documentation, and export subsidies. Non-tariff barriers have become increasingly used in recent years, despite their negative effect on total welfare.

non-voting shares. *See* SHARES.

normal-cost pricing. Setting price by adding a mark-up to MARGINAL COST, the mark-up varying with the level of demand. (The term normal cost is perhaps a misnomer, since the term full cost pricing is more commonly used.)

normal curve. *See* NORMAL DISTRIBUTION.

normal distribution. A probability distribution whose continuous distribution (the normal curve) has a bell-shaped symmetrical pattern that extends indefinitely at both ends.

The normal curve can be defined in terms of its mean and standard deviation, and from these it is possible to calculate the height of the curve (the frequencies) corresponding to any numerical value. It is also possible to estimate the probability of getting a numerical value between two numbers by the corresponding area under the curve.

normal goods. *See* INCOME ELASTICITY OF DEMAND.

normal profit. The profit required for a firm to remain in its existing line of business. Normal profit is subjective, and may differ from one firm to another and, for a given firm, from one period to another.

normative economics. *See* ECONOMICS.

numeraire. A monetary unit used as the basis for denominating on a common basis a class of international transactions, e.g. the US dollar is used as the numeraire for international trade in oil.

O

obsolescence. The fall in value of an asset for reasons other than wear and tear. A machine might lose value because a more efficient machine comes on to the market; if one firm buys the new machine and is thereby able to sell its output at a lower price, its rivals may be forced to follow suit, and the existing machines may then become virtually worthless. Consumer goods may also become obsolescent because superior alternatives are marketed, or simply because of changes in fashion. Planned obsolescence denotes that producers make changes in design, colour, etc. in order to reduce the satisfaction derived from existing goods, so that consumers will replace these goods earlier than they would otherwise have done.

occupational immobility. The inability of workers to move from one occupation to another. This may be due partly to differences in the skills and abilities required by the two occupations, and partly to barriers to entry into the new occupations erected by trade unions, professional associations, etc.

occupational pension scheme. An arrangement organized by an employer, or on behalf of a group of employers, to provide pensions and other benefits in respect of employees on leaving employment or on death or retirement. In recent years the position of employees has been improved in a number of respects: membership of schemes has become optional, benefits can be transferred between employers, and the rights of people leaving a scheme early have been improved. Almost one in two workers is now in an occupational pension scheme. Most schemes require payments to be made by employees although some, e.g. in the civil service, are non-contributory.

off-balance-sheet financing. Obtaining the use of facilities without the need to increase liabilities as recorded in the balance sheet, e.g. equipment might be hired or leased rather than purchased.

offer for sale. *See* NEW ISSUE MARKET.

offer price. The price at which securities, e.g. units in UNIT TRUSTS, can be bought by investors.

Office of Electricity Generation. OFFER regulates the privatized electricity generating industry.

Office of Fair Trading. *See* COMPETITION POLICY.

Office of Gas Supply. OFGAS regulates the privatized gas supply industry.

Office of Telecommunications. OFTEL regulates the privatized telecommunications industry.

Office of Water Services. OFWAT regulates the privatized water authorities.

official development assistance. Government assistance to developing countries on concessionary (non-commercial) terms. The United Nations set a target for ODA of 0.7

per cent of gross national product, but most countries, including the UK, have failed to reach this target.

official financing transactions. In the BALANCE OF PAYMENTS the requirement for official financing transactions is given by the sum of the current and capital accounts, and may therefore be positive or negative. These transactions comprise movements of capital that involve the Bank of England, namely drawings on (or additions to) official reserves, and other official financing through borrowing in foreign currencies.

official reserves. In April 1992 the UK official reserves comprised gold (10 per cent), special drawing rights (3 per cent), reserve position with the INTERNATIONAL MONETARY FUND (4 per cent) and convertible currencies (83 per cent).

offset. *See* COUNTERTRADE.

oligopoly. A market in which a large proportion of output or sales is accounted for by a few firms. Many markets are of this type, but marginal analysis, used extensively in the theory of the firm, does not provide a satisfactory theory of oligopoly, since it cannot explain how the going price is determined. Moreover empirical evidence suggests that prices in oligopoly are less sticky than is suggested by the KINKED DEMAND CURVE model. Other models using marginal analysis have been constructed, but the conclusions derived from these models vary, depending upon the assumptions made. One model assumes complete co-operation among firms in price and output decisions, the outcome being the same as in a single firm monopoly. Another model assumes that there is no co-operation and that each firm believes that its rivals will react to a price change by keeping their prices unchanged. This leads to the same outcome as in perfect competition. Between these two extremes other models make assumptions that lead to predicted outcomes between the monopoly and perfect competition outcomes.

on-cost. Another term for overhead cost.

open-access resource. A resource on whose use no limitation is placed; an example would be a river which could be polluted at will.

open economy. An economy of a country which engages in international trade.

open market. A market in which there are no or few restrictions on the interplay of market forces. Open markets are characterized by (a) a high degree of uncertainty, at the time that production decisions are taken, about future prices; (b) an extreme difficulty in co-ordinating the activities of producers.

open-market operations. *See* MONETARY POLICY.

open price agreement. An INFORMATION AGREEMENT relating to prices.

opening prices. The prices at which trading in a market first occurs.

operating costs. Another term for variable costs.

operating profit. *See* PROFIT.

operations research. Operations or operational research is the analysis of business problems or situations in order to identify the optimal solution. For example if a firm wished to supply 95 per cent of orders from stock, the analysis of the past pattern of orders, together with the application of statistical theory, would give the minimum level of stock required.

opportunity cost. *See* COSTS.

opportunity cost ratio. *See* COMPARATIVE ADVANTAGE.

optimal externality. *See* EXTERNALITY, OPTIMAL.

optimal-growth theory. Theory which attempts to identify the rate of economic growth that would maximize social welfare. If the costs of economic growth, such as pollution, are ignored, the problem becomes one of identifying the growth rate that maximizes consumption per head over time.

optimal scale. *See* MINIMUM EFFICIENT SCALE.

optimal tariff. If one country accounts for a significant proportion of world imports of a good, the higher that country's demand, the higher will be the world price, i.e. the supply curve to that country will be upward sloping. Decisions on importing are made by individuals (or firms) and the quantity imported will be such that the cost to the individual of the last unit imported, i.e. the world price, equals the benefit derived from that unit. However, because the country faces an upward sloping supply curve, i.e. marginal cost exceeds average cost (world price), the cost to society will exceed the private benefit of each unit. Society will gain by restricting imports to the level at which the benefit from the last unit equals the social cost. The tariff which would bring this about is known as the optimal tariff. If the quantity imported by a country does not affect the world price, the optimal tariff is, of course, zero.

optimum. The position in which the aims of an economic agent are being met as far as is possible given the constraints that exist. For example the optimum pattern of expenditure is that which maximizes the UTILITY of a consumer with a given level of income.

optimum order quantity. The optimum or economic order quantity is the size of order which minimizes the costs of holding stocks or inventories. It balances the administrative costs of placing orders (which favour placing few, large orders) against the financing costs of inventories (which favour placing a large number of small orders).

optimum output. The output at which profit is maximized. (This assumes that the firm wishes to maximize profit. The optimum output might be different with other objectives, e.g. an increase in market share.)

optimum population. The simplest definition of the optimum population is the population which would enable the output of goods and services per head to be maximized. The optimum population will change as the amount of capital changes. Moreover the increased possibility that some resources may become exhausted due to population growth might also affect the optimum position.

option. (1) An agreement whereby a sale or purchase can be made at a specified price within a given period. On the stock exchange the right to sell securities is known as a put option, and the right to purchase as a call option. Markets in options can be used either for speculation or to spread risk. (2) Senior executives are sometimes given the option to buy shares in their company at the price ruling at the time the option is granted, an option that can be exercised during a period of several years. This provides an incentive to the executives to try to improve the performance of their company so that the shares rise in price and the value of their options increases.

option values. *See* TOTAL ECONOMIC VALUE.

ordinal utility. *See* UTILITY.

ordinary shares. *See* SHARES.

Organization for Economic Co-operation and Development. An organization, with twenty-four members in Europe, North America and other parts of the world, whose aims are to encourage economic growth and world trade. It produces regular reports on the world and individual economies, and provides a forum in which the industrialized nations discuss international economic problems.

Organization of Petroleum Exporting Countries. A group of thirteen major producers and exporters of crude petroleum. OPEC was formed in 1960 but did not have a marked impact on oil markets until the 1970s when it imposed a number of substantial price increases. It was able to maintain the higher prices since it accounted for about two-thirds of world output of oil, and about 90 per cent of exports. Political factors were also important, insofar as a common antipathy towards Israel encouraged OPEC members to keep to the output quotas needed for higher prices. Since then the influence of OPEC has declined for a number of reasons. The higher prices led to a fall in OPEC's market share as alternative sources of oil (and other fuels) were developed, e.g. North Sea oil and gas. The higher prices also stimulated energy-saving measures. Finally, differences of view arose about the market shares of members. Several countries exceeded their quotas to finance military expenditure or to support economic development. The unity of OPEC was also damaged by members' political hostility.

organizational slack. *See* BEHAVIOURAL THEORY OF THE FIRM.

original income. *See* INCOME.

other things being equal. *See* CETERIS PARIBUS.

output. When analysing a market or a firm, output is defined as the quantity of goods or services produced in a given period. (To simplify the analysis it is assumed that in a multi-product firm the output of each product can be separately identified.) But when analysing the economy allowance has to be made for the fact that the goods and services produced by some firms are used as inputs by other firms. In measuring output these intermediate goods are disregarded, output being defined as total VALUE ADDED.

output approach. *See* NATIONAL INCOME ACCOUNTING.

output gap. (1) The difference between actual output and trend output. (2) In models of national income determination an output gap is said to exist when the equilibrium level of output is less than the full-employment level.

output quota. A limit to output, accepted by members of a CARTEL or COMMODITY AGREEMENT.

outsiders. People who are not employed and who do not therefore influence wage negotiations.

overdraft. *See* BANK ADVANCES.

overfunding. *See* FUNDING.

overhead cost rate. The rate at which overhead costs are charged (i.e. added to prime costs) to each unit of output. The rate is calculated by dividing budgeted total overhead costs by budgeted total output.

overhead costs. *See* COSTS.

overheated economy. Denotes that aggregate demand is judged to be too high, given the level of economic capacity.

overmanning. Employing more workers than is required to produce a given output. This is one form of ORGANIZATIONAL SLACK, of X-INEFFICIENCY, and of DISGUISED UNEMPLOYMENT.

overseas investment. *See* FOREIGN INVESTMENT.

overseas sector. Individuals, firms and other organizations in other countries. The BALANCE OF PAYMENTS accounts identify three types of transactions with the overseas sector: those arising from exports and imports of goods and services; those arising from the overseas ownership of property, defined to include both financial and physical assets; transfers, e.g. payments to and receipts from the European Economic Community.

overshooting. Overshooting occurs when an economic variable responds too much to a stimulus, e.g. when an increase in demand results in price increasing beyond the equilibrium level, requiring a subsequent downward adjustment.

over-subscription. When applications for NEW ISSUES of securities exceed the number of securities offered. If the excess is substantial, trading in the securities usually opens at a premium, i.e. the market price exceeds the issue price. This indicates that the firm raised less money by the issue than would have been possible.

over-the-counter market. A market in securities outside the orbit of the stock exchange. Such markets are particularly well developed in the USA.

overtime. Work in excess of the hours worked at the agreed standard rate of pay. Workers benefit (provided that the overtime is voluntary) since the additional hours worked usually attract a higher rate of pay. Employers benefit from the flexibility; even at higher rates of pay it is cheaper than constantly changing the number of workers employed. However when overtime is worked regularly it may be at the expense of additional jobs.

overtrading. A firm which has insufficient working capital to meet the needs of its business is said to be overtrading.

overvalued currency. A currency whose current value in the foreign exchange markets is above its equilibrium level. This may be due to the fact that the government has fixed the rate at too high a level or, in a free market, because the rate does not fully reflect the influence of longer-term market forces.

ownership rights. *See* PROPERTY RIGHTS.

P

Paasche index. *See* INDEX NUMBER.

paid-up capital. That part (often 100 per cent) of the issued capital of a company that has been paid up by shareholders.

Panel on Takeovers and Mergers. *See* CITY CODE.

paper profit. An unrealized profit on an asset. If one person owns a large proportion of the asset, e.g. the shares in a company, it may be difficult to realize the paper profit, since sales of the asset would lead to a fall in its price.

par value. The nominal or face value of a stock or share.

paradox of thrift. An increase in the propensity to save leads to a fall in national income, leaving the level of saving unchanged. (A decrease in the propensity to save would lead to a rise in national income, again leaving the level of saving unchanged.)

paradox of value. Refers to the fact that the price of a necessity, e.g. water, may be lower than the price of a product that is much less useful, e.g. diamonds. The paradox is resolved when it is understood that price reflects relative SCARCITY and MARGINAL UTILITY which diminishes as consumption increases.

paradox of voting. Consistency in decision-taking by individuals does not guarantee that the decisions taken in a democratic society will be consistent. In this context consistent means transitive, i.e. if an individual or group prefers A to B and B to C, it will also prefer A to C.

parallel imports. Imports through channels of distribution other than those officially supplied by the manufacturer of the product concerned. The manufacturer has much less influence (if any at all) on the price at which parallel imports are sold or distributed to the public.

parallel money markets. *See* MONEY MARKET.

parallel pricing. When suppliers of a product make identical price changes at roughly the same time they are said to engage in parallel pricing. The price changes may reflect a change in costs that affects all suppliers to the same extent. Alternatively they may be the result of COLLUSION.

parameter. The value (or values) in a mathematical function that remain constant against movements in the variables of the function. For example in a consumption function of the form $C = a + b(Y)$, where C is consumption and Y is disposable income, a and b are parameters or constants.

Pareto efficiency. Pareto efficiency, sometimes known as economic efficiency, is a situation in which it is impossible to make someone better off without making someone else worse off. A Pareto efficient allocation of resources requires that markets should not be distorted in any way (the first-best allocation). But if a distortion does exist (and all economies have many distortions), it may be possible to improve the allocation of resources by introducing further distortions (the second-best solution). For example if some markets are monopolistic, resource allocation may be improved if perfectly competitive markets also become monopolistic.

partial-correlation coefficient. A measure of the strength of the relationship between two variables when the values of other influencing variables are held constant.

partial-equilibrium analysis. The study of a market that ignores the fact that changes in that market could have effects on other markets which would then feed back into the initial market. It is assumed that the feedback is of no significance, and that it can safely be ignored in order to simplify analysis. A good example would be where a reduction in the price of a product led to an increase in real income that was insignificant as a proportion of the incomes of consumers. Partial-equilibrium analysis would be less valid if the price reduction led the suppliers of other products to protect their markets by increased advertising and this drew customers away from the initial market.

participation discrimination. The term used by certain economists to describe a situation in which differences in annual earnings between majority and minority workers are a consequence of differences in participation in the labour force in terms of time in employment over the year. These differences in participation are a function of hours of work and of time spent unemployed or out of the labour market.

participation rate. The participation or activity rate is the proportion of the population of working age who are in work or seeking work. (Working age is defined as the period between the minimum school leaving age and the age at which the state retirement pension becomes payable.) Participation rates for various age cohorts are also calculated.

partnership. An unincorporated business, of from two to twenty people (or more in certain professions such as accountancy and the law). All the partners (with the exception of sleeping partners, if any) take part in the running of the business, and each partner is personally responsible for any debts incurred by the partnership (except in the few limited partnerships that have been formed).

patents. Firms or individuals who invent new processes or products can apply for a patent which prevents others from copying the invention for a specified number of years. The patent system provides an incentive to spend money on research and development. On the other hand patents can impede the diffusion of new discoveries, once made.

pay-as-you-earn. The deduction of income tax by employers, acting on behalf of the Inland Revenue, from the weekly or monthly pay of staff.

payback. The payback method of investment appraisal ranks products in accordance with the length of time required for the sum of the net cash inflows derived from a project to equal the initial cash outflow. The shorter the payback period, the higher the ranking. Of the three projects shown in Table 19, A would be ranked first. The main deficiency of the payback method is that it ignores (a) the total profits expected to be generated by projects, and (b) the time pattern of these profits. The circumstances most favourable to this method are when future economic conditions are highly uncertain and the firm wishes to limit its risks.

pay leapfrogging. When different groups of workers attempt to justify pay claims by reference to pay differentials. If group A achieves a wage increase in order to bring their pay up to (or above) that of group B, group B then seeks higher wages in order to restore the previous differential with A.

Table 19   Payback method of investment appraisal

Net cash flow	Project		
	A	B	C
Year 0	−1000	−1000	−1000
1	100	150	500
2	250	250	250
3	500	250	150
4	150	250	50
5	−	250	50
6	−	200	−

pay-out ratio. The dividends paid by a company as a proportion of its earnings (which may be expressed gross or net of tax).

payment in kind. Payment in goods and services.

payroll tax. A tax on employers related to the size of the wage and salary bill. There is no payroll tax in the UK, although employers' national insurance contributions have a similar effect.

peak load pricing. A system of pricing in which peak time users of a product pay higher prices to reflect the higher cost of supply at such times. This higher cost may be due to the use of less efficient production units, e.g. electricity supplied from older generating stations.

pendulum arbitration. *See* ARBITRATION.

penetration pricing. Charging a low price in order to gain rapid penetration of a market. If average cost falls as output increases, the penetration price may then yield normal profit.

pension funds. Contributions to occupational and perscnal pension schemes. The contributions are mostly placed in managed invested funds, and the managers of these funds are among the most important institutional investors, being the largest shareholders in many prominent companies.

pensions. Income received by retired people which is related to their working life. There are several types of pension in the UK. The state retirement pension depends upon an individual's record of national insurance contributions over his or her working life. At present it is payable from age sixty for women and sixty-five for men, but the government is considering moving to a common age for payment. Retirement pensions may include an earnings-related element (state earnings-related pension schemes), but it is possible for members of an OCCUPATIONAL PENSION SCHEME which meets certain conditions to contract out of the SERPS. PERSONAL PENSIONS first became available in July 1988 and in the first year nearly 3½ million people applied for personal pension plans. Government encouragement of personal pensions reflects the increasing burden of state retirement pensions, due largely to demographic changes. The number of people of pensionable age was expected to rise from 9½ millions in 1989 to 13 millions in 2025. The number of people of working age for each person of pensionable age was expected to fall from 3.4 to 2.6.

perfect competition. A perfectly competitive market is one in which there are a large number of perfectly informed buyers and sellers of identical products, and in which there are no barriers to entry or exit. Because products are identical and there is perfect information, each supplier is able to sell as much as it wishes at the going market price, but can sell nothing at a higher price, i.e. each supplier faces a horizontal demand curve, and average revenue equals marginal revenue. In order to maximize its profits the firm produces to the point at which MARGINAL COST equals MARGINAL REVENUE. It is possible that this output will yield supernormal profits in the short run, but since there are no barriers to entry, supernormal profits will attract new firms into the market. The additional output from these new suppliers will cause the price to fall so that only NORMAL PROFIT is earned in the long run. Conversely, if subnormal profits are earned in the short run, some suppliers will leave the market and the fall in supply will lead to a rise in price so that normal profit is earned in the long run.

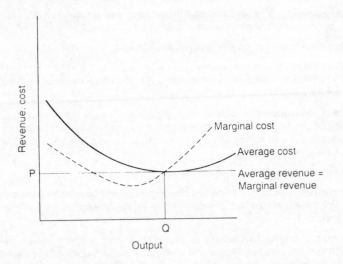

Figure 10   Long-run equilibrium in perfect competition

Perfect competition is not to be seen as an exact description of markets in practice (probably the markets in some financial assets, e.g. shares, come closest to the conditions required for perfect competition). Rather it should be seen as an ideal, a market form that is consistent with PARETO EFFICIENCY and therefore a benchmark against which other market forms can be judged. It is, however, a very imperfect benchmark. If there are a large number of producers, costs may well be higher because of the inability to take advantage of ECONOMIES OF SCALE. Moreover, freedom of entry and perfect information are unlikely to be conducive to INNOVATION. (Neither of these factors figures in the Pareto calculus, despite their considerable practical importance.) This is not to deny that the model of perfect competition has produced useful insights, but it seems that these insights may be more fruitful when incorporated in other models, e.g. the model of CONTESTABLE MARKETS.

permanent income hypothesis. A hypothesis advanced by Milton Friedman who argued that consumption depends upon average long run (permanent) income. Consumption will respond fully to changes in income only when people believe that the change will be maintained. This hypothesis may help to explain why cross-section studies have revealed lower propensities to consume than those found in time-series studies of long-run consumption functions.

perpetuities. Bonds that are never repurchased by the issuer, who continues to pay interest for ever, e.g. CONSOLS.

personal allowance. An offset against income tax, which means that the first portion of a person's income (£3445, or more for older people, in 1993/4) is not taxable.

personal disposable income. *See* INCOME.

personal equity plan. Introduced in 1986 to encourage direct investment in shares, the scheme was subsequently extended to cover holdings in unit and investment trusts. Up to £6000 can be invested in any year and, provided that the securities are held from the start of the plan until 31 December of the following year, gains from selling the securities are free of capital gains tax, and dividends are free of income tax if re-invested.

personal loan. *See* BANK ADVANCES.

personal pension. Under the Finance Act 1988 employers can no longer make membership of an occupational pension scheme compulsory. Employees are given the option of subscribing to a personal pension scheme of their own choice. (More than a hundred insurance companies, friendly societies, unit trusts and building societies offer schemes.) The schemes are portable, i.e. employees changing employers can take their accumulated pension rights with them. The ultimate value of the pension depends upon the contributions paid and the return on them when invested, in contrast to occupational pensions which are usually linked to final salary. Personal pensions are the only form of pension available to the self-employed. Contributions attract tax relief up to specified limits.

personal saving. Personal disposable income minus consumers' expenditure. Personal disposable income includes: employers' contributions to the National Insurance Fund and occupational pensions funds; the income earned on the assets of pension funds; the imputed rental value of owner-occupied housing; the income of unincorporated businesses. Changes in any of these items will cause a change in the recorded level of personal saving if consumption is unchanged.

personal savings ratio. Personal saving as a proportion of personal disposable income.

personal sector. The personal sector comprises households, unincorporated businesses and non-profit making organizations such as charities and trade unions.

personal wealth. The assets of the personal sector both financial, e.g. shares, pension rights, and physical, e.g. houses.

petrocurrency. A currency whose exchange rate is significantly higher than it would otherwise be because of the country's exports of oil.

petroleum revenue tax. A tax levied at 75 per cent on a field-by-field basis on profits from oil and gas production in Britain and from the UK Continental Shelf. Expenditure on exploration and the appraisal of potential fields can be offset against tax, and companies are allowed a slice of tax-free production. The tax can be seen as an indirect form of payment for the government licences giving exploration rights, which often yield very high profits.

Phillips curve. From a study of the UK economy in the period 1861 to 1957, A.W. Phillips found that there was an inverse relationship between the rate of unemployment and the rate of change of money wages. Plotting the data on a graph with unemployment on the horizontal, and changes in wages on the vertical axis, yielded a well-defined curve. Since changes in money wages often lead to price changes, Phillips's findings led to the conclusion that there was an inverse relationship between the rate of unemployment and the rate of inflation. The policy implication of this analysis was that the government could influence the rate of inflation by changing unemployment by means of demand management policies. However, this apparent trade-off between unemployment and inflation seemed no longer to apply from the 1970s onwards. It appeared that if the Phillips curve was still valid, it must lie much further to the right than Phillips suggested, meaning that a given rate of unemployment was associated with a much higher rate of inflation than expected.

Phillips curve, expectations-augmented. Whereas the PHILLIPS CURVE, as originally formulated, sloped down from left to right, the expectations-augmented curve is vertical, cutting the horizontal axis at the NATURAL RATE OF UNEMPLOYMENT. The expectations-augmented curve is sometimes called the long-run Phillips curve, being distinguished from downward sloping short-run curves.

physical controls. Direct controls on production or consumption, e.g. regulations specifying the types of buildings that can be erected, and the forms of activity than can be undertaken, in a given area.

piece-rates. A wages system under which workers are paid in accordance with the work done. Piece-rates can act as an incentive to workers and as a means of risk-reduction for employers.

Pigou effect. *See* REAL BALANCE EFFECT.

placing. *See* NEW-ISSUE MARKET.

planned economy. *See* COMMAND ECONOMY.

planned investment. The amount of investment expenditure that firms plan to undertake, given the level of national income. In simple models the equilibrium level of income is that at which planned investment equals PLANNED SAVING.

planned saving. The amount of saving planned at a given level of national income.

plant bargaining. Wage bargaining conducted at the plant (office, factory, etc.). Sometimes minimum wage rates are determined centrally, and these are supplemented by amounts negotiated at the level of the plant, which is more sensitive to conditions in the local labour market.

ploughing-back. Retaining profits for use in the further development of the business.

point elasticity. Elasticity at a point on a demand or supply curve. An accurate measure of point elasticity requires the use of calculus but a good approximation for small changes in price is given by the expression:

$$e = \frac{\text{the percentage (or proportionate) change in quantity}}{\text{the percentage (or proportionate) change in price}}$$

For example if price fell from 100 to 99 and the quantity demanded increased from 100 to 102, the elasticity of demand would be -2.

poison pill. *See* TAKEOVER.

polarization. Under the Financial Services Act 1986 each registered insititution has to state clearly whether it is acting as salesmen or agent for only one intermediary, e.g. one insurance company's endowment policies, or as an independent advisor. An institution acting as an advisor, e.g. a bank, cannot recommend its own services (life insurance, etc.), although clients can expressly request information about those services.

poll tax. *See* LUMP-SUM TAX.

population. (1) The number of people living in a given area. (2) A term applied to any class of data of which a count is made or a sample taken, e.g. the unemployed.

population, census of. A count of all the people living in the UK, taken every ten years. The information obtained enables details to be published of the age and sex structure of the population, occupations, living conditions, etc. The census data is also used to make predictions of future population changes.

population structure. The proportion of the population in various age-groups, and the proportion of males and females.

population trap. A rate of population growth greater than the rate of growth of economic activity, leading to a decline in income per head.

portability. The ease with which a currency can be transferred within the banking and financial system.

portable pension. *See* PERSONAL PENSION.

portfolio. The collection of assets held by an investor. The term is most commonly applied to financial assets.

portfolio balance approach. An explanation of the EXCHANGE RATE which emphasizes the importance of capital flows which are independent of changes in the balance of payments current account. Capital flows may be the result of changes in investors' preferences concerning (a) the form of assets held and (b) the currency in which those assets are denominated.

portfolio investment. A term applied particularly to investment overseas, where it denotes expenditure on the purchase of financial assets, as opposed to direct investment.

portfolio theory. Portfolio theory attempts to identify the factors influencing investors' choices of assets, and the characteristics of an efficient portfolio. Investors are assumed to prefer a higher to a lower expected return, but also to dislike risk, defined as variability in the return of the portfolio as a whole. If all investors are risk-averse, the more risky assets will have to offer a higher expected return. In this situation, provided that the returns on different assets are not correlated, diversification, i.e. the purchase of a range of assets, can enable investors to reduce their risk without any reduction in the portfolio's expected return.

positional goods. The significance of positional goods was demonstrated by Fred Hirsch who defined them as goods that are either (a) scarce in some absolute or socially imposed sense or (b) subject to congestion or crowding through more extensive use. Since positional goods, e.g. old masters, beautiful landscapes, are virtually fixed in supply, their price tends to rise over time relative to other goods whose supply can be increased to meet an increased demand.

positive economics. *See* ECONOMICS.

post-Keynesian economics. Post-Keynesian economics has its origins in the work of J.M. Keynes and of the classical economists (including Marx). Three sub-groupings can be distinguished: (a) The American post-Keynesians, e.g. L. Tarshis and J. Weintraub, emphasize in their writings the integration of money (including international money) with the real aspects of the economy, and explore how these relationships are affected by uncertainty. The micro-foundations of their macroeconomics are usually imperfectly competitive. (b) The neo-Ricardians emphasize long-period aspects of the economy. They have developed the long-period aspects of Keynes's theory of effective demand and combined this with the long-period theory of value and distribution of the classical economists and Marx, as modernized under the heading of the surplus approach by P. Sraffa and others. (c) The third sub-group, which might be called Robinsonians/Kaleckians, reject conventional equilibrium analysis and the long-period approach, at least for explanations of processes at work in actual economies. They are attempting to produce models of cyclical growth which incorporate endogenous theories of institutions and technical change, as well as monetary factors. They have developed empirical models of the US and UK economies which reflect the post-Keynesian approach to the theory of accumulation, the pricing of manufactured products and the macro-distribution of the product between profits and wages.

potential competition. In their price and output decisions many firms have to take into account not only existing competitors but also firms which could easily enter the market. This potential competition may cause firms to forego higher short-run profits that would induce new entry.

potential output. *See* CAPACITY.

potential Pareto improvement criterion. *See* COST BENEFIT ANALYSIS.

poverty. Poverty is usually defined in a relative rather than an absolute sense. People are said to be poor when they do not enjoy what is deemed by society to be the minimum acceptable standard of living (in terms of food, accommodation, etc.). Poverty may be due to a variety of causes, including unemployment, low pay, and large family size.

poverty trap. A combination of income tax and means-tested state benefits may mean that poor people keep an extremely small fraction of any increase in earnings, i.e. the effective marginal rate of tax may be extremely high. When the costs of working, e.g. transport to and from work, are taken into account, some people may be better off unemployed than working.

precautionary motive. *See* MONEY, DEMAND FOR.

pre-commitment. An arrangement, entered into voluntarily, which restricts one's future options.

predatory pricing. Setting prices intended to force competitors out of business or the market.

preference shares. *See* SHARES.

preference-similarity theory. An explanation of INTRA-INDUSTRY TRADE. It is assumed that producers supply models or versions of products with characteristics that appeal mainly to domestic consumers, but that a minority of customers in overseas markets also desire products with these characteristics. Since this form of product differentiation occurs especially in developed countries, intra-industry trade mainly takes place between such countries.

preferential duty. A TARIFF imposed at a lower rate on imports from some countries than from others.

premium. (1) A regular payment in return for an insurance policy. (2) A security whose market price exceeds its issue price (or its nominal price) is said to be selling at a premium. (3) An addition to the normal or list price of a product because of special circumstances, e.g. very quick delivery.

prescriptive economics. Another term for NORMATIVE ECONOMICS.

present value. The discounted value of a sum arising in the future. If the rate of interest was 10 per cent, the present value of £110 received in one year's time would be £110 divided by 1.1, which equals £100. A person would be indifferent as between these two alternatives (assuming that the rate of interest is an accurate measure of his rate of time preference) since he could invest £100 today and receive £110 in a year's time. An investment project usually yields a stream of cash inflows, but the same principle applies in estimating the present value.

price. What must be given in order to obtain a good or service. Price is normally expressed in terms of a quantity of money per unit of the commodity.

price as indicator of quality. When consumers are unable to judge the quality of a product, e.g. because they cannot test it before purchase, they may see its price as an indicator of quality. For such products a higher price might lead to a greater quantity demanded.

price ceiling. The maximum price at which the government allows a product to be sold or supplied, e.g. limits have been imposed on the rents charged for accommodation. Price ceilings are usually imposed to ensure that poorer people are able to purchase the product in question. But to ensure that this happens an appropriate system of rationing is required, since demand is likely to exceed supply at the ceiling price.

price-consumption curve. *See* INDIFFERENCE-CURVE ANALYSIS.

price control. *See* PRICES AND INCOMES POLICIES.

price differentiation. Charging different prices for a given product to different customers or groups of customers.

price discrimination. Charging different prices for a given product to different customers or groups of customers when the price differences do not reflect differences in the costs of supply. Price discrimination leads to higher profits provided that the different markets (groups of customers) supplied have different PRICE ELASTICITIES OF DEMAND, and that there is no leakage between the markets. This second condition requires that customers are unable to buy in one market and re-sell in another, and that they are unable to transfer from one market to another. The term discriminating monopoly may seem to imply that only monopolists can practise price discrimination, but this is true only in the sense that the demand curve must be less than perfectly elastic in at least one of the markets. In some situations price discrimination can benefit both producers and consumers. If there is no uniform price at which a profit could be made, the producer might cease production. However, price discrimination might enable the producer to earn a profit and so continue in production.

price-earnings ratio. The price of a share divided by the most recent year's earnings per share.

price effect. A change in price has both a substitution and an income effect, as demonstrated for product markets by INDIFFERENCE-CURVE ANALYSIS. If the price of a factor of production increases, other factors whose relative prices have fallen are likely to be substituted for it. However the cost and therefore the price of the product may still increase so that less is demanded. The consequence of this price effect may be a reduction in the demand for all the factors of production, including those whose relative prices have fallen.

price elasticity of demand. The proportionate (or percentage) change in the quantity of a product demanded, divided by the proportionate (percentage) change in its price.

Demand is said to be (price) elastic when elasticity is greater than (negative) one, and inelastic when it is less than (negative) one. (Because price elasticity of demand is almost always negative, it is conventional to omit the negative sign. For example if, following a change in price from £100 to £101, the quantity demanded fell from 100 to 98, elasticity would be given as two, rather than the true value of negative two.) For many products demand tends to become more elastic, in response to a given price change, as more opportunities for SUBSTITUTION arise over time.

price elasticity of supply. The proportionate (or percentage) change in the quantity of a product supplied, divided by the proportionate (percentage) change in its price. Supply is said to be (price) elastic when elasticity is greater than one, and inelastic when it is less than one. Elasticity of supply tends to be higher for manufactured goods than for primary (and especially agricultural) products whose supply is governed by natural conditions. But for all products elasticity, in response to a given price change, tends to increase as more opportunities arise over time to make adjustments in the use of FACTORS OF PRODUCTION.

price fixing. Agreements among competitors concerning prices to be charged.

price flexibility. Prices are said to be flexible when they respond freely to changes in the balance between demand and supply. In classical economics markets were considered to be always in equilibrium because of price flexibility. This proposition was denied by J.M. Keynes. Taking an example from Keynes, real wages are not sufficiently flexible to ensure that there is no excess supply in the labour market.

price floor. The level below which price is not allowed to fall. In an attempt to protect producers' incomes, commodity agreements may specify that buying by the central organization should always prevent price from falling below the floor.

price index. *See* INDEX NUMBER and INFLATION.

price leadership. When one firm's lead in changing price is followed by its rivals. Price leadership can be seen as evidence of collusive behaviour and therefore anti-competitive. Alternatively it could indicate that all firms in the market are affected by cost changes to roughly the same extent, but that one firm reacts before the others. In some instances the dominant firm in the market has been accepted as the price leader for a considerable period of time. In other instances different firms have led on different occasions; this situation is sometimes known as barometric price leadership, the firm making the first move having acted as a barometer for the rest of the industry.

price level. The average price of all goods and services. It is a useful concept in macroeconomic models. It cannot be precisely calculated in practice, but various INDEX NUMBERS give some indication of changes in the price level.

price lining. Selling a range of heterogeneous products at the same price, e.g. articles of clothing of various colours, styles and sizes.

price maintenance. *See* RESALE PRICE MAINTENANCE.

price maker. A firm which sets a price for its product and sells what it can at this price. Price making is usually associated with firms which are dominant on account of their size or high market share.

price mechanism. In a free market economy resources are allocated via the price mechanism. When the owners of resources decide to which producers they should make inputs available, they are influenced by the rewards offered by the various producers. Producers, when deciding which goods and services to produce, are influenced by the prices offered for the various goods and services, and also by the rewards that they have to offer to obtain the inputs required to produce these goods and services. Finally, the price mechanism helps to determine which consumers are able to buy particular goods and services and, looking at the matter from a slightly different viewpoint, which goods and services each consumer buys.

price-minus costing. This refers to the situation when firms who are PRICE TAKERS, finding that the market price does not yield satisfactory profits, respond by reducing their costs through increased efficiency.

price squeezing. An anti-competitive practice that might be undertaken by a vertically integrated firm in competition with non-integrated firms. For example if it controlled the supply of raw materials it might sell these to non-integrated firms at a high price so that it could undersell them in the market for final products.

price stickiness. A failure of prices to respond quickly to changes in the CONDITIONS OF DEMAND OR SUPPLY. Several possible explanations of price stickiness in product markets have been advanced, including price making or administered pricing by dominant firms, and the existence of the KINKED DEMAND CURVE in oligopoly. These explanations emphasize the advantages of price stickiness to producers. But other explanations also take account of advantages to consumers. For example, the model of shopping developed by A. Okun assumes that because shopping is a constantly repeated activity, the relationship between shopper and store (or between any customer and supplier) is similar to that between employee and employer, with advantages to both parties from a continuing relationship. A continuing relationship reduces the amount of resources devoted by the supplier in seeking out consumers, and reduces the resources devoted by consumers to acquiring information about products, prices, etc. Okun argues that price stability may help to develop this type of relationship.

price support. The maintenance of price above the free market level, achieved through purchases by a central organization.

price system. A form of economic organization in which resources are allocated through the PRICE MECHANISM.

price taker. A firm which accepts the market price and plans its output in the light of that price.

price theory. The branch of economics concerned with the formation of market prices. Price theory using MARGINAL ANALYSIS explains how prices are determined in perfect competition, monopoly and monopolistic competition. Marginal analysis can also be used to show why prices might be sticky in oligopoly. The conclusions derived from this approach, and especially from a comparison of perfect competition and monopoly, have important implications for welfare economics. However, these conclusions depend heavily upon the assumptions underlying the models concerning firms' motivations and the amount of information available, and empirical studies suggest that these assumptions seldom apply in practice. Consequently, alternative theories have been formulated, based on observation of business behaviour. These theories relate both to pricing procedures, e.g. FULL-COST PRICING, and to more comprehensive accounts of behaviour, e.g. BEHAVIOURAL and MANAGERIAL THEORIES OF THE FIRM. A third approach has involved the application of GAME THEORY to pricing decisions in markets characterized by interdependence among suppliers.

price war. A situation in which rivals keep undercutting each other's prices in an attempt to win sales.

prices and incomes policies. Prices and incomes policies have been used in an attempt to counteract both DEMAND-PULL and COST-PUSH INFLATION. A comprehensive policy involves controls on both prices and incomes, but since the costs of implementing such a policy are high, governments have sometimes adopted a less comprehensive approach, trying to control either prices or incomes. However this has proved difficult politically. Trade unions have been reluctant to accept wage controls when the absence of price controls could allow firms to increase their profits. Firms have been reluctant to accept price controls when the absence of controls on wages, and thus on costs, could cause profits to fall to unacceptable levels. Whether a more or a less comprehensive policy is adopted, numerous questions arise concerning the details of the policy. Should a figure, e.g. for changes in prices, be stated as a guideline or norm or as a maximum? Should it be expressed in absolute or percentage terms? On what criteria, if any, should departures from the figure be allowed, e.g. should a shift to working unsocial hours justify an increase in wages? Should price controls take account of changes in costs? If so, should the price be allowed to reflect all increases in costs or should the firm be expected to absorb part of those increases? What prices should firms be allowed to charge for new products? What wages or salaries should be paid for new jobs? These questions indicate the difficulties that can arise in the implementation of prices and incomes policies. Furthermore, by inhibiting changes in relative prices, the policies impede the re-allocation of resources. Finally, it seems that the long-term effect on the rate of inflation is negligible, any ground gained while the policies are operating soon being lost once the policies are relaxed. The strongest case for the policies are when they are applied rigidly for a short period of time in order to break an inflationary (price-wage or wage-price) cycle. The deficiencies of conventional prices and incomes policies have led to proposals for a different form of incomes policy, in which taxation would be used to influence changes in earnings. Under a scheme proposed by Richard Layard any employer paying above the pay norm would pay tax equal to the tax rate times the excess growth of pay. Firms awarding pay increases below the norm would pay a negative tax, i.e. would receive a subsidy.

pricing season. Marginal analysis suggests that prices change with every change in demand or cost. However, price changes give rise to costs, e.g. reprinting price lists, and to added uncertainty for customers. Consequently many firms set prices that they hope to maintain for a season, e.g. six or twelve months.

primary sector. The primary sector of the economy comprises firms engaged in agriculture, forestry, fishing and the extractive industies.

prime costs. *See* COSTS.

prime rate. The rate charged by US commercial banks to first-class corporate customers for short-term loans.

principal – agent relationship. The essence of this relationship is that the principal engages an agent to perform some service on the principal's behalf which involves delegating some decision-making authority to the agent. When there is a separation of ownership from control in firms, the shareholders act as principals and the directors and senior executives as agents. Professionals (lawyers, architects, etc.) act as agents, and their clients as principals. Agency theory has been extensively applied to the relationship between employers (principals) and workers (agents). Agency theory suggests that the principal, e.g. an employer, will try to limit the divergence from his interests by establishing incentives, by monitoring, measuring and observing the agents, and by devising budgetary restrictions and operating rules. Agents will demonstrate that they will not act in a way that will harm the principal's interests. One way in which workers can do this is by investing in their relationship with their employer, for example by undergoing training in skills that are required only by the principal, thus showing that they would have something to lose should the relationship be broken.

principle of comparative advantage. *See* COMPARATIVE ADVANTAGE.

principle of exclusion. The consumption of a private good by one household means that another household cannot consume that good.

principles of taxation. *See* CANONS OF TAXATION.

prior charges. The holders of DEBENTURES and PREFERENCE SHARES have priority over the holders of ordinary SHARES to payments out of profits or capital repayments. These payments are known as prior charges.

prisoner's dilemma. A situation in game theory in which a group of economic agents, unaware of how the other agents are going to act, act independently, and the outcome is less favourable than it would have been if they had acted in conjunction. For example in the absence of a strong competition policy it might be possible for the firms in an OLIGOPOLY to collude in setting a price that would maximize their joint profits. However each producer, not being sure that the other producers will adhere to the agreement, may reason that it will maximize its profits by setting a lower price. But when all producers reduce price, no producer maximizes profits.

private benefits. The benefits received by the parties to a market transaction, i.e. it does not include EXTERNAL BENEFITS. Examples of private benefits are the satisfaction obtained from a product by the purchaser, and the goods which a firm can produce with the resources which it purchases.

private company. A company which can raise finance by the issue of shares, but which cannot make a public issue of shares. Most of the companies in the UK are private, and almost all of these are LIMITED COMPANIES.

private costs. Costs incurred by firms during the production and distribution of goods and services, i.e. it does not include EXTERNAL COSTS.

private enterprise. Economic activity in the private, as opposed to the public, sector.

private good. A good which if it is consumed by one household cannot be consumed by another household.

Private Investors Authority. LAUTRO and FIMBRA are due to merge in July 1994 to form the PIA.

private sector. *See* SECTORS OF THE ECONOMY.

privatization. Two aspects of privatization can be distinguished, both of which lead to a switch of resources from the public to the private sector. The first is a transfer of ownership from the private to the public sector, e.g. the sale of shares in the former nationalized industries to the general public, the sale of council houses to tenants. The second is opening to private sector suppliers markets previously reserved for public sector suppliers, e.g. competitive tendering for work previously done by the direct works departments of local authorities, franchises which allowed independent television companies to compete with the BBC. The objectives of the privatization programme undertaken in the UK, and especially of the transfer of nationalized industries to the private sector, appear to have included: to increase producers' exposure to competition and so to provide an incentive to increased efficiency; to raise revenue for the government and thus reduce the public sector borrowing requirement; to widen share ownership; to enable the firms concerned to compete more freely for funds in the capital market; to ease problems of pay determination in the public sector; to redistribute income and wealth; to free producers from detailed government intervention. These objectives have sometimes proved to be incompatible, and most economists believe that too little weight has been given to the first objective listed above. The government seldom took full advantage of the opportunity to split the industry into competing units, possibly because it believed that important ECONOMIES OF SCALE would thereby be lost. (The prices charged in the electricity, gas, telecommunications and water industries are subject to approval by government appointed regulators, and price controls may act as an incentive to increased efficiency.)

probability. If an event has n out-turns of which r have a particular characteristic, the probability of that characteristic occurring in a single out-turn is $r \div n$. The best known example is a toss of a coin where the probabilities of getting a 'head' or a 'tail' are equal ($r = 0.5$).

probability distribution. A theoretical frequency distribution showing the expected frequency with which a particular event will occur on average. For example the probability distribution of getting a 'head' from a single toss of a coin would be

number of heads	probability
1	0.5
0	0.5

producer price index. An index of the prices of CAPITAL GOODS. The index is obtained by deflating total fixed capital formation at current prices by the constant price total.

producer's surplus. The excess of the revenue received by the producer of a given quantity of a product above the minimum the producer would require in order to supply that quantity.

product differentiation. Measures adopted by producers to convince customers that their products are distinct from the products of competitors. These measures range from the production of heterogeneous, i.e. physically distinct, products, to branding and advertising designed to create a distinctive image for one brand of a homogeneous product. In some instances an important part of product differentiation relates not to the product itself, but to other aspects of the supplier's offer: length of delivery date, period of guarantee, after-sales service, etc. The effect of product differentiation is to make the demand for the firm's product less price elastic. It may also lead to an increase in demand.

product life cycle. Many products exhibit a fairly distinct pattern of sales and profitability: growth, maturity and decline. Firms take this into account in their policies relating to prices, investment, R & D expenditure, etc.

product mix. The mix of products supplied by a firm. Firms often attempt to have a mix which includes products at differing stages in the PRODUCT LIFE CYCLE. They may also seek to minimize their risk by having products which sell in markets which behave differently during the BUSINESS CYCLE.

production, census of. Information is obtained each year from all firms employing 100 or more people in manufacturing, construction, utilities and the extraction industries, and from a sample of firms in these industries employing from 20-99 people. The information includes the volume and the value of output, costs, and labour employed.

production, factors of. *See* FACTORS OF PRODUCTION.

production, theory of. *See* THEORY OF PRODUCTION.

production externalities. *See* EXTERNALITY.

production function. The production function shows the maximum output that can be produced in a given period from specified inputs in the existing state of technical knowledge. The function is usually expressed in mathematical terms. The function may exhibit constant, increasing or diminishing RETURNS TO SCALE. The Cobb-Douglas production function achieved notoriety because it appeared to show that the shares of total output accruing to labour and capital were constant over time. However this finding would no longer receive support statistically.

production possibility frontier. A production possibility frontier, boundary or curve shows the various combinations of two products that could be produced in a given period of time. (The quantity of one product is measured on the *y* axis, the quantity of the other on the *x* axis.) The frontier is usually assumed to be concave to the origin, reflecting the fact that some resources are better suited to the production of one good and other resouces to the production of the other good. As the output of one good is increased, resources are employed that are relatively less efficient in that use than those already employed; the rate of technical substitution declines as more of a good is produced. If the products measured on the two axes are capital and consumption goods, the production possibility frontier indicates the level of economic capacity. An increase in capacity, due to an increase in the quantity of inputs available or to technological advances, would be shown by an outward shift of the frontier.

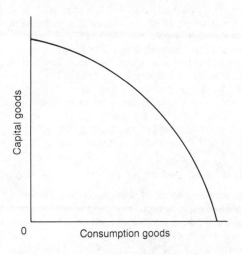

Figure 11   A production possibility frontier

production quota. *See* OUTPUT QUOTA.

productive efficiency. *See* ECONOMIC EFFICIENCY.

productivity. Productivity is the relationship between output and the inputs used to produce that output. Since the quantity of resources, and especially of labour, grows only slowly, increases in productivity are usually the main source of increases in output. In the UK total factor productivity is estimated to have increased by about 1½ per cent a year in the 1960s and 1980s but scarcely at all in the 1970s. Labour productivity is estimated to have increased by over 2 per cent a year in the 1960s and 1980s and by around 1 per cent in the 1970s. Productivity grew faster in the UK in the 1980s than in other major industrialized nations (the exception being a faster growth of labour productivity in Japan). But UK labour productivity is still lower in the UK than in the USA, Canada, France and Germany. Many possible causes of labour productivity growth have been identified, although none can be shown to have made a significant contribution to the increased rate of growth in the UK. These include new technology, e.g. the spread of computer controlled machinery and computer aided design; the closing of less efficient units; labour hoarding by employers which enabled output to be increased to meet higher demand without hiring additional workers; a decline in the power of trade unions enabling the introduction of more flexible working practices.

profit. (1) *See* ECONOMIC PROFIT. (2) Accountants provide several definitions and measures of profit, but unfortunately these definitions and measures are subject to different conventions and procedures. For example gross profit can be defined as revenue from sales minus the cost of sales; for manufacturing companies the cost of sales might include all costs except depreciation and interest, these being subtracted from gross profit to give net profit. But for retailers the cost of sales would be restricted to the cost to them of the goods purchased from manufacturers and wholesalers; to arrive at net profit it would be necessary to deduct all other costs, e.g. labour, rent, depreciation and interest. Under US accounting conventions the gross profit of a manufacturing company would be calculated after subtracting only some of the costs subtracted under UK conventions. Costs may be valued on a historic, current or replacement basis, and each yields a different figure for profit. Finally net profit, however calculated, can be expressed either before tax, or after the payment of corporation tax in the case of companies and income tax in the case of unincorporated businesses. Alternative measures also exist at the aggregate, national, level. Gross trading profits as defined in the UK NATIONAL ACCOUNTS are only about half of the wider definition which covers all gross domestic product other than employment income, and which is used in calculating shares in national income and in estimating changes in PRODUCTIVITY.

profit and loss account. *See* TRADING AND PROFIT AND LOSS ACCOUNT.

profit sharing. An arrangement whereby employees share in the profits earned by the business. Profit sharing may occur whether or not there are outside shareholders; in both instances the motive is to provide an incentive and a reward for effort. However it is by no means easy to relate changes in profits to changes in the effort of individual workers. Where there are outside shareholders, the employee's profit share usually takes the form of a bonus, either a given amount, or a percentage of earnings. The profit-related element of the remuneration of some senior executives can be a substantial part of their total remuneration when the firm does well.

profit-sharing contracts. If workers are no more risk averse than employers, and if they have equal access to information, they may accept a contract which guarantees employment but not their income. Such profit-sharing contracts tend to be found especially in the financial sector and in some of the service trades where many workers are, in effect, self-employed.

profit taking. Selling shares on the stock exchange in order to realize capital gains. The term is associated particularly with speculative share trading.

programme, planning, budgeting system. PPBS is a method of trying to optimize the allocation of resources, subject to political constraints, in the public sector. Programme refers to the main areas of public expenditure, e.g. education. Each programme is broken down into sub-programmes and an attempt is made to measure the output of these sub-programmes and evaluate the resources required to produce this output. This information helps to identify the way in which government objectives might be met at the least resource cost. It also helps to identify the OPPORTUNITY COST of trying to achieve one particular objective, e.g. the building of a given number of new schools might require the building of a college to be deferred.

progress payments. Payments made by the client during the progress of a contract. It is a common feature of large engineering projects, where the contractors have a large financial outlay before the contract is completed.

progressive system of taxation. A system under which the proportion of income paid in tax increases as income increases. In the UK income tax is progressive partly because the first segment of income is not taxed, and partly because taxable income is taxed at higher rates (currently 20, 25 and 40 per cent) as income increases. A progressive rate of taxation can be justified on the grounds of vertical equity, or on the assumption that the marginal utility of money diminishes so that the pain felt by a millionaire when paying one pound in tax is less than the pain felt by a poorer person.

promissory note. A legal document stating that a person promises to pay a certain sum, e.g. in repayment of a loan, on a certain day. It is very similar to a BILL OF EXCHANGE.

property income from abroad. Property income from abroad is the sum of interest, profits and dividends received from assets held overseas. As an item in gross national product, payments received from abroad are included net of payments to overseas holders of assets in the UK.

property rights. The aspect of property or ownership rights that has received most attention in economics is the rights of the owners of assets to charge for the use of these assets. If assets that yield benefits can be used free of charge this is because property rights have not been established in those assets, or because the owners choose not to exercise their property rights, for one reason or another. A landowner may allow walkers free access to his land either because he feels well disposed towards walkers or because he believes that to install and maintain a system of charges would incur more costs than it would yield revenue. The exercise of property rights is seen as an important means of conserving resources.

property tax. A tax levied on the ownership of property, e.g. the council tax.

proportional tax. A tax levied as a constant proportion of income.

protection. The imposition of TARIFFS, QUOTAS or other barriers to trade, with the aim of protecting domestic producers against competition from imports. Although the producers may benefit, the country as a whole may not do so, since the higher prices resulting from protection reduce consumers' real incomes.

provisions. Money set aside to cover bad and doubtful debts.

proxy vote. Only a minority of shareholders choose to attend the annual general meeting of the companies in which they hold shares. Of the remainder, many authorize the existing board members to vote on their behalf. The board is, therefore, given power well in excess of their own shareholdings.

prudential standards of liquidity. Banks hold a certain proportion of their assets in liquid form so that they can meet demands for the withdrawal of deposits whenever they arise.

public dividend capital. Capital of nationalized industries subscribed by the government on which a variable dividend is paid instead of interest.

public enterprise. Economic activity conducted by state owned or state controlled enterprises.

public expenditure. Government spending on goods and services (approximately 55 per cent) and on TRANSFER PAYMENTS (45 per cent). Planned spending is detailed in estimates presented to Parliament together with the budget. Actual spending is reported in the appropriation accounts prepared at the end of the financial year.

public finance. The branch of economics concerned with the analysis of the impact of government expenditure and taxation.

public goods. Public goods have two essential characteristics. The first is non-excludability, denoting that if the good is provided for one citizen it is provided for all. The second is non-rivalness, denoting that the consumption of the good by one person does not impede its consumption by others. The best example of a public good is probably national defence. Because of their characteristics, it is not possible to establish a market in public goods. Instead they are provided by the state, the cost being met out of taxation.

public issue by prospectus. *See* NEW ISSUE MARKET.

public limited company. A LIMITED COMPANY which has a minimum capital of £50 000 and can raise permanent capital by issuing shares to the general public.

public ownership. State ownership of assets.

public saving. The difference between the public sector's current receipts and current expenditure. It is broadly equivalent to public sector net investment minus public sector borrowing.

public sector. *See* SECTORS OF THE ECONOMY.

public sector borrowing requirement. The excess of the expenditure of the public sector over its receipts. (If receipts exceed expenditure public sector debt repayment occurs.) If the PSBR is financed by the sale of liquid assets to the banking system this is likely to be inflationary. If it is financed by longer-term borrowing this will raise interest rates and may cause CROWDING OUT. Consequently governments have often sought to limit the size of the PSBR. (When Chancellor of the Exchequer, Nigel Lawson expressed the intention to move to a zero PSBR, taking one year with another.) However, critics have argued that the actual PSBR is a poor indicator of the government's fiscal stance, i.e. of the impact of fiscal policy on output, employment and prices. Three alternative indicators have been proposed: (a) The demand-weighted PSBR, which shows the result of weighting different forms of government expenditure and revenue according to their respective MULTIPLIERS. (b) The cyclically-adjusted PSBR, which attempts to remove the impact of cyclical variations in activity from the budget balance. It is a measure of what the PSBR would be at given tax rates etc., if the economy were, in some sense, 'on trend'. (c) The inflation-adjusted or real PSBR, defined as the actual PSBR minus the erosion by inflation of the real value of the stock of public sector debt.

public sector debt repayment. *See* PUBLIC SECTOR BORROWING REQUIREMENT.

public sector financial deficit. The PUBLIC SECTOR BORROWING REQUIREMENT minus the proceeds of capital transactions, e.g. from privatization.

public utilities. Industries supplying basic services, e.g. gas, water, electricity. These industries are often nationalized or subject to public supervision and regulation.

pump priming. Public expenditure which, it is hoped, will stimulate economic activity in the private sector.

purchasing power parities. In comparing output and productivity levels in different countries it is necessary to deflate national output measures to a common base. An appropriate method is to use purchasing power parities which equalize the purchasing power of different currencies in their domestic economies. For example if a standard basket of goods cost $2000 in the USA and £1000 in the UK the PPP exchange rate would be $2 = £1.

purchasing power parity theory. This theory considers the PURCHASING POWER PARITY exchange rate to be the equilibrium exchange rate.

pure inflation. Pure inflation exists when the prices of all products and factors of production rise at the same percentage rate.

pure public good. A public good of which all citizens must necessarily consume the same amount, i.e. the aggregate quantity supplied.

put option. A contract giving the right to sell a security at a specified price within a given period.

Q

quantity discounts. Reductions in price for buying in large quantities. The discount may relate to the size of a single order or to orders aggregated over a period of time. It may relate to the number of articles purchased or to the value (especially common when a purchaser buys several different articles from one supplier).

quantity rationing. Quantity rationing occurs when demand exceeds supply at the going price, leaving the wants of some potential purchasers unfulfilled. Quantity rationing is a sign that prices are not flexible.

quantity theory of money. The quantity theory of money states that a change in the nominal money supply leads to an equivalent change in the price level but does not affect output or employment. The Fisher equation is $MV = PT$, where M is the money supply, V the velocity of circulation, P the price level and T the number of transactions. The quantity theory assumes that both V and T are constant, the constancy of T being due to the fact (or rather the assumption) that the economy is operating at the full employment level. The quantity theory fell out of favour as an explanation of the behaviour of the economy when Keynesian economists showed that in practice changes occurred in both V and T. However the theory re-emerged in a more sophisticated form in the doctrines of monetarist economists. They recognize that the economy might not be operating at the full employment level but believe that in the longer term employment, and hence the number of transactions, can be increased only by SUPPLY-SIDE measures, not by an increase in the money supply.

quasi-markets. Situations in which the state funds goods and services but these are purchased by a variety of sellers competing with each other, e.g. vouchers for education and training, a system of self-governing schools, budgets for general practitioners and hospital trusts.

quasi-money. Another term for NEAR MONEY.

quasi-rent. This originally applied to the difference between the price of a product and avoidable cost. Avoidable cost (usually confined to direct labour and materials) is the amount necessary to keep the firm in production, and the excess over this amount is analogous to ECONOMIC RENT. But the term quasi-rent is used because this is a short run situation; in the long run the firm needs to cover other costs in addition to those that are avoidable in the short run. Quasi-rent is now applied to any payment in excess of what is required to keep a factor of production in its present use in the short run but not in the long run.

queue. A manifestation of QUANTITY RATIONING, a queue denotes that the wants of some customers cannot be immediately satisfied, e.g. waiting lists for admission to hospital.

quotas. (1) Restrictions on the quantity of imports. The main purpose of import quotas is to protect domestic producers, and the quotas may take account of the capacity of these producers and the size of the market. Quotas may be global, specifying the quantity to be imported from all countries, or they may be applied only to imports from certain countries. (2) Quotas on output are usually imposed by a CARTEL or as part of a COMMODITY AGREEMENT. The aim of output quotas is to restrict supply and so maintain or increase prices. (3) Restrictions on the quantity of exports. Export quotas are usually agreed as part of COMMODITY AGREEMENTS. See also VOLUNTARY EXPORT RESTRAINTS.

quoted company. A company that has obtained a STOCK EXCHANGE QUOTATION.

G

R

RPI-X pricing formula. When the electricity, gas, telecommunications and water industries were privatized, the price changes that they were allowed to make were related to the RETAIL PRICE INDEX. X, denoting the required deviation from the RPI, can vary between industries and over time. It is usually positive, meaning that price rises less than inflation (and may even fall), but its initial value was zero for the regional electricity industries. Moreover the privatized water companies were able to raise their prices faster than the general rise in prices (RPI+K) because of the need to increase capital expenditure, partly to meet higher environmental standards.

random sample. A sample selected by chance, so that every member or item of the population has an equal chance of being included.

random walk. *See* EFFICIENT MARKETS HYPOTHESIS.

range. A measure of variation between a group of numerical observations. It is the difference between the highest and lowest values taken by the observations.

rank correlation coefficient. A measure of the strength of relationship between pairs of sample observations, based on their ordinal ranking within the sample. If the ordinal rankings are identical, denoting a perfect positive relationship, the coefficient $(r) = 1$.

rank-order tournament. A situation in which a prize, e.g. promotion, is awarded to an employee whose performance is judged better than that of other employees. (This contrasts with piece work where an employee's reward does not depend upon an interpersonal comparison.) It is hypothesized that the effort made by employees to achieve the prize will depend upon the size of the prize and the costs involved in trying to obtain the prize.

rate cap. In order to meet its aim of controlling public expenditure, the central government may wish to limit the spending of local authorities. One way of doing this is to limit the amount that the LAs can raise from local taxes, a procedure known as rate capping.

rate of interest. *See* INTEREST.

rate of return. There are various ways of calculating the rate of return, but all are measures of the profit earned on invested capital. Profit may be defined before or after payment of tax, interest or depreciation. Capital may be defined to include or exclude loan capital or working capital. As a method of investment appraisal the rate of return is deficient in not taking account of the time pattern of cash outflows and inflows.

rate-of-return regulation. Setting a limit to the rate of profit earned by a monopoly supplier or other dominant firm. This form of regulation is commonly applied to privately owned utilities in the USA.

rate of technical substitution. *See* PRODUCTION POSSIBILITY FRONTIER.

rate support grant. A grant made by central government to local authorities.

rates. Until replaced by the community charge, rates were the main source of local finance for local authorities. The only form of rates payable now is the UNIFORM BUSINESS RATE.

rational expectations. People's expectations of the future are said to be rational if they do not incorporate any systematic bias or error. If expectations are not fulfilled it must be because of a random, non-systematic error that could not have been foreseen when the expectations were formed. An important implication of rational expectations is that people will not suffer MONEY ILLUSION. If, in an attempt to increase demand, output and employment, the government adopts policies that are expected to cause a price rise of 5 per cent, workers will adjust their wage claims accordingly. Real wages will therefore be unaffected, and policies which were designed to operate via a fall in real wages will be ineffective. The assumption of rational expectations also underlies the EFFECTIVE MARKETS HYPOTHESIS.

rational behaviour. For decision-takers' behaviour to be described as rational it would usually be assumed that they can order the outcome of decisions (they can decide whether they prefer A to B or B to A or are indifferent between them), that these preferences are transitive (if A is preferred to B, and B to C, A will be preferred to C), and that they attempt to maximize their utility (they make the decision that leads to the preferred outcome). But this is a short-term framework. Intransitive preferences are not incompatible with rational behaviour if they are the result of learning and the acquisition of new information in the longer term. Moreover the assumption of utility maximization can be challenged if it is considered to be incompatible with altruistic behaviour, as it seems to be in many traditional models of ECONOMIC MAN.

rationing. The allocation of resources or products by means other than the price system. In wartime the government rationed food on the basis of equal shares for all adults. If firms find that demand for their products exceed supply, they may give preference to existing customers or they may adopt some other rationing procedure, e.g. first come first served.

reaction function. The way in which a firm in OLIGOPOLY reacts to a change (in price or output) made by a rival.

real balance effect. The real balance or Pigou effect refers to the effect on the value of wealth of price changes. As originally formulated by A.C. Pigou it related to an increase in wealth, due to declining prices, that led to an increase in consumption and so in output and employment. The real balance effect has been suggested as part of the explanation of the large swings that have recently occurred in the SAVINGS RATIO.

real exchange rate. The UK's real exchange rate in relation to another currency, e.g. the US dollar, can be defined as: (the sterling price of UK goods divided by the dollar price of US goods) multiplied by the dollar-sterling exchange rate. For example if a basket of goods cost £1000 in the UK and $1500 in the USA and the nominal exchange rate was $2 = £1, the real exchange rate would be (1000 ÷ 1500) x 2, = 1.33.

real income. *See* REAL VARIABLES.

real money supply. *See* REAL VARIABLES.

real rate of interest. *See* REAL VARIABLES.

real variables. A distinction can be made between nominal and real variables, both of which may be expressed in pounds, dollars, etc. per unit. A change in the real variable is calculated by adjusting the change in the nominal variable by the change in a general price index, e.g. the Retail Price Index. For example, if the actual, nominal price of a car increased by 20 per cent (from £10 000 to £12 000) and the RPI increased by 10 per cent (from 100 to 110), the real price of the car would have risen by almost 10 per cent, (120 ÷ 110). Real variables that are calculated in this way and are of especial importance in economics are the real money supply, rate of interest, wages and the various measures of national income, expenditure and output.

real wages. *See* REAL VARIABLES.

recession. (1) Technically defined as two successive quarters of negative growth. (2) A phase of a BUSINESS CYCLE.

reciprocity. The granting by two countries of mutual concessions in international trade.

recognized banks. *See* BANK OF ENGLAND.

recommended retail price. The price at which a manufacturer recommends its products should be sold by retailers. The practice of recommending retail prices may provide retailers and consumers with useful information, although it has been argued that in markets in which retailers generally follow the manufacturer's recommendation, the practice can inhibit price competition. In other markets it acts as mis-information, as the product is seldom, if ever, sold at that price.

recovery. *See* BUSINESS CYCLE.

recycling. Reclaiming materials for re-use in the production process. Governments have attempted to encourage recycling, e.g. by the provision of central collection points. However, government subsidies to the users of recycled materials may be required if recycling is to have a more significant role in the conservation of resources.

redeemable securities. Securities that are repayable at their PAR VALUE at a specified date. Most fixed interest securities are redeemable.

redemption date. The date at which a loan is repaid.

redemption yield. *See* YIELD.

rediscounting. The purchase of securities, and especially bills, between the date of issue and the maturity date. For example 3 months Treasury bills to the value of £100 000 might initially be purchased for £97 000, a discount of approximately 12 per cent. After 1 month they might be purchased (rediscounted) for £98 000.

reducing balance. *See* DEPRECIATION.

reflation. Government measures to increase aggregate demand and hence employment and output. These measures might involve reductions in taxation, an increase in government expenditure, and a cheap money policy.

refusal to supply. Some manufacturers have attempted to enforce the prices at which their goods were re-sold by refusing to supply distributors selling at lower prices. The practice would now generally be considered to be illegal.

regional development grant. *See* REGIONAL POLICY.

regional policy. Measures to influence the location decisions of firms and, less importantly, movements of workers. The aim of regional policy is to reduce regional inequalities, especially in employment opportunities and income. The justification advanced for government intervention in location decisions is that market forces would fail to reduce regional differentials in an acceptable time period. Governments can intervene by preventing development in areas of relatively low unemployment or by encouraging development in areas of high unemployment. This encouragement might take several forms:

subsidies related to the cost of inputs; the provision for individual firms of advice and facilities, especially factories, to rent or to purchase; the provision of facilities that might benefit more than one firm, e.g. central training facilities, an improved communications network. Subsidies may take the form of tax concessions, low-cost loans or grants. The current pattern of assistance dates back to 1984. In November of that year the government announced its intention of improving the effectiveness of regional policy by linking assistance more directly to job creation, and restricting the amount of grant going to large capital-intensive firms. To this end the phasing out of the existing regional development grant, one of the main forms of assistance, was announced, and a revised RDG scheme (RDGN) was introduced. Under the revised scheme the maximum grant assistance was to be 15 per cent of eligible capital expenditure or £3000 for each new job created. (To restrict the amount of grant payable, a grant-per-job limit of £10 000 was imposed in most cases.) The operation of regional selective assistance, the other main form of assistance, was also revised in 1984. Since that date there has been a stricter economic appraisal of projects and a more stringent grant-per-job limit. Moreover, transfers to the assisted areas which do not create extra jobs no longer qualify for assistance. This was a major shift in policy, which had previously sought to encourage such re-locations. There are two types of assisted area: development and intermediate areas. RSA is available in both, but RDGN is confined to development areas. The coverage of the assisted areas was considerably reduced in 1984, with a view to concentrating assistance in areas of greatest need. It was recognized when the new policy was introduced that better targetting was likely to be accompanied by a reduction in the scale of assistance, and this is exactly what happened. During the 1980s expenditure in real terms fell by about a half.

regional selective assistance. *See* REGIONAL POLICY.

regional trade grouping. A number of countries which come together to form a COMMON MARKET, FREE-TRADE AREA or some other form of association in which mutual concessions on trade are agreed.

regional unemployment. The rate of unemployment calculated for each of eleven regions of the United Kingdom.

regionalism. A tendency to form REGIONAL TRADE GROUPINGS.

registered labour force. *See* LABOUR FORCE.

registered unemployment. The number of people registered as claimants for unemployment benefit.

regression analysis. A statistical technique for estimating the PARAMETERS of an equation from data of observations of DEPENDENT and INDEPENDENT variables. A series of points are plotted, each point denoting a pair of values of the variables. For example, in trying to estimate a CONSUMPTION FUNCTION, we plot the levels of disposable income and consumption in each year. A line of best fit to the data is then fitted, so that the sum of the squares of the deviations (vertical distances) of the points from the line is minimized (the ordinary least squares method). The goodness of fit of the regression line to the sample observations is measured by the correlation coefficient. From the regression line we can derive the parameters of an equation representing the relationship between the variables. From the regression line shown in Fig. 12 we obtain a consumption function of the form $C = a+bY$ where C is consumption and Y is disposable income; a is determined by the position of the line and b by the slope.

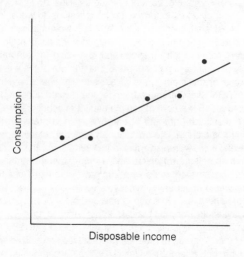

Figure 12   Regression analysis

When it is felt that more than one independent variable influences the dependent variable, multiple linear regression is employed (assuming, of course, that the relationships are again linear). However if there is a correlation between the independent variables (known as a multicollinearity), least squares regression cannot be used. Regression equations normally include an error term, reflecting the fact that estimates based on a sample do not perfectly represent the relationship in the population as a whole. If there is correlation in a series of error terms (a situation known as auto-correlation), an alternative method of analysis to least squares regression must be used.

regressive tax. A tax which takes a decreasing proportion of income as income rises, e.g. a POLL TAX.

regulation. The supervision and control of the activities of private enterprise by the government or a government appointed body. A broad distinction can be made between structure regulation, deciding which firms or types of firms can engage in which activities, and conduct regulation, deciding the permitted behaviour of firms in their chosen activities. Structure regulation often involves a LICENSING system. For example the Bank of England is responsible for licensing some institutions to act as banks and others to act as licensed deposit takers. LAUTRO has withdrawn the licences of some institutions that previously conducted life assurance business. PRIVATIZATION may involve both structure and conduct regulation. When a nationalized industry is privatized, decisions are made concerning the number and shape of the new private-sector enterprises. After privatization the electricity, gas, telecommunications and water industries have been subject to regulation with respect to prices charged, standards of service, etc. The theory of CONTESTABILITY emphasizes the significance for efficiency of easy entry to and exit from an industry. Overall the privatization programme in the UK has done little to facilitate contestability, more reliance having been placed on conduct regulation as a means of ensuring efficiency. However, conduct regulation can itself increase contestability as when OFGAS ordered British Gas to increase its bulk sales of gas to other suppliers who in effect compete with British Gas as retailers of gas.

regulatory capture. When a body set up to regulate an industry gives greater weight to the interests of the firms in the industry than of the customers of those firms.

re-intermediation. The return within the banking system of lending that had been forced out of the system by official controls on bank lending.

related goods. Goods whose demand is interdependent, i.e. SUBSTITUTES and COMPLEMENTS.

relative-income hypothesis. James Duesenberry advanced the hypothesis that an individual's consumption is influenced by the relationship between current and previous peak income and also by other people's consumption. Peak income is important because if income falls, although consumption may decline, it will remain above what its level would have been had income not previously reached that peak. If people spend in order to maintain consumption in line with that of others with similar incomes, an increase in average income need not lead to a fall in the average propensity to consume.

relative price. The price of a product expressed in terms of the amount of other products that must be given up in order to buy one unit of that product.

removal costs. When a firm moves into an area, existing firms and households may suffer additional costs due to congestion, pollution, etc. However, these firms and households may stay in the area rather than move elsewhere because the additional costs incurred in the area are less than the removal costs: the cost of searching for a new site or home, moving machines or furniture, engaging new labour or finding new friends, etc.

renewable resources. *See* NATURAL RESOURCES.

rent, economic. *See* ECONOMIC RENT.

rent seeking. This term has been applied both to entrepreneurship, which can yield rent via efficiency gains, and to the pursuit of income transfers. But it is now usually restricted to the latter context, i.e. to activities which do not increase efficiency or productivity, and indeed may reduce it, but which result in a special position or monopoly power, and thus raise income. An example of rent seeking is the formation of a CARTEL in order to raise prices, thus transferring income from consumers to producers. Another example would be lobbying designed to persuade the government to introduce IMPORT QUOTAS.

rental rate. The rental rate for capital is the cost of using capital services.

rentier. A person whose income is derived from the ownership of capital.

replacement-cost accounting. A form of INFLATION ACCOUNTING in which assets are valued at the prices that would have to be paid to replace them.

replacement investment. *See* GROSS INVESTMENT.

replacement rate. The ratio of net income out of work to net income in work. A very similar concept to the REPLACEMENT RATIO, but the replacement rate takes account of any income in addition to unemployment benefit.

replacement ratio. The ratio of the unemployment benefit received by unemployed workers to the average after-tax earnings of employed workers.

repressed inflation. *See* INFLATION.

reputational policy. The theory of reputational policy states that a country's ability to reduce its inflation rate, and the cost of doing so, depends upon its ability to establish a good reputation. When a government with a good reputation announces anti-inflationary intentions, these are believed. Because they are believed, inflationary expectations are reduced, and the cost of reducing inflation, in terms of higher unemployment, is reduced. The UK's decision to join the exchange rate mechanism of the European Monetary System could be seen as an attempt to establish a good reputation, an attempt that failed when membership was suspended in 1992. Reputational policy has also been applied to the analysis of firms' behaviour.

required rental. The required rental on capital is the rental rate that just allows the owner to cover the OPPORTUNITY COST of owning the capital.

resale price maintenance. *See* COMPETITION POLICY.

research and development. In principle a distinction can be made between research and development. The aim of research is to extend knowledge, while development involves the application of knowledge with the aim of improving the production process. Improvements might take the form of new materials, labour-saving machinery, more effective methods of health care, etc. R & D is undertaken in a wide range of institutions. Universities tend to concentrate (although not entirely) on research, firms tend to concentrate (not entirely) on development, and government laboratories come in between. It was estimated that in the 1980s the government funded, directly or indirectly, about half of total spending on R & D in the UK. Internationally the UK is seen as being strong in research, as indicated by the number of Nobel Prize winners, but less strong in development, as indicated by the number of British inventions that have been developed most fully by other countries.

reservation wage. The lowest wage that will be accepted by a job seeker.

reserve assets. Liquid assets kept by the banks so that they can meet demands for the repayment of deposits or the requirements of the monetary authorities.

reserve assets ratio. The percentage of total assets held in liquid form. This percentage is normally maintained for prudential purposes, but governments sometimes specify a reserve assets ratio as part of a policy to control the growth of the money supply.

reserve currency. A currency which countries and international institutions are willing to hold as part of their foreign currency reserves and which finances a significant part of international trade, e.g. the dollar, Deutschmark.

reserve price. The lowest price at which a supplier is willing to sell an article.

resource allocation. A great deal of economics is concerned with the analysis of how resources are allocated. Households have to decide how to allocate their time between work and leisure, how to allocate their income between current consumption and saving (future consumption), how to allocate current consumption among various products. Firms have to decide which goods and services to produce and which resources they should acquire in order to produce these goods and services. The government has to decide how to spend tax revenues, whether to introduce measures to re-allocate resources so as to reduce external costs, etc. The electorate has to decide how involved government should be in the process of resource allocation.

resources. *See* NATURAL RESOURCES.

restraint of trade. All agreements in restraint of trade, unless held by a court not to be unreasonable or against the public interest, are illegal. An example would be where an employee, as a condition of his employment, has to promise never to set up in competition with his employer.

restrictions on entry. *See* BARRIERS TO ENTRY.

restrictive agreement. Under the Restrictive Trade Practices Act 1956, a restrictive agreement is defined as an agreement between two or more persons carrying on business in the production or supply of goods, under which restrictions are accepted by the parties in respect of the prices to be charged, the terms or conditions of sale, quantities or types to be produced, the process of manufacture, the persons or areas to be supplied or the persons or areas from which the goods are to be acquired. All such agreements should be registered with the Office of Fair Trading.

restrictive labour practices. Practices which prevent the maximization of productivity. The term usually denotes concerted action by a group of workers, often initiated or sanctioned by a trade union. Restrictive practices include overmanning, demarcation rules which reduce labour flexibility, an unnecessarily long period of apprenticeship, and a failure to co-operate with management in the introduction of new machinery or processes.

Restrictive Practices Court. *See* COMPETITION POLICY.

Restrictive Trade Practices Act. *See* COMPETITION POLICY.

retail banking. *See* BANK, COMMERCIAL.

Retail Price Index. The RPI measures the average change from month to month in the prices of goods and services bought by the majority of households. The weights attached to the various products are revised annually in the light of the spending patterns revealed by the Family Expenditure Survey. (The expenditure of higher income households and households dependent on state pensions are excluded.) The prices of a representative selection of more than 600 products are regularly monitored in 180 towns, yielding more than 120 000 items of price information. An important use of any price index is as a measure of INFLATION, and there has been considerable debate as to the adequacy of the RPI for this purpose.

Table 20   Retail Price Index: weights, 1990

Food	158
Catering	47
Alcohol	77
Tobacco	34
Housing	185
Fuel, light	50
Household goods	71
Household services	40
Clothing, footwear	69
Personal goods and services	39
Motoring expenses	131
Fares, travel	21
Leisure goods	48
Leisure services	30
Total	1000

Source: *Annual Abstract of Statistics*

retail trade. The final link in the distribution chain by which goods move from producers, often via wholesalers, to consumers. Retailers break bulk, i.e. split large consignments into units suitable for purchase by consumers, display merchandise, and sometimes offer other services such as the provision of credit, delivery, maintenance of equipment, etc. Multiple retailers have taken an increasing share of trade, largely by offering a wide range of products at lower prices than charged by smaller retailers, unable to take advantage of ECONOMIES OF SCALE. Many smaller retailers have tried to gain some scale economies, especially in buying, by joining voluntary groups. Department stores have maintained a modest share of the market by stocking a wide range of products, and offering a high level of service. (However in the retail trade in general an increasing number of shops have reduced their labour requirements by means of self-service and self-selection.) The main appeals of mail order retailers have been the convenience of examining catalogues and goods at home, and the offer of extended credit. This second factor has become less important as other sources of consumer credit have been introduced.

Table 21 Retail Trade, 1989

	No. of businesses	% of outlets	% of turnover
Single-outlet retailers	215 613	61.6	27.6
Small multiples (2-9 outlets)	25 779	19.4	11.8
Large multiples	895	19.0	60.6
Total	242 287	100	100

Source: *Annual Abstract of Statistics*

retained earnings. Profits or earnings retained for investment in the business.

retention ratio. The proportion of earnings retained for investment. The retention ratio is one minus the pay-out ratio.

retentions. Another term for retained earnings.

return on capital employed. *See* RATE OF RETURN.

return on investment. *See* RATE OF RETURN.

returns to scale. The increase in output that occurs when the SCALE OF ORGANIZATION is increased by increasing all inputs in the same proportion. Output may increase more than proportionately to inputs (increasing returns), in the same proportion (constant returns) or less than proportionately (decreasing returns).

revaluation. An increase in the official rate at which a country's currency is exchanged for other currencies. Whereas currency appreciation is the result of market forces operating on a floating exchange rate, revaluation occurs by government edict in a FIXED EXCHANGE RATE SYSTEM. Some writers, possibly feeling that revaluation might be taken to mean either an increase or decrease in the exchange rate, prefer the term upvaluation. When a currency is revalued (or appreciates) exporters have to increase their foreign prices if they are to maintain their prices in terms of the domestic currency. For example if a UK car manufacturer sold in the USA at a price of $22 500 with an exchange rate of £1 = $1.50, it would receive £15 000 per car. If sterling was then revalued to £1 = $2.00, the manufacturer would have to increase price to $30 000 to continue to receive £15 000 per car. (In practice the manufacturer might increase price by less than this to avoid a large fall in the number of cars sold.)

revealed preference theory. The revealed preference theory claims that it is possible to explain consumer behaviour, and in particular how consumers respond to changes in price, on the basis of only two types of information. The first is observations of how consumers spend their money in different price-income situations, thus revealing their preferences. The second is the information (or assumption) that consumers behave rationally, i.e. that their choices demonstrate TRANSITIVITY. This information is sufficient to allow a partial INDIFFERENCE MAP to be constructed. As with indifference analysis, the revealed preference theory explains the response to a price change as a combination of a substitution and an income effect.

revenue. The amount earned by a firm in a given period from the sale of goods and services. For each product, revenue is price times quantity sold.

reverse income tax. Another term for NEGATIVE INCOME TAX.

reverse takeover. (1) The takeover of a public company by a private company. (2) The takeover of a larger company by a smaller company.

reverse yield gap. *See* YIELD GAP.

revolving credit. An arrangement under which someone borrows a specified sum of money and has the option, having repaid some of the loan, of increasing the amount borrowed up to the sum initially specified.

Ricardian equivalence. The idea, originally put forward by David Ricardo and revived by Robert Barro, that there is a relationship between government and personal sector finances. If the government runs a deficit this, it is assumed, will increase citizens' future tax liabilities, and so reduce the present value of private net wealth. Individuals with perfect foresight will respond by increasing their savings. The implication is that a given increase in government expenditure need not have a greater impact on aggregate demand if financed by borrowing than by tax increases, contrary to what is argued by Keynesian economists.

rights issue. *See* NEW-ISSUE MARKET.

risk. A state in which the number of possible future outcomes exceeds the number that will occur, but where there is evidence enabling one to attach probabilities to each outcome. There are two characteristics of such a state, the likely outcome and the degree of variation in all possible outcomes. For example, a project requiring an investment of £1000, might have a 50 per cent chance of yielding a profit of £500, and a 50 per cent chance of yielding a loss of £500. A large number of such projects would on average yield zero profit. Another project, also requiring an investment of £1000, might have a 50 per cent chance of yielding a profit of £1000 and a 50 per cent chance of yielding a loss of £1000. A large number of such projects would also yield zero profit, i.e. the same outcome. But because the degree of variation in outcomes is greater in the second than in the first situation, the second project would be considered to carry the greater risk. People may be risk-averse, risk-lovers or risk-neutral. Risk-averse people invest only if the odds are favourable, e.g. a 60 per cent chance of a profit of £500 and a 40 per cent chance of a loss of £500. It is assumed that most people are risk-averse because, since the marginal utility of money diminishes, the reduction in utility resulting from a loss of £500 would outweigh the increased utility resulting from a profit of £500. (Diminishing utility also means that a risk-averse person would invest £1000 in a project that was certain to yield a profit of £100 rather than in a project with equal chances of yielding a profit of £150 and £50. This example helps to explain why investors normally have to be offered a higher expected yield on ordinary shares than on debentures, given that the yield on shares is subject to more variation.) Risk-neutral people also require favourable odds to invest. But they are not affected by the degree of dispersion of the possible outcomes. In choosing whether to invest in ordinary shares or debentures, they would be concerned only with the respective yields. Finally, risk-lovers will invest even at unfavourable odds, e.g. if there is a 40 per cent chance of a profit of £500 and a 60 per cent chance of a loss of £500. (This is not, of course, to say that they prefer the odds to be unfavourable.)

risk-averse. *See* RISK.

risk-bearing economies. *See* ECONOMIES OF SCALE.

risk capital. *See* VENTURE CAPITAL.

risk-lover. *See* RISK.

risk-neutral. *See* RISK.

risk-pooling. The pooling of independent risks is the principle underlying insurance. The principle is effective only when the risk can be spread over a very large number of individuals.

risk-sharing. The bearing of a given risk by more than one individual or institution. A good example is the LLOYD'S syndicates, where many people may each have a very small share of a given risk.

rivalry. Another term for competition, which might be manifested in various ways: the introduction of a new product, advertising, price reduction, etc.

Robinson-Patman Act. *See* ANTI-TRUST.

Rooker-Wise Amendment. An amendment incorporated in the Finance Act 1977 whereby personal allowances for income tax are automatically indexed unless Parliament decides otherwise.

royalties. Payments made for the right to use a process or supply a product. For example a firm may allow another firm to manufacture a product protected by a patent on the payment of a royalty for each article manufactured.

S

salaried contract. A contract between a trade union and an employer that stipulates both the wage and the number to be employed. Salaried contracts are most likely to be found where workers are more risk-averse than employers, and employers find it difficult to hire and train workers.

sales maximization. W.J. Baumol advanced a theory of the firm in which firms attempted to maximize their sales revenue in the long run, subject to a minimum profit constraint. Profit in excess of the minimum required was used to fund marketing activities and product development.

sales promotion. Measures to increase sales: advertising, competitions, coupons offering temporary price reductions, etc.

sales revenue. Price multiplied by the quantity sold in a given period.

sales tax. A tax levied as a proportion of the retail price at the point of sale. Single point sales taxes are levied in the USA and other countries, but not in the UK. (However the term sales tax is sometimes used loosely to refer to all expenditure taxes.)

sample. Obtaining data on some members of a population for the purpose of identifying the relevant characteristics of the population as a whole. Statistical methods make it possible to specify the size of the sample that will enable conclusions about the population to be drawn with a given degree of confidence.

satisficing. *See* BEHAVIOURAL THEORY OF THE FIRM.

save-as-you-earn. An arrangement whereby, under schemes approved by the Inland Revenue, tax concessions are given to people who arrange for regular deductions to be made from their wages or salaries for the purchase of shares.

saving. Income minus consumption. Saving may be undertaken by households (PERSONAL SAVING), the corporate sector (COMPANY SAVING), the public sector (PUBLIC SAVING) and the nation as a whole (NATIONAL SAVING). The economy is in equilibrium when planned saving equals planned investment. An excess of planned saving would cause the economy to contract; an excess of planned investment would cause the economy to expand (assuming that there is spare capacity).

savings function. The savings function shows the level of planned saving at each level of disposable income. A theoretical concept, it is the inverse of the consumption function.

savings ratio. The proportion of disposable income that is saved. It usually refers to PERSONAL SAVING.

Say's law. A principle advanced in the early nineteenth century by J.B. Say, this law can be summarized as 'supply creates its own demand'. Say suggested that an increase in the number of people seeking work would force down the level of real wages until the excess labour became employed. The value of the additional output would be exactly matched by the value of the additional factor payments. Say's arguments are reflected in modern SUPPLY-SIDE ECONOMICS.

scale of organization. The scale of organization refers to the maximum output that the firm could produce in a given period. With a given scale of organization there is a limit to output because there is at least one input, one factor of production, whose quantity is limited. The longer the time period under consideration, the greater the opportunity for increasing the quantity of the limiting factor, i.e. for increasing the scale of organization.

scarcity. A situation in which there are insufficient resources to enable all the wants of consumers to be met. It is because of scarcity that the analysis of RESOURCE ALLOCATION is so important in economics.

scatter diagram. A diagram showing the values of a dependent variable that are found to be associated with given values of an independent variable.

screening. When an employer selects employees on the basis of a qualification not directly concerned with the work to be done by those employees.

scrip dividends. Additional shares allocated to shareholders instead of dividends. A small but increasing number of companies offer the option of scrip dividends, which appeal to shareholders who wish to increase their holdings without incurring the costs of buying more shares on the stock exchange.

scrip issue. A scrip issue (also called a bonus issue), comprises shares issued free to shareholders in proportion to the number of shares already held. The issue of additional shares leads to a fall in their price, but the value of each shareholding may increase slightly because (a) a scrip issue is often taken as a sign of confidence in the company's future prospects, with favourable implications for the share price; (b) at the lower price the shares may be somewhat more marketable.

seasonal adjustment. The elimination from a time series of fluctuations that exhibit a regular pattern at particular times of the year, e.g. unemployment regularly rises in winter and falls in summer. The elimination of these fluctuations enables a clearer picture of the trend in unemployment to be obtained.

seasonal unemployment. *See* UNEMPLOYMENT.

second best. *See* PARETO EFFICIENCY.

Second World. The phrase that used to be applied to the communist countries of Eastern Europe, the Soviet Union and China.

secondary bank. A bank that plays a relatively minor role in the UK banking system, e.g. the UK branches of overseas banks.

secondary benefits. Indirect benefits arising from an investment project. For example, an irrigation scheme would lead to increased crop yields (direct benefits), plus additional output in the food processing and distribution industries.

secondary market. A market in which assets are resold, as distinct from being sold for the first time. There are secondary markets in securities, mortgages, life assurance policies and many durable goods.

sectors of the economy. The division of the economy into sectors is a primary feature of a national accounting system. Each sector is a group of transactors, and the UK NATIONAL ACCOUNTS classifies transactors in several alternative ways, each classification being useful for a particular purpose. (1) (a) The enterprise sector, which includes all firms, organizations and institutions which supply goods and services at a price intended to cover the cost of supply and yield a profit. (b) The personal sector, comprising households and non-profit making institutions such as charities and trade unions. (c) The government sector, comprising central and local government institutions whose services are provided free or at heavily subsidized prices. (2) (a) The private sector, comprising households, unincorporated businesses and companies. (b) The public sector, comprising central government, local authorities, nationalized industries and other public corporations. (c) The overseas or foreign sector, comprising the private and public sectors of other countries. (3) (a) The personal sector, comprising households, unincorporated businesses, charities, trade unions and pension funds. (b) The corporate enterprise sector, comprising industrial and commercial companies, financial companies and public corporations. (c) The general government sector, comprising central government and the local authorities. Industries are sometimes grouped into the primary sector, e.g. agriculture and the extractive industries, the secondary or manufacturing sector, and the tertiary sector, e.g. retailing, hairdressing, banking and insurance.

secular stagnation. Long-term or secular stagnation is a situation in which consumption ceases to increase because many of the population's wants have been satisfied.

secular trend. A long-term trend.

securities. Financial assets that can be traded or used as COLLATERAL SECURITY, e.g. stocks and shares, bills of exchange, life assurance policies. The term is sometimes used as a synonym for stocks and shares.

Securities and Exchange Commission. A US government agency which oversees the operations of the American securities industry. People who believe that the British system of self-regulatory organizations headed by the Securities and Investments Board lacks teeth, sometimes point to the SEC as a more effective vehicle.

Securities and Futures Authority. A self-regulatory organization formed in 1991 by a merger of the Securities Association and the Association of Futures Brokers and Dealers. The Authority oversees the activities of bodies trading in various forms of securities and futures.

Securities and Investment Board. Set up under the Financial Services Act 1986, the SIB is responsible for the conduct of the other self-regulatory organizations which oversee the activities of various types of financial institutions. Originally there were five SROs, but a merger between two reduced the number to four in 1991 and further mergers seem likely.

securitization. Bundling together separate illiquid investments into a package which can be actively traded in a second-hand market. For example individuals who do not wish to continue contributing to a life assurance policy can sell their policies to an institution which re-sells them wholesale to investors.

selective distribution. Selling only through distributors who fulfil certain criteria, e.g. the provision of adequate showroom space.

self-employment. Self-employment rose rapidly during the 1980s, partly due to a fall in the number of jobs for employees and partly because of various government incentives. Today, of the total workforce, about one person in eight is self-employed, working as one man businesses, other sole proprietors and members of partnerships.

self-financing. Meeting the financial requirements of a company from its retained earnings (undistributed profit). In recent years internal sources of finance have accounted for over two-thirds of the total funds of industrial and commercial companies.

self-liquidating. A self-liquidating transaction involves the provision of finance for an activity that will yield the means for repayment, e.g., a bill of exchange drawn to finance imports of goods in the expectation that the goods will be sold by the time the bill matures.

self-regulatory organizations. *See* SECURITIES AND INVESTMENT BOARD.

selling costs. Selling costs, such as advertising and the costs of operating a sales force, have received a great deal of attention in microeconomic theory. It has been argued that selling costs are undesirable since at least some of the resources could have been used in more 'productive' activities. Moreover they can lead to imperfections in the market which have two undesirable consequences: (a) supernormal profits can be earned in the short run in MONOPOLISTIC COMPETITION and in both the short and long run in MONOPOLY; (b) in monopolistic competition the long-run equilibrium output is less than that at which average cost would be minimized. On the other hand activities giving rise to selling costs have some advantages. They provide information to potential customers. If they lead to an increase in sales they enable more advantage to be taken of ECONOMIES OF SCALE. They may reduce fluctuations in sales between one period and another and so provide a sounder basis for investment.

semi-variable costs. *See* COSTS.

seniority model. A model of trade union behaviour. The model assumes that the union is most concerned to further the interests of its senior members. Consequently when demand falls, the union resists wage cuts, since less senior members will bear the brunt of the consequential unemployment. (This will be true only when redundancies are limited, and it may not even be true then.) When demand increases, the union presses for wage increases rather than additional employment.

separation of ownership from control. In the majority of large firms the directors and senior managers frequently account for only a small proportion of the total shareholding. The largest shareholders are usually INSTITUTIONAL INVESTORS who play little or no part in the running of the firm. The separation of ownership from control might allow directors and managers to adopt policies that serve their own interests rather than those of shareholders as assumed, for instance, in the SALES MAXIMIZATION theory. But they are, of course, constrained by competition. Moreover if the rewards to shareholders become out of line with those offered by similar firms the share price will fall, making the firm vulnerable to a takeover bid. Finally, many firms offer senior executives incentives, e.g. bonuses, share option schemes, whose value depends upon the firm's profitability.

sequestration. Holding part of the assets of parties involved in a dispute. Sequestrators are sometimes appointed by the courts as a means of imposing fines on trade unions in breach of the law.

services. Intangible, non-transferable, economic goods as distinct from commodities. (Many writers use goods as a shorthand expression for goods and services.) As nations become richer an increasing proportion of expenditure tends to be accounted for by services, supplied by both the public sector, e.g. many educational and medical services, and the private sector, e.g. tourism and other leisure activities. In the UK about 40 per cent of consumers' expenditure is accounted for by services. Overall, international trade is less important for services than for commodities, although there are clear exceptions, e.g. financial services (banking, insurance, etc.), air and sea travel. In general, labour productivity has risen faster in manufacturing than in services, but again there are exceptions; developments in information technology have enabled the commercial banks to make big reductions in staffing.

set aside. Paying farmers either to grow nothing on part of their land, or to switch production into certain other crops. Set aside is being used increasingly as a way of reducing crop surpluses within the European Community.

settlement day. Another term for ACCOUNT DAY.

sex discrimination. The Sex Discrimination Act was passed in 1975 to protect and improve the status of women in ways not covered by equal pay legislation. But the Act was deemed by the European Court to be inadequate in some respects. Two women employed by Lloyds Bank successfully argued that the bank's occupational pension scheme discriminated in favour of men. In another case a female employee of the National Health Service who had been forced to retire at sixty-two, successfully argued that the retirement age should be the same for both sexes. The UK subsequently introduced legislation to this effect, and it seems likely that this will eventually lead to state retirement pensions being payable to both sexes at the same age (probably sixty-five).

shadow economy. *See* BLACK ECONOMY.

shadow price. A price which represents the estimated OPPORTUNITY COST to society of engaging in an activity. It is used in COST BENEFIT ANALYSIS, being applied to situations where prices are not charged or where the prices charged do not reflect the true cost of the activity concerned.

shareholders. The owners of shares in companies. It is estimated that in the UK INSTITUTIONAL INVESTORS hold 60 per cent of shares and private investors 20 per cent, (the remaining 20 per cent being held by the government and other British and overseas investors).

share indices. Index numbers showing changes in the prices of shares traded on stock exchanges. The FINANCIAL TIMES SHARE INFORMATION SERVICE includes a large number of indices.

share options. *See* OPTIONS.

shares. The nominal capital of a company is divided into a number of shares of equal value. There are two main types of shares: preference shares which usually attract a fixed rate of dividend, and ordinary shares on which the dividend is variable. Preference shareholders are paid in full before ordinary shareholders (but after debenture holders), and the holders of cumulative preference shares also receive any arrears of dividends before payments are made to ordinary shareholders. Finally, should the firm go into liquidation leaving a residual value after the payment of debtors, preference shareholders again take precedence in payment over the holders of ordinary shares. Against these disadvantages can be set the fact that, taking one year with another, the return on ordinary shares exceeds that on preference shares. Since companies have issued far more ordinary shares, investors presumably consider that the higher return outweighs the additional risk. Most ordinary shares attract voting rights, but some companies restrict voting rights to certain classes of share so that the holders of these shares (who may be members of the family that founded the company) can retain control. However, non-voting shares do not meet with general approval, and they are now issued by only a small minority of companies.

shell company. A company quoted on the stock exchange that is trading at a very low level or is not actively trading. Such a company may be the subject of a reverse takeover by a company wishing to acquire a stock exchange listing.

Sherman Act. *See* ANTI-TRUST.

203

H

shocks. Events which change the autonomous components of aggregate demand and so shift the aggregate demand schedule. The shock may initially affect the supply side of the economy, e.g. the OPEC-inspired increase in the price of oil in 1973 which led to a fall in real aggregate demand.

shoe-leather costs. Higher rates of inflation usually lead to higher nominal rates of interest. This induces people to reduce money balances which means that they must incur more costs in undertaking transactions, e.g. travelling to the bank more often to withdraw cash. These additional costs are known as the shoe-leather costs of inflation.

shop steward. A shop-floor employee elected by members of a trade union to represent them in negotiations with management at the workplace.

short-dated securities. Securities whose redemption date is near.

short run. The short run or short period is that period within which at least one variable cannot change. For example in the theory of the firm it is the period in which the quantity of at least one input is fixed. It follows that in the short run a change can occur in the cost of variable factors only. As output increases in the short run, average variable cost may rise, fall or remain constant, but average fixed cost must fall.

short-termism. Short-termism exists when more attention is given to the short-term performance of a firm than to its longer-term prospects. Short-termism can be manifested in the behaviour of investors, e.g. when they accept a takeover bid to realize an immediate profit on their shares (although this is not necessarily a sign of short-termism). It can also be manifested in the behaviour of firms, e.g. when they reduce spending on R & D in order to boost current profits.

shortage. An excess of quantity demanded over quantity supplied at the market price.

sight deposits. Sight deposits or sight accounts are bank deposits that can be withdrawn on demand. Often called current accounts in the UK.

signalling, theory of. The theory of signalling suggests that it may be rational to invest in costly education even if the education adds nothing directly to the person's productive capacity. The completion of the education is a signal of the person's capacity to persevere, understand complex arguments, etc.

simulation. Building an economic model, attaching values to the variables and running the model (usually using a computer) to discover the out-turn.

single capacity system. Before the BIG BANG it was possible to act as a stockbroker or a stockjobber, but not as both.

Single European Act. The Act that set the targets for completing internal harmonization and the establishment of a single market within the EUROPEAN ECONOMIC COMMUNITY.

single market. *See* EUROPEAN ECONOMIC COMMUNITY.

single-union deal. An arrangement by which a company grants sole negotiating rights to one trade union. Such arrangements, which have been favoured by Japanese firms setting-up in Britain, avoid inter-union disputes and simplify negotiations. They do, however, run counter to the intention of the BRIDLINGTON RULES.

sinking fund. *See* AMORTIZATION.

skimming price. A high price which, the supplier recognizes, will be paid only by the minority of consumers who value the product most highly. A skimming price is often set by the first supplier of a product, who gradually reduces price as competitors enter the market.

slump. *See* BUSINESS CYCLE.

social accounting matrices. A development of input-output analysis, SAMs extend the analysis of intersectoral flows in the production account to the government, financial and personal sectors. This forces consistency in the different parts of the national accounts, linking them to household survey data. It also aids understanding of the relationship between changes in economic activity, income distribution and saving. SAMs generally provide the basic starting point against which COMPUTABLE GENERAL EQUILIBRIUM MODELS are calibrated or validated.

social benefits. PRIVATE plus EXTERNAL BENEFITS.

social capital. *See* CAPITAL.

social costs. PRIVATE plus EXTERNAL COSTS.

social indicators. Dissatisfaction with national income as a measure of welfare has led to the development of alternative social indicators which take account of material and non-material factors, e.g. the HUMAN DEVELOPMENT INDEX.

social net benefit. The change in social benefits minus the change in social costs arising from some form of economic activity.

social security. Government assistance to people with particular needs or in particular circumstances, e.g. unemployment benefit, retirement pensions, child benefit, death benefit. In most social security systems citizens' contributions finance, at least in part, benefits paid currently. Benefits may be means-tested, i.e. available only to those whose income or wealth falls below a certain level, or they may be universal, i.e. payable to all who meet specified conditions such as being available and willing to work or being aged 65 and having retired from work. The foundation for the UK social security system is the BEVERIDGE REPORT, published in 1942 and implemented in legislation beginning in 1945. After that initial legislation the system grew steadily, often in ways not foreseen or intended by Beveridge, until by the mid 1980s social security spending accounted for almost one-third of all public expenditure. Social security benefits grew from less than 10 per cent of personal incomes in the mid 1950s to over 20 per cent by the mid 1980s. These changes were mainly due to three developments. The first development was the increase in the proportion of elderly people. At the beginning of the 1950s the proportion of the population aged 65 and over was just under 11 per cent, but by the middle of the 1980s it had risen to just under 15 per cent (and is forecast to exceed 18 per cent in 2020 and 28 per cent in 2050). The second development was the increase (by 100 per cent between 1961 and 1985, with a further increase since then) in the proportion of people living in one-parent families. The third development was the steep rise in unemployment, including the long-term unemployed who qualified for supplementary benefit (now income support), having exhausted their right to unemployment benefit. These three developments help to explain the increase in the relative importance of social security payments, despite the fact that the real value of some benefits fell during this period. This increased spending was the background to the Social Security Act passed in 1986 and fully implemented in 1988. The Act made modifications to the STATE EARNINGS-RELATED PENSION SCHEMES aimed at reducing the cost for future generations. The Act also simplified the system by establishing a common basis for entitlements to the three main income-related benefits: income support, family credit and housing benefit. For people not in employment, income support offers a personal allowance plus increases for dependents. Family credit offers supplements to low-income families in full-time work and with children to support. The government expected these benefits to account for an increasing proportion of social security spending, in line with its aim of directing spending to meet the greatest needs. However the TAKE-UP rate for means-tested benefits remains relatively low, and this has led a number of economists to advocate the introduction of a negative income tax. This would combine social security benefits and income tax payments in a single system of redistribution.

Table 22 Selected items of social security expenditure, 1991

	£ 000 million
Retirement and widows' benefits	26 399
Family benefits	6 032
Income support	11 155
Unemployment benefit	1 445

Source: *United Kingdom National Accounts*

social welfare. The total welfare of a nation.

social-welfare function. A function expressing society's rankings of alternative national economic states. Serious problems arise in trying to specify such a function. In practical terms it would require far more information than could be gathered and collated. In theoretical terms the first problem is that a given economic state could be associated with many alternative patterns of distribution among individuals, and each of these patterns would produce a different level of total welfare unless all individuals are considered to be the same in every way. This means that an observer must decide how to weight the interests of each citizen, i.e. the social-welfare function is influenced by a VALUE JUDGEMENT of the observer. Another problem lies in the fact that considering the social-welfare function to be simply the sum of individual welfare functions ignores the existence of interdependence. Further problems arise in the theory of implementation. One possibility is that the government imposes the social-welfare function on society. But this would itself distort the function unless government by dictat had already been taken into account. (Would social welfare have any meaning if it involved refusing votes to people who would prefer to be able to vote?) The alternative method of implementation would be to devise a voting system that could turn the individual rankings into a single social ranking. However Kenneth Arrow showed in the so-called impossibility theorem that it is not possible to devise a voting system that can be guaranteed to provide consistent and decisive results.

socialism. The essence of socialism is the state ownership of productive assets, but it is also frequently characterized by the allocation of resources through central planning.

soft currency. A currency whose exchange rate is falling or is expected to fall. Countries are reluctant to hold soft currencies as part of their foreign exchange reserves.

soft loan. A loan made at a concessionary, non-commercial, rate of interest. Soft loans are normally confined to the less (and least) developed countries.

sole proprietorship. The ownership of a business by a single person, the sole proprietor or trader.

sole trader. *See* SOLE PROPRIETORSHIP.

Solow economic-growth model. The HARROD-DOMAR model of economic growth assumes a fixed capital-output ratio. By contrast the model formulated by R. Solow assumes that the long-run rate of growth and the natural growth rate of the labour supply will be brought into equality by an adjustment of the capital-output ratio. Increased saving increases the growth rate in the short run but not in the long run, since it is then balanced by an increase in the capital-output ratio. Long-run growth in output per head is possible only if there is TECHNOLOGICAL CHANGE.

sources and uses of funds statement. An accounting statement (also known as a funds-flow statement) which shows the sources from which a firm derives its cash and the uses to which it puts this cash. The main source is usually sales revenue, but other sources may include the sale of assets, loans and share issues. The cash is used for the purchase of inputs, – labour, machinery, materials, etc., – interest payments, dividends, taxes, etc.

sovereign debt problem. If a country is unable to pay the interest due on international loans, the lenders may feel obliged to re-schedule the loans, or even to make new loans, in the hope that the country will eventually be strong enough economically to repay the original debts.

special deposits. Deposits which commercial banks have in the past been required to make with the Bank of England. They are not included in the banks' cash or reserve assets, and so a call for special deposits could form part of a restrictive MONETARY POLICY.

special drawing rights. A device for increasing international liquidity, SDRs are issued by the INTERNATIONAL MONETARY FUND. They are allocated to members in proportion to their IMF quotas and are included within members' foreign exchange reserves. SDRs were at first based on the weighted values of sixteen currencies, but in 1981 this was reduced to five: the dollar (42 per cent) the Deutschmark (19 per cent), the franc, the yen and the pound sterling (13 per cent each).

specialization. Another term for the DIVISION OF LABOUR. But whereas the term division of labour is most commonly applied to the operations of firms, specialization is also applied to regions and to countries.

specific human capital. Workers' skills and abilities that are of use only to one firm, a factor which can account for many of the features of an INTERNAL LABOUR MARKET. When a firm incurs screening costs and workers incur search costs, and when both subsequently invest in knowledge specific to the firm, it means that employment has considerable fixed costs. It is important that employer and workers share both the costs and the returns, and to ensure that this happens, premature quits and dismissals should be avoided. This requires long-term (implicit) contracts and the self-selection of stable employees.

specific tax. An indirect tax levied as an absolute amount per unit, e.g. 50 pence per kilo.

speculation. Buying in the hope of being able to sell subsequently at a higher price, and selling in the hope of being able to buy subsequently at a lower price.

speculative motive. *See* MONEY, DEMAND FOR.

spillover effect. Another term for EXTERNALITY.

spot market. A market in which commodities are bought for immediate delivery.

spot price. The price of a commodity bought for immediate delivery.

stabilization policy. Policy aimed at reducing fluctuations in economic activity. These policies were adopted in the UK (and other Western countries) in the 1950s and 1960s. Although empirical tests provided little evidence that the overall effect had been to reduce fluctuations, there was no repetition of the steep fall in economic activity and rise in unemployment that had occurred between the wars. However it seemed that stabilization policy had led to higher rates of inflation, and eventually short-term stabilization was abandoned as a policy aim, being replaced by the MEDIUM-TERM FINANCIAL STRATEGY. It may be that the long recession experienced in the early 1990s will cause more attention to be given once again to stabilization policy.

stabilization programmes. A term associated especially with the INTERNATIONAL MONETARY FUND, which often provides assistance on condition that such a programme is adopted. This involves the attempt to correct a balance of payments difficulty and excess demand by changing the real exchange rate, liberalizing trade and tightening fiscal policy.

stable equilibrium. If an equilibrium is disturbed by a shock, and forces exist which cause the equilibrium to be re-established, it is said to be stable.

stag. An investor who subscribes to new issues of shares in the hope of re-selling them to make a quick profit.

stagflation. A situation in which prices are rising but output is not.

stakeholders. Groups towards whom the managers of a firm have a responsibility: owners, creditors, workers and customers.

stamp duty. A form of indirect taxation which involves the fixing of pre-paid stamps to legal and commercial documents, e.g. when the ownership of property is transferred. Stamp duty is levied at a rate of 1 per cent on purchases of land and buildings above £30 000, and at one-half per cent on purchases of shares. But this latter duty is due to be abolished, possibly when a new system of recording stock exchange transactions is introduced.

standard cost. The estimated cost of production given efficient working under normal conditions. Standard costs are often used as the basis for prices under cost-plus pricing procedures. They are also used in monitoring the firm's performance, actual cost being compared with standard.

standard deviation. A measure of the spread of observations of a variable around its mean.

Standard Industrial Classification. A system of classifying economic activity, used in compiling official statistics. The system is numerical: single-digit classification distinguishes broad sectors of the economy, e.g. manufacturing, construction; two-digit classification distinguishes industrial sectors within these broad sectors, e.g. chemicals, textiles, within manufacturing; further disaggregation occurs until five-digit classification covers individual product classes. (In the USA sub-division continues to the seven-digit level.) The SIC follows the same principles as the International Standard Industrial Classification, issued by the United Nations. The basis for the classification is similarity on the production side and not substitutability on the demand side, and this reduces the usefulness of the SIC in the analysis of product markets.

standard of deferred payment. *See* MONEY.

standard of living. The national accounts provide several possible measures of the standard of living: national income, gross national product, gross domestic product, etc. However, it is recognized that a number of deficiencies are common to all these measures. They do not take account of: the amount of leisure time, including the proportion of people not in paid work; the range of choice offered to consumers; the division of output between that intended for military and for civilian purposes;

environmental factors such as the amount of green space for recreational activities; economic bads such as pollution; non-material factors such as the amount of crime, the mortality rate and the divorce rate. These are all important aspects of the standard of living, and various SOCIAL INDICATORS, which take some of these factors into account, have been developed as additional measures of living standards.

state earnings-related pension schemes. *See* PENSIONS.

static efficiency. *See* ECONOMIC EFFICIENCY.

statistical inference. A process by which conclusions are drawn about a POPULATION from which a SAMPLE has been drawn.

steady-state growth. Economic growth in which all variables, e.g. the labour force, the capital stock, vary at a constant rate (although the rate may differ for the different variables).

sterilization. An open market operation between domestic money and bonds whose sole purpose is to neutralize the effect on the money supply of balance of payments surpluses and deficits.

sterling exchange rate index. An index measuring changes in the value of sterling against other countries as a whole. The index is calculated by taking a weighted average against seventeen other currencies, the weights reflecting the relative importance of the currencies in the UK's trade.

stochastic process. A process subject to random influences.

stock appreciation. An increase in the value of stocks of raw materials, components, etc. due to an increase in market prices. Firms are not liable to pay corporation tax on profits arising from stock appreciation.

stock cycle. *See* INVENTORY INVESTMENT CYCLE.

stock exchange. A market in which securities are bought and sold. Many large cities have stock exchanges; the British exchange comprises London plus branches in seven provincial cities (including Dublin). The London Stock Exchange is one of the largest in the world, coming after only New York and Tokyo in the volume of business transacted. Over six thousand securities are listed on the main market (i.e. excluding the unlisted securities market) of the London exchange, of which around two-thirds are company securities and the remainder public sector and Eurobond securities. Around two thousand UK registered and around five hundred overseas companies are listed. Following the agreement in 1986 to merge the International Securities Regulatory Organization and the British Stock Exchange, the full title of the body became the International Stock Exchange of the United Kingdom and the Republic of Ireland. Companies wishing to raise capital can make NEW ISSUES of securities on the stock exchange. However most transactions are in securities issued previously (second-hand securities), buying and selling prices for which are quoted by market makers. The existence of this second-hand market encourages investors to subscribe to new issues.

Stock Exchange Alternative Trading Service. Introduced in November 1992, SEATS comprises (a) market making in stocks by a single trader and (b) a 'bulletin board' on which investors are able to post for public display orders to buy or sell shares. When market makers trade they are obliged to fulfil orders on the bulletin board which are at the same or better prices than their proposed trading prices.

Stock Exchange Automated Quotation. A screen-based securities dealing system in which market makers on the London Stock Exchange report their prices and trading volumes to users of the system. SEAQ has enabled transactions on the exchange to be conducted by telephone instead of on the trading floor. SEAQ International is the largest institutional cross-border exchange in Europe.

stock exchange quotation. A company granted a stock exchange quotation has the prices of its securities included in the stock exchange official list (LISTED SECURITIES). Companies must fulfil certain requirements to obtain a quotation; lower standards apply to the UNLISTED SECURITIES MARKET.

stock-sales ratio. *See* INVENTORIES.

stock split. An issue to shareholders of new shares, without increasing the capital of the company. Increasing the number of issued shares causes their price to fall and improves their marketability.

stockbroker. Someone who buys and sells securities on behalf of clients, who are charged commission, or on his own account.

stockpiling. Building up stocks or inventories in excess of the level required for normal levels of trading or consumption.

stocks. (1) Fixed interest securities. (2) Accumulations of assets; also known as INVENTORIES. (3) In the USA stocks has the same meaning as shares in the UK. (4) The quantity of something at a point in time, as contrasted to a flow which occurs over a period of time, e.g. the stock of capital as contrasted to the level of investment.

stop-go. Economic policy which alternates between dampening and boosting economic activity.

store of value. *See* MONEY.

strategic entry deterrence. A STRATEGIC MOVE or moves taken in order to prevent new entry into a market.

strategic move. In GAME THEORY a strategic move is defined as an action of one player (e.g. a firm) which influences the decisions of other players in a manner favourable to the first player, by affecting the other players' expectations about how the first player will act. For example if two firms were engaged in a contest to take over a third, and one firm arranged a large borrowing facility, the second firm, taking this as an indication of a determination to win the contest whatever the cost, might drop out of the bidding.

stratified sample. A SAMPLE that is obtained by dividing the POPULATION into a number of distinct sub-groups, e.g. age brackets, and selecting a proportionate number of items from each sub-group.

structural adjustment programme. A term associated especially with the INTERNATIONAL BANK FOR RECONSTRUCTION AND DEVELOPMENT, which may provide assistance on condition that such a programme is adopted. A structural adjustment programme involves the measures involved in a STABILIZATION PROGRAMME together with the liberalizing of internal markets and a reduction in the role of the state.

structural unemployment. *See* UNEMPLOYMENT.

structure-conduct-performance paradigm. The hypothesis that market structure (number of sellers, market shares, degree of vertical and horizontal integration, etc.) influences conduct (pricing, the output produced, level of investment, etc.) which in turn influences performance (profit rates, mark-ups, the functional distribution of income, etc.). The evidence relating to this hypothesis is at best descriptive, linking variables in a correlative manner. This is a serious weakness since it is possible that causal relationships might run in the opposite direction to that hypothesized. For example, if some firms are more efficient than others, they may be able to earn above average profits which can then be invested in activities, e.g. advertising, new product development, which enable them to increase their market share.

structure regulation. *See* REGULATION.

subdivision of market. (1) If PRODUCT DIFFERENTIATION is very successful, the market may in effect be split into a number of sub-markets, each having very few suppliers. (2) Regardless of product differentiation, a market may be subdivided on the basis of geographical space (most feasible in international or large domestic markets such as the USA), time (services are especially likely to be valued more highly at some times than at others), and by the type of customer (children, retired people, etc.).

subjectivism. The view that economic agents make decisions on the basis of how they imagine they would affected by a particular state of affairs. For example, consumers allocate their incomes on the basis of the satisfaction that they would expect to obtain from the consumption of alternative bundles of products.

subnormal profits. Profits that are less than is required for a firm to remain in its existing business.

subsidiaries. *See* HOLDING COMPANY.

subsidiarity. Subsidiarity means that in a hierarchical system a decision is taken at a higher level of authority only if to do so would be more efficient than if the decision were taken at a lower level. There is currently intense debate about the practical implications of subsidiarity for the division of authority between member countries of the European Community and Community institutions.

subsidy. *See* GOVERNMENT SUBSIDIES.

subsistence level. The minimum income required to sustain the labour force. For Karl Marx this was the minimum required to enable people to work efficiently. For the classical school of economists it was related to a standard of living accepted by custom.

substitutes. Products which meet, at least partially, the same needs of customers. Substitutes are often physically similar, but need not be so. For example, for households deciding how to spend their leisure time, beer consumed in a pub and the hire of a video film may be substitutes. The value of the CROSS-PRICE ELASTICITY OF DEMAND is the best objective measure of the extent to which two products act as substitutes. The higher its value, the better substitutes for each other the products are deemed to be.

substitution effect. A change in relative prices causes an increase in the quantity demanded of the variable whose relative price has fallen, and a fall in the quantity demanded of the variable whose price has risen. In other words the substitution effect is always negative. The variables might be two products, two factors of production, leisure and consumption, etc. A price change has an effect on real income, but the substitution effect excludes any effect on demand of the change in income. In INDIFFERENCE-CURVE ANALYSIS, the substitution effect of a change in price is shown by a swivelling of the budget line around a given indifference curve; the income effect is shown by a shift of the budget line to become tangential to a different indifference curve.

sunk costs. *See* COSTS.

sunrise industries. Emerging industries, especially those involving new technology.

sunset industries. Industries in long-term decline.

superneutrality of money. When the only effect of a change in the growth rate of the money supply is a change in the rate of inflation.

supernormal profit. Profit in excess of that required for a firm to remain in its existing business. Supernormal profit can be earned in the long run only if there are barriers to the entry of new firms, and in these situations it may be called monopoly profit.

supplementary costs. *See* COSTS.

supply. The ability and willingness to produce and distribute a product. (See also AGGREGATE SUPPLY.) This willingness depends primarily upon the price of the product and the cost of production and distribution.

supply curve. A line showing the quantity of a product that would be supplied in a given period at various prices. A market supply curve is obtained by aggregating horizontally the supply curves of all the firms in that market. The shape of the curve, the elasticity of supply, depends upon the time period under consideration. In approaches to the THEORY OF THE FIRM that use marginal analysis it can be shown that in perfect competition the firm's short-run supply curve is that segment of the marginal cost curve that lies on and above the average variable cost curve. Since marginal cost rises beyond this point it follows that the supply curve is upward sloping. In the very short run it may not be possible to increase supply at all, i.e. the supply curve may be vertical. (An example would be when a given amount of food has been delivered to a wholesale market and no further deliveries can be made that day.) In the long run existing firms can vary the quantities of all inputs and new firms can enter the market. Consequently supply is more elastic than in the short run. Indeed if the new entrants are as efficient as the existing firms, marginal cost need not rise as output increases, i.e. the supply curve could be horizontal (supply is infinitely elastic). It is not possible to derive a supply curve from the marginal cost curve in other markets. It can be shown that in these markets the shape of the supply curve is influenced by the shape of the demand curve, and the assumption underlying models incorporating marginal analysis is that demand and supply are determined independently. Since markets tend not to be perfect, explanations of the shape of supply curves other than those derived from marginal analysis must be sought. If, in order to increase output, firms have to incur higher costs in order to obtain additional inputs, they will require higher product prices if they are to increase output. However, the bigger the output, the more opportunity to take advantage of ECONOMIES OF SCALE and the greater the LEARNING EFFECT. These factors will counteract the higher costs per unit of input, and supply will therefore become more elastic. Indeed the supply curve could be horizontal or even downward sloping. If an increase in output does not require an increase in input prices, the supply curve may well be horizontal; it is certainly likely to be so if firms adopt COST-PLUS PRICING procedures and set prices for a PRICING SEASON.

supply schedule. A table showing the quantity of a product that would be produced in a given period at various prices.

supply-side policies. Policies whose aim is to shift the AGGREGATE SUPPLY CURVE to the right, so that an increase in aggregate demand could be satisfied without an increase in the price level. Central to the policies are various measures intended to make markets more flexible and efficient. Measures to increase the flexibility of the labour market include lower rates of taxation on income, the taxation of unemployment benefits, subsidies to training, encouraging more flexible patterns of apprenticeship, curtailing the powers of trade unions. Measures to increase the flexibility of the capital market include the abolition of controls on foreign exchange transactions, dividends, bank lending and hire purchase contracts. The aim of these measures is to enable savings to go to where there is the best combination of risk and return, i.e. where the most efficient use is made of capital. Aggregate supply is also affected by changes in the efficiency with which goods and services are produced. Increased efficiency is one of the aims of privatization and competition policy.

suppressed inflation. *See* INFLATION.

surplus. An excess of supply over demand at the going price.

surplus capacity. Another term for EXCESS CAPACITY.

surplus value. *See* MARXIAN ECONOMICS.

survivor technique. A technique for estimating the relative efficiency of different sizes of firms. If there are ECONOMIES (or DISECONOMIES) OF SCALE and the industry is reasonably competitive, one would expect larger (or smaller) firms to increase their market share over time. An increase in share implies efficient size, a fall in share implies inefficient size. The main deficiency of the technique is that it ignores the many other factors which are known to affect market share.

sustainable development. The development of economies to the benefit of present generations but not at an unacceptable cost to future generations.

swap facilities. Agreements made between CENTRAL BANKS whereby a country may temporarily exchange its currency for another currency in greater demand. Such agreements are often made through an international body such as the BANK FOR INTERNATIONAL SETTLEMENTS.

swaps. *See* INTEREST SWAPS.

T

take-home pay. Another term for PERSONAL DISPOSABLE INCOME.

take off. One of the five stages of economic growth identified by W.W. Rostow. At the take-off stage the economy begins to generate sufficient investment to ensure self-sustaining growth.

take-up. The take-up rate is the proportion of people eligible for a state benefit who receive that benefit. Low take-up rates are thought to be due to the complexity of the social security system and the stigma which may be attached to the receipt of MEANS-TESTED benefits.

takeover. The acquisition of one company by another. The shares of the company taken over may be acquired for cash or in exchange for shares in the bidding firm. A takeover implies that the initiative is taken by the bidder, and the threat of takeovers is an incentive to firms to pursue efficiency and profitability when there is a SEPARATION OF OWNERSHIP FROM CONTROL. The motives for takeover bids are varied. In some instances the bidding firm believes that it could manage the assets of the other company more efficiently. This might be because the combined firm could obtain ECONOMIES OF SCALE or other advantages (sometimes termed synergy) which could not be obtained by the two firms operating separately. Alternatively it might be because the bidding firm has superior management skills. In these instances, a takeover could lead to an increase in economic efficiency (although it could also lead to social costs if it gives rise to redundancies). In other instances the main reason for the bid is to split the firm acquired into smaller businesses and sell these to other buyers. These bids occur when the bidder believes that the other company is under-valued by the stock market, and the main direct effect of successful bids of this type is redistribution of income. (However the change in ownership could subsequently affect economic efficiency.) A third motive, that appears to have become more important in recent years, especially in the USA, has been to make a profit from the bid itself, i.e. even if the bid does not succeed. This can occur if the bid causes the price of the shares to rise above the bid price, perhaps because another bidder puts in a higher offer. The original bidder then sells the shares that he bought previously at a lower price. A variation on this theme is when someone buys shares in a company, but is persuaded not to make a bid by an offer from the company to buy in the shares at a higher price. When individuals buy shares with this outcome in view, the term greenmail is used. A company that receives, or feels that it may receive, an unwelcome takeover bid, may adopt a number of defensive strategies. It may itself merge with another firm in order to make itself financially or structurally unattractive to bidders (the poison pill tactic). Alternately it may sell assets that it believes make it especially attractive to bidders. It may enter into contracts which make it extremely expensive to dismiss senior personnel (the golden parachute tactic). If an unwelcome bid has been made, it may search for a more suitable partner, a white knight.

tangible wealth. Physical assets, i.e. CAPITAL and LAND, make up the tangible assets or wealth of a firm or a country.

tap issue. An issue of securities for purchase direct from the issuing authority, i.e. without going through the market. Marketable stocks which are issued on tap include some funded stocks which after issue can be traded on the stock exchange. Tap issues of Treasury bills are usually regarded as non-marketable although some pass into the market as a result of the operations of the Issue Department of the Bank of England. Non-marketable securities issued on tap include National Savings Certificates and Premium Bonds.

target price. (1) Most COMMODITY AGREEMENTS have a target price which is sustained by purchases and sales by the central authority. (2) The price which firms adopting COST-PLUS PRICING hope to achieve.

target-return pricing. Setting a price that will yield the firm's desired rate of return on capital employed if output is at the estimated level.

tariffication. The conversion of all restrictions on agricultural imports into fixed tariffs. Starting from a common form of protection would, it is suggested, facilitate agreement on reducing protection.

tariffs. A TAX levied on imports, either on an AD VALOREM or a SPECIFIC basis. By raising the price of imports, tariffs have the following effects: the government obtains revenue; the incomes of domestic producers of competing goods rise because they increase their prices, their sales volume or both; the real incomes of consumers fall because of the higher prices of goods, including domestically produced goods which use dearer imported materials or components. The overall effect on economic welfare of the country depends upon the balance of these three effects. The impact of tariffs also depends upon whether countries on whose exports the tariffs are imposed retaliate by imposing countervailing tariffs (or some other form of protection). Retaliation is least likely if it is believed that the tariffs have been imposed to meet a particular need and will be removed in the not too distant future. The need might be to protect an INFANT INDUSTRY, to facilitate an orderly run down of a domestic industry, or to overcome a temporary BALANCE OF PAYMENTS deficit.

tatonnement. A process which illustrates how equilibrium might be reached in perfect markets. The first stage is the presentation of SUPPLY and DEMAND SCHEDULES. These schedules are revised wherever there is excess supply or demand. The revised schedules are then re-presented, and the process continues until there is equilibrium in all markets. Trading then takes place at these equilibrium prices.

Taurus. A system due to be introduced in 1993, under which stock exchange transactions would be documented and certified by electronic messages and accounts instead of paper certificates, but abandoned as too expensive.

tax. *See* TAXATION.

Tax and Price Index. An index number which measures changes in the Retail Price Index (and hence in indirect taxation), in direct taxation and in employees' national insurance contributions. A change in the TPI shows the percentage change in gross income that would be required to maintain the real income of taxpaying workers.

tax avoidance. Measures taken by firms and individuals to legally reduce their liability to taxation.

tax base. The categories in respect of which taxation is levied. For example corporation tax is levied on the profits of all incorporated businesses, but not on unincorporated businesses, (their owners pay income tax).

tax-based incomes policy. *See* PRICES AND INCOMES POLICIES.

tax bracket. A range of incomes on which tax is levied at a specified rate.

tax burden. The amount paid in tax, plus any cost incurred by the taxpayer in calculating this amount.

tax evasion. Failing to meet tax liabilities, especially by failing to record all income.

tax exempt special savings account. The government introduced TESSAs in 1991 in order to encourage longer-term saving. Provided that the account (which may be with a building society, bank, etc.) is held for five years, all capital gains and re-invested dividends are exempt from tax.

tax expenditures. Concessions granted by the Inland Revenue which reduce tax liability. These include concessions relating to: contributions to personal and company pensions, mortgage interest payments, tax exempt special savings accounts, personal equity plans, and save-as-you-earn employee share schemes. All tax expenditures can be seen as deviations from a COMPREHENSIVE INCOME TAX.

tax haven. A country that imposes low rates of personal and corporate taxation, and which consequently attracts wealthy individuals and the headquarters of companies.

tax yield. The revenue raised by a tax, minus the costs of collection.

taxable income. Income minus tax concessions and allowances.

taxation. A compulsory transfer of money from individuals or groups to the government. Taxes may be levied on income or wealth (direct taxation) or on expenditure (indirect taxation). Taxation (and individual taxes) may be PROGRESSIVE, REGRESSIVE or PROPORTIONAL. Total taxation, including local taxes, royalties, national insurance and other social security contributions, accounts for 94 per cent of total government receipts.

Table 23   Tax and other government receipts

	Budget forecasts for 1992-3 Percentages*
Inland revenue:	
Income tax	25.9
Corporation tax	7.3
Other	1.8
Total Inland revenue	35.0
Customs and excise:	
Value added tax	17.4
Oil, tobacco and alcohol duties	10.3
Customs duties	0.8
Other	0.8
Total Customs and Excise	29.3
Rates	6.1
Other taxes and royalties	3.4
Total tax and royalty receipts	73.9
Social security receipts	16.8
Community charge receipts	3.5
Interest, dividends, trading surplus, rent	4.0
Other receipts	1.7
General government receipts	100

(*Figures have been rounded to nearest decimal place)

taxation, incidence of. *See* INCIDENCE OF TAXATION.

team production. Team production occurs when output is produced by the simultaneous co-operation of several team members. This means that the individual contribution of each member of the team to the final output cannot be measured by management, and this could provide opportunities for shirking.

technical change. Innovations in production processes that allow a given output to be produced with fewer inputs than previously, and the diffusion of these new or modified processes.

technical economies. *See* ECONOMIES OF SCALE.

technical efficiency. *See* ECONOMIC EFFICIENCY.

technical progress. Another term for TECHNICAL CHANGE.

technical substitution, rate of. *See* PRODUCTION POSSIBILITY FRONTIER.

technique. A particular method of combining inputs to produce output.

technological change. Usually considered to comprise both process and product innovation and diffusion. Technological change is an extremely important factor in economic growth.

technological-gap theory. An attempt to explain changes over time in the pattern of international trade. Countries that are early adoptors of a technology export products utilizing or embodying that technology. But this pattern of trade changes as other countries adopt the technology.

technological unemployment. *See* UNEMPLOYMENT.

technology. The sum of all known TECHNIQUES.

technology transfer. Production techniques pioneered in one firm, industry or sector are adopted by other firms, industries or sectors. One of the justifications advanced for public expenditure on military contracts or space exploration is that techniques developed for these purposes are subsequently adopted for uses of more immediate benefit to mankind.

tender. An offer to supply or buy at a fixed price. Contracts for large construction projects are often awarded on the submission of tenders. Discount houses specify the price at which they will take up an issue of Treasury bills.

term loan. A loan made for a specific number of years at a fixed rate of interest.

term structure of interest rates. The relationship between the rates of interest available on securities with different maturity dates. If interest rates are expected to rise, longer-dated securities will offer a higher rate of interest than shorter-dated ones. The reverse will apply if interest rates are expected to fall.

terms of exchange. *See* EXCHANGE.

terms of trade. The terms of trade express the relationship between the average prices of exports and of imports. The average price is a weighted average, the weights being the relative importance of the different categories of goods in the base year (which has a value of 100). This weighted index is sometimes known as the income terms of trade, as opposed to the unweighted, net barter, terms of trade. If the price of exports increases in relation to the price of imports the index rises; if the relative price of exports falls, the index falls. A rise in the index is known as an improvement in the terms of trade, since a larger quantity of imports than previously can be purchased with the proceeds of a given volume of exports. But the increase in relative price is likely to cause a fall in the volume of exports relative to imports, and the net effect on the BALANCE OF PAYMENTS could be either favourable or unfavourable. The direct effect on unemployment is likely to be unfavourable.

theory choice. Any economic theory is a simplified version of reality, but in many areas of economics one must choose from among competing theories. The existence of competing theories reflects differences in assumptions about the reality that these theories seek – in a simplified form – to represent. The choice of theory is made difficult by the absence of generally accepted objective criteria by which competing theories may be compared, ranked and evaluated.

theory of distribution. An attempted explanation of the incomes of the FACTORS OF PRODUCTION.

theory of income determination. Simple models of income determination are based on the idea of the circular flow of income: producers offer rewards to the owners of inputs who use this income to finance purchases of goods and services supplied by the producers. The volume of transactions, the level of real income, expands as a result of injections into the circular flow: investment, government expenditure and exports, but contracts as a result of withdrawals: saving, taxation and imports. (This process of expansion or contraction is amplified by the operation of the MULTIPLIER and the ACCELERATION PRINCIPLE.) The national income reaches equilibrium when planned expenditure in one period equals income in the previous period (assuming that the expenditure plans are fulfilled). Equilibrium can also be explained using the concepts of injections and withdrawals; the equilibrium national income is that at which planned injections equal planned withdrawals. If equilibrium is disturbed by an injection it will be re-established when income has increased to the level at which the injection is matched by an equal withdrawal. There has been a long-standing controversy concerning the relationship between equilibrium and full employment income. Classical economics assumed that equilibrium would be established at the full employment level. Keynesian economists believe that this is unlikely to happen in a free market economy, and argue that the government may need to adopt measures to increase aggregate demand. New classical economists take a position very similar to classical economists, and argue that these measures do nothing to increase employment even in the short term. Monetarists admit that equilibrium below full employment is possible in principle, but they believe that government attempts to increase employment via higher demand will be successful only temporarily at best, and that supply-side policies are more likely to reduce unemployment in the longer term.

theory of price. All approaches to the theory of price agree that price is determined by the interplay of the forces of demand and supply. On the demand side, application of the law of diminishing marginal utility, indifference curve analysis, and the revealed preference approach all lead to the conclusion that for most products the DEMAND CURVE is downward sloping, indicating a negative relationship between price and quantity demanded. (Exceptions to this conclusion are Giffen goods, products whose price is seen as an indicator of quality, and products which are bought for conspicuous consumption.) There is less unanimity concerning the likely shape of the SUPPLY CURVE between the different theories: those based on marginal analysis, those incorporating full-cost pricing procedures, the behavioural theories and managerial theories. Short-run supply curves are seen as likely to be upward sloping in some theories, horizontal in others.

theory of production. The analysis of how inputs are transformed into output. The factors taken into account are the techniques or technical relationships as shown, e.g., by ISOQUANTS, the relative prices of inputs, and the relative prices of goods and services.

theory of second best. *See* PARETO EFFICIENCY

theory of the firm. The main concern of the theory of the firm, and especially of models using MARGINAL ANALYSIS, has been to explain price and output decisions. These models are not intended to represent the actual behaviour of firms, and it has been said that they constitute a theory of markets rather than of the firm. Theories based on early empirical studies, e.g. those conducted by R. Hall, C.J. Hitch and P.W.S. Andrews, also concentrated on pricing decisions, although they did consider other issues, such as the impact of changes in interest rates on investment decisions. These studies led to the formulation of the FULL-COST or normal cost pricing theory. The theory of the firm has subsequently expanded to give greater attention to: (a) other aspects of firms' behaviour (advertising, R & D expenditure, investment in human capital, etc.); (b) motives other than profit maximization (growth, satisficing, etc.); (c) the nature of the relationships within firms (principal–agent, coalitions, monitoring, etc.).

theory of valuation. A branch of financial economics concerned with the valuation of risky assets.

theory of value. Alternative theories have been advanced to explain the value of goods and services. One approach has emphasized utility; the greater the utility derived from a product, the greater its value. Another approach has emphasized cost; the greater the cost incurred in supplying a product, the greater its value. Within the cost approach, the labour theory of value was once especially influential. The theory originated with David Ricardo and became the centrepiece of MARXIAN ECONOMICS. Subsequently in mainstream economics a distinction has not been made between the theory of value and the theory of price. Market prices have been seen as indicators of value, of the benefit derived from products (although it is recognized that EXTERNALITIES may mean that private and social benefits diverge). More recently the measurement of value in assets in which there is no market has become an important issue in ENVIRONMENTAL ECONOMICS. Two of the questions currently under debate in this branch of economics are the usefulness of valuations derived from studies of attitudes and opinions rather than behaviour, and the extent to which valuations can be transferred from one context to another.

third parties. Groups or individuals who are external to an economic transaction or activity but are affected by it, e.g. non-smokers who contract lung-cancer through inhaling the smoke of other people's cigarettes.

third world. The LESS DEVELOPED COUNTRIES.

Tiebout model. *See* INVISIBLE FOOT.

tied loan. A loan which is made on condition that the money is spent on the products of the lender nation.

tie-in sales. A requirement that a purchaser can buy one product only if he buys another product or products from the same supplier. An anti-competitive device, it is disallowed in many countries.

tight money. *See* DEAR MONEY.

time deposits. Bank deposits which can be withdrawn only after a period of notice has expired.

time preference. The extent to which people prefer immediate to future consumption. This will depend upon a number of factors, including those underlying the LIFE-CYCLE theory of consumption, people's expectations of future changes in the range of products available, and the RATE OF INTEREST. If the rate of interest is taken as a measure of the reward to saving (deferring consumption), rational consumers will save provided that the interest rate exceeds their time-preference rate.

time rates. Payments to workers based on the amount of time at work. It is argued that time rates fail to provide an incentive to effort or to conscientious working, a deficiency that is especially important when the outcome of individual workers' effort cannot be observed.

time series. A sequence of measurements of a variable at different points in time.

time-series analysis. The application of statistical methods to time-series data in order to explain the behaviour of variables over time.

token money. A means of payment whose value as money greatly exceeds its cost of production or its value in other uses.

total costs. *See* COSTS.

total economic value. The total economic value of an environmental asset comprises: (a) its use value, e.g. timber cut from a tropical forest; (b) its option value, i.e. the value attached to the forest even though it is not currently used; if it contains plants that could be used in the production of medicines, we may wish to leave these plants undisturbed to reproduce themselves so that they will be available should the sources being used at present become exhausted; (c) its existence value, the value that would be attached to the forest if there was never an intention to use its products.

total expenditure. Another term for AGGREGATE DEMAND.

total output. Another term for AGGREGATE SUPPLY.

trade association. An organization representing the interests of member-firms drawn from a particular industry. Typical activities include the collection and publication of statistics on the industry and lobbying governments on behalf of members.

trade barriers. Obstacles to international trade. Some barriers are natural, e.g. high transport costs, poor communications. Others are artificial, e.g. TARIFFS, QUOTAS, VOLUNTARY EXPORT RESTRAINTS.

trade bill. *See* BILL OF EXCHANGE.

trade creation. *See* CUSTOMS UNION.

trade credit. It is common practice for manufacturers to allow distributors to pay for goods some time after delivery, e.g. 7, 14 or 28 days or more. BILLS OF EXCHANGE are another form of trade credit. Trade credit is an important source of finance, and cannot be easily controlled by the monetary authorities.

trade cycle. Another term for BUSINESS CYCLE, the latter now being used more often.

trade deficit. A shorthand expression for a balance of payments current account deficit.

trade discount. The percentage below the recommended retail price at which a manufacturer sells to wholesalers or retailers, or at which a wholesaler sells to retailers. Conventional rates of discount apply to different groups of products, the rates reflecting the functions of the wholesalers and retailers of those products: transporting, storing, displaying and demonstrating products, giving advice, providing after-sales service, etc.

trade distortion. Interference with international trade so that it does not take place in accordance with the principle of COMPARATIVE ADVANTAGE.

trade diversion. *See* CUSTOMS UNION.

trade gap. A deficit on the BALANCE OF TRADE.

trade intensity coefficient. The share of a market (product or group of products) in a country's exports, in proportion to the share of that market in world exports.

trade investments. Shares held by one company in another. The term usually indicates that the shares are held for the return that they yield, as opposed to being used as the basis for a takeover bid.

trade liberalization. Eliminating or reducing TRADE BARRIERS.

trade multiplier. *See* FOREIGN TRADE MULTIPLIER.

trade-off. A trade-off exists when having more of one thing means having less of another.

trade price. An alternative method of quoting a TRADE DISCOUNT.

trade surplus. A shorthand expression for a balance of payments current account surplus.

trade unions. Associations of workers who represent their members in negotiations on wages and salaries and on other conditions of employment. A great deal of research effort has been expended in trying to identify the impact of unions on pay, productivity, financial performance and employment. British labour economists are generally agreed that around 1980, workplaces with unions had higher pay, lower productivity and worse financial performance than workplaces without unions. But during the 1980s productivity increased more in unionized than in non-union workplaces. In analysing the labour market a distinction is sometimes drawn between closed and open unions. Closed unions organize skilled workers who have served an apprenticeship, have a commitment to their occupations and who have a high level of union membership. Open unions organize unskilled workers who often move relatively frequently from job to job. The British trade union movement has since 1979 experienced its longest ever continuous decline. This is due to several factors, including lower employment in heavily unionized sectors, an increase in the proportion of females in the work-force, and legislation curbing the powers of unions. Mergers between unions have led to the emergence of some very large unions, such as the Amalgamated Engineering and Electrical Union with over a million members. This has facilitated the making of SINGLE-UNION DEALS. It has also brought into question the usefulness of the TRADES UNION CONGRESS.

tradeable permit. *See* ENVIRONMENTAL POLICY.

Trades Union Congress. The central body of the British trade union movement. When Labour governments were in power the leaders of the TUC were regularly consulted about government economic policy. But the TUC's influence waned with the advent of Conservative governments, the decline of trade union membership, and the growth of very large unions.

trading and profit and loss account. This is really two accounts, the main revenue accounts of a business, with a combined heading. The trading account shows the firm's gross profit (the excess of sales revenue over the cost of goods sold). In the profit and loss account other expenses, such as administrative and selling costs, are deducted from gross profit to give the net profit.

trading profit. Another term for GROSS PROFIT.

trading stamps. Stamps given by retailers in proportion to the value of the purchase. When stamps to a certain value have been acquired they can be exchanged for money or, more usually, for goods. Trading stamps are equivalent to a price reduction, they are intended also to generate long-term customer loyalty to the retailer or the product concerned.

Training and Enterprise Councils. *See* LABOUR MARKET POLICIES.

Training for Work. *See* LABOUR MARKET POLICIES.

transactions costs. The costs of obtaining information required for exchange to take place, and of enforcing the agreed terms of exchange. A number of mechanisms help to reduce transactions costs. Money permits a series of bilateral exchanges which in effect constitute a multilateral system, without the enormous costs involved in arranging multilateral barter. State intervention may reduce transactions costs by standardizing legal and financial procedures, and by undertaking projects that would not otherwise be undertaken because, e.g., of the high costs of gaining the agreement of a large number of small producers concerning their respective contributions. The FIRM has also been seen as a mechanism for reducing transactions costs by internalizing exchanges that would otherwise have been transacted via markets.

transactions motive. *See* MONEY, DEMAND FOR.

transfer earnings. The minimum earnings required for a factor of production to remain in its present use. For a firm, transfer earnings are the same as NORMAL PROFIT.

transfer payments. Payments by the government to individuals without requiring any service in return, e.g. retirement pensions. Transfer payments are not included in calculations of national income.

transfer pricing. The pricing of products (which may be components, finished goods, services, etc.) as they pass from one division or department of a firm to another. Transfer pricing may be conducted at arm's length, i.e. divisions have complete freedom of action in price negotiations. Arm's length transfer pricing is often used to help to measure the efficiency of divisions or departments that operate as profit centres. It also enables the firm to decide whether to manufacture part of a product internally or to buy that part from another supplier. Alternatively, transfer pricing may be conducted in accordance with a formula laid down centrally. In multinational enterprises formula transfer pricing may be used to minimize the enterprise's tax liability, internal prices being set so that the greatest profit is earned in those countries with the lowest rates of company taxation. (This practice is, of course, politically unpopular.)

transfers in kind. Payments other than in cash. Transfers in kind are said to be less efficient than cash transfers which the recipients can spend as they wish. However, gifts of food and clothing can help to ensure that the basic needs of very poor people are met.

transformation curve. *See* PRODUCTION POSSIBILITY FRONTIER.

transitional unemployment. *See* UNEMPLOYMENT.

transitivity. Transitivity exists if a person prefers A to B, B to C, and A to C. Transitivity is said to be a characteristic of rational behaviour, but if the possibility of learning is allowed for, intransitivity cannot be a proof of irrational behaviour.

transmission mechanism. The process whereby an increase in the money supply leads to an increase in AGGREGATE DEMAND. A distinction can be made between direct and indirect transmission mechanisms. Monetarists argue in favour of a direct mechanism, emphasizing the fact that an increase in the money supply causes the ratio of money to other assets to become higher than desired, leading people to increase their consumption in order to restore the ratio to the desired level. Indirect mechanisms are favoured by Keynesian economists. Some Keynesians emphasize the fact that some of the additional money is used to purchase bonds. This causes an increase in the price of bonds, equivalent to a fall in the rate of interest. Lower interest rates stimulate investment spending. Other Keynesians (and international monetarists) emphasize the fact that an increase in the money supply tends to lead to a reduction in the exchange rate.

Treasury. The government department with the main responsibility for macroeconomic policy.

Treasury bills. Instruments for short-term government borrowing. Bills have a maturity date 91 days after the date of issue. Each week tenders for bills are invited from discount houses (who together undertake to cover the entire issue), bankers and brokers. Bills are also available on TAP to government departments. The Bank of England operates in the money market by dealing in Treasury bills.

Treaty of Rome. The Treaty signed in 1957 by France, West Germany, Italy, Belgium, Holland and Luxembourg, establishing a customs union. By this Treaty the European Economic Community came into being on 1 January 1958.

trend. The long-term movement of a variable, observable when short-term fluctuations have been eliminated from data.

Treuhandanstalt. The body established to take over, restructure and privatize the state-owned enterprises of what was formerly East Germany.

turnkey project. A construction project undertaken on a one-off basis by a foreign firm or consortium.

turnover. Total sales revenue.

turnover tax. A turnover or cascade tax is levied as a proportion of the price of a commodity on each sale in the chain of production and distribution.

two-part tariff. A system of pricing under which a standing charge is made designed to (approximately) cover the fixed costs of the firm, and a unit charge is made to cover the variable cost of producing the amount consumed. Industries using two-part tariffs include telecommunications, gas, electricity and water.

two-tier board. A board of directors of a company comprising (a) a supervisory board, which includes worker representatives, responsible for formulating general policy; (b) a management board which is concerned with the day-to-day implementation of policy. This structure is found in large German companies and is a model of governance favoured by the European Community.

U

U-form enterprise. A term applied by Oliver Williamson to firms organized along unitary lines, i.e. having a single chief executive and functional divisions – finance, sales, etc. – responsible to the chief executive for their functions as applied to all company products. Although this is a common structure for small and medium size companies, it can lead to 'control-loss' in large companies due to difficulties in transmitting information reliably and in co-ordinating operations. To minimize these problems many large firms are structured as M-FORM ENTERPRISES.

unavoidable costs. *See* COSTS.

uncalled capital. The balance of issued shares not paid-up, which the company can call on if it wishes to raise finance.

uncertainty. A state in which the number of possible future outcomes exceeds the number that will occur, and where there is no evidence enabling one to attach probabilities to each outcome. Economic theory now pays more attention to the existence of uncertainty than was once the case. For example it is one of the central themes of the AUSTRIAN SCHOOL of economics, and in the theory of ENTREPRENEURSHIP.

undated securities. *See* IRREDEEMABLE SECURITIES.

underemployment. *See* DISGUISED UNEMPLOYMENT.

underfunding. *See* FUNDING.

underlying inflation. *See* INFLATION.

undersubscription. When the number of shares applied for is less than the number on offer, the issue is said to be undersubscribed. Firms raising capital by the issue of shares arrange for the UNDERWRITING of the issue in case of undersubscription.

undervalued currency. A currency whose exchange rate is below what its current level would be in a free market or below its expected long-run equilibrium level.

underwriting. The business of insuring against RISK. In return for a fee or commission, underwriters agree to bear all or part of the cost of specified damage or loss. Underwriters at LLOYD'S insure against a wide variety of risks: loss of ships and their cargoes, fire, explosion, etc. Most NEW ISSUES of shares are underwritten by financial institutions who guarantee to take up any shares not bought by the general public. The company issuing the shares is thus protected against the risk of not obtaining the money required to finance its planned expenditure. Since shares that are undersubscribed usually open at a discount when trading begins, the underwriters take the risk of making a capital loss.

undistributed income. Another term for RETAINED EARNINGS.

unearned income. Dividends, interest and other investment income.

unemployment. A situation in which some members of the labour force are unable to find jobs. Unemployment can be measured in various ways. The current basis of measurement in the UK is the registration of people as claimants for unemployment benefits, but there are proposals to change to using data from the quarterly Labour Force Survey. Economists have distinguished several types of unemployment (some of which may overlap): demand-deficient (also known as cyclical or Keynesian) unemployment results from a general deficiency in demand affecting virtually all industries; structural unemployment arises when there is a long-term decline in the demand for the products of a particular industry, and other industries are unable to absorb the redundant workers; technological unemployment is due to the introduction of new machines or processes which reduce the need for workers of a given type; frictional or transitional unemployment arises when a worker leaves one job and finds another but after a short period of time rather than immediately; seasonal unemployment occurs when the demand for workers is seasonal, as in tourism, catering and parts of agriculture. Although it is impossible in practice to identify precisely these various forms of unemployment, an awareness of their relative importance can aid policy-making. For example, structural and technological unemployment are likely to be more responsive to increased training opportunities than to measures intended to boost aggregate demand. There has been a long debate among economists as to whether unemployment can persist and, if so, why this is. In classical economics, unemployment was seen as being due entirely to too high a level of real wages; flexibility of wages would ensure that unemployment would not persist. Monetarist and neo-classical economists also see inflexible wages as a major cause of unemployment. It is recognized that some workers might be willing to take jobs at less than the going wage rate but are prevented from doing so by institutional factors (minimum wage legislation and trade union power); these workers are said to be unemployed involuntarily. There may in addition be some workers who are unemployed voluntarily, perhaps because they are holding back from employment in the hope of finding a higher-paid job, or because they prefer a combination of greater leisure and social security benefits to working at the going wage rate. Although Keynesian economists recognize that too high real wages can lead to unemployment, they emphasize inadequate demand as a major cause.

unemployment, natural rate of. The natural rate of unemployment is the rate of unemployment when the labour market is in equilibrium. In this situation any unemployment is VOLUNTARY. (Since this is the minimum rate of unemployment that can be sustained without an increase in inflation, it is sometimes known as the non-accelerating inflation rate of unemployment or the minimum sustainable rate of unemployment.) Monetarist and neo-classical economists argue that the natural rate of unemployment can be reduced by SUPPLY-SIDE POLICIES, but not by policies to boost aggregate demand. Widely differing estimates of the natural rate of unemployment have been given, a fact which reduces its value as a guide to policy decisions.

unemployment trap. The availability of social security benefits reduces the incentive to seek work.

unfunding. *See* FUNDING.

uniform business rate. A tax on business properties, paid in the first instance to the central government. When the revenue is subsequently transferred to local authorities some degree of redistribution from richer to poorer local authorities occurs. The UBR is based on property values as assessed in 1990, and rises in line with inflation.

unincorporated businesses. Sole proprietorships and partnerships. There are around one and a quarter million unincorporated businesses in the UK, making this the most important form of business numerically. However most are very small, and together they account for only about one-tenth of the capital expenditure undertaken by all businesses.

union density. The percentage of employees in a trade union. In the UK union density is around two-thirds in the public sector but less than 30 per cent in the private sector.

union mark-up. The percentage addition to the wage rate estimated to be due to the unionization of the workforce. A mark-up of around 10 per cent is a generally accepted figure for the UK.

unit banking. A system under which a bank can have only one outlet or branch.

unit of account. *See* MONEY.

unit tax. Another term for a SPECIFIC TAX.

unit trust. An organization which invests money subscribed by the public in securities, and in return issues units which it will repurchase on demand. The units represent equal shares in the trust's portfolio, and hence investors are enabled to spread their risks. Units yield income, which in some instances is automatically re-invested. The value of the units varies in accordance with the value of the portfolio. The management of the trust derives its income from (a) annual charges, levied as a percentage of the income of the trust's investments, and (b) the margin between the price at which it buys units (the bid price) and the price at which it sells them (the offer price, which includes an initial charge). Trusts may be highly specialized or very general, may emphasize growth or income, and may be fixed (unchanging portfolio) or flexible (portfolio changing as market conditions change).

unitary taxation. Taxation levied on a multinational enterprise by a country or state on the basis of a proportion of the company's worldwide income rather than the profit earned in that country or state. Unitary taxation might be adopted in response to attempts by companies to minimize tax liabilities, especially through TRANSFER PRICING procedures. But this method of taxation must involve the arbitrary calculation of tax liabilities, and may well lead to DOUBLE TAXATION.

United Kingdom National Accounts. An annual publication by the Central Statistical Office containing details of national income, output, expenditure, etc.

United Nations Conference on Environment and Development. A meeting, popularly known as the Earth Summit, held in Rio de Janeiro in 1992 to consider improved ways of protecting the environment.

United Nations Conference on Trade and Development. A conference that met in 1964 and on several subsequent occasions, to discuss ways in which the gap between the developed and the less developed countries might be narrowed. UNCTAD has a permanent secretariat and regularly publishes papers on economic development issues.

universal benefit. A benefit that is available regardless of income or financial circumstances, i.e. it is not means-tested.

unlimited liability. The owners of unincorporated businesses are liable to meet the debts of those businesses out of their personal assets.

unlisted securities markets. Many countries have second-tier markets on which securities are traded which may not meet the requirements for listing on the main market of the country's stock exchange, e.g. because they have not have been in existence for a long enough period. A USM was established in London in 1980 when the small number of companies seeking a STOCK EXCHANGE QUOTATION was felt to be at least partly due to the requirements imposed.

unstable equilibrium. If an equilibrium is disturbed by a shock, and no forces exist which cause the equilibrium to be re-established, it is said to be unstable.

upswing. A period of rising economic activity following a recession or slump.

upvaluation. *See* REVALUATION.

urban policy. A major shift in government policy occurred in the late 1970s when inner-city problems, traditionally diagnosed as environmental and social deprivation, were seen to be linked to local economic decline, and in particular to the rapid erosion of manufacturing in the conurbation cores. Urban policy became the responsibility of the Department of the Environment and since then public funds, often in conjunction with private capital, have been provided through a variety of channels, including Urban Development Corporations covering the London and Merseyside docklands, the Cardiff Bay area, Sheffield, Central Manchester etc., enterprise zones, and a multiplicity of agencies sponsored by local authorities.

use values. *See* TOTAL ECONOMIC VALUE.

utilitarianism. The belief that the task of government is to maximize the aggregate UTILITY of citizens.

utility. The satisfaction or happiness derived from a situation or activity such as consumption. The law of DIMINISHING MARGINAL UTILITY is based on the assumption of a cardinal measure of utility, i.e. that the person concerned can give a value to the satisfaction derived. For indifference-curve analysis, on the other hand, it is sufficient to assume an ordinal measure of utility, i.e. the person concerned can rank the satisfaction obtained from alternative situations or choices. In both cases utility is subjective.

V

valuation ratio. The ratio of a company's stock market value to its capital employed.

value. *See* THEORY OF VALUE.

value added. Total revenue minus the sum of purchases of raw materials, components and services. Value added can be calculated for individual firms, and a high value added is often an indication that the firm has particular skills or expertise. The concept of value added is used in national income accounting in order to prevent DOUBLE COUNTING.

value-added tax. A tax applied at every point, within the chain of production and distribution, at which an exchange of goods or services takes place. In calculating their tax liability, firms offset the tax included in the price of goods purchased (input tax), against the tax included in the price of goods sold (output tax). In effect suppliers act as tax collectors, the tax being borne entirely by consumers. The standard rate of tax at present is 17½ per cent, but a large range of essential items, accounting for almost half of total consumers' expenditure, are relieved of tax, either by being zero-rated, e.g. most food bought for consumption at home, children's clothes, books, public transport and newspapers, or by being exempt from VAT, e.g. financial services. The difference between these two forms of relief is that any input tax can be deducted with zero rating but not with exemption. Consequently only with zero rating does the final price contain no tax element. VAT accounts for more than a sixth of total government revenue from TAXATION.

value judgement. A statement which incorporates the values held by the person making the statement, e.g. 'the distribution of wealth is too uneven'. It is impossible to test empirically the truth of such statements. Since some statements could be taken either as value judgements or of objective descriptions, it should always be made clear which is intended.

value maximization. Empirical studies suggest that firms are more likely to attempt to maximize the present value of profits earned over a number of years than to maximize short-run profits.

value of physical increases in stocks. In calculating the value of physical increases in stocks and work in progress, an adjustment is made for price increases. Physical stock changes are part of investment expenditure.

variable. A term that can take a range of numerical values.

variable costs. *See* COSTS.

variance. (1) A measure of variation within a group of numerical observations. It is the average of the squared deviations of the observations from the group mean. (2) Deviations of actual performance, e.g. output, costs, from planned or budgeted performance.

vehicle excise duty. Popularly known as the road tax, this is an excise duty levied at different rates on different types of vehicle, e.g. £115 a year on private cars, and from £130 to £5000 a year on goods vehicles.

velocity of circulation. The speed with which money turns over as it is spent on goods and services. Technically the velocity of circulation is the ratio of annual output or income to the money stock. Its value depends, of course, upon which measures of income, output and money are used. The velocity of circulation is affected by changes in LIQUIDITY PREFERENCE, changes in the rate of interest, and by innovations in the financial system affecting the transmission of money.

venture capital. Venture or risk capital is provided on a long-term basis for projects whose likely profitability is especially difficult to assess. Typical uses would be to finance the establishment of new firms, capital expenditure by small firms wishing to grow or to enter new markets, and management buy-outs.

vertical equity. *See* EQUITY.

vertical integration. *See* GROWTH OF THE FIRM.

vertical restraints. Conditions imposed by a manufacturer on the distributors of its products, e.g. resale price maintenance, full-line forcing, exclusive supply.

visible balance. *See* BALANCE OF PAYMENTS.

visible trade. International trade in goods (but not services).

voluntary exchange. *See* EXCHANGE.

voluntary export restraints. Agreements between two parties, which may be governments or industries, whereby one party agrees to restrict the volume of its exports to the other country to a specified amount over a given period of time. Agreements restricting exports to the UK have been negotiated for cars (from Japan), footwear, pottery, colour televisions, cutlery, etc.

voluntary groups. Associations of retailers and wholesalers who combine some of their activities, and in particular purchasing, in order to obtain ECONOMIES OF SCALE.

voluntary unemployment. *See* UNEMPLOYMENT.

voting shares. *See* SHARES.

W

wage bargaining. *See* BARGAINING.

wage contracts. A term used in labour economics referring to contracts which specify the wages or salaries to be paid, but not the numbers to be employed. A number of factors favour wage contracts (as opposed to salaried or profit-sharing contracts). Employers may offer such contracts if they can hire workers easily and the cost of training workers is low. Workers may be willing to accept the contracts if they are more risk-averse than employers, and if they can offset the loss of wages through unemployment benefits. Unions will be more inclined to accept the contract if it contains a SENIORITY rule.

wage drift. Wage or earnings drift is the difference between wage rates set by national negotiations and earnings. Earnings can exceed nationally negotiated rates because of overtime working at premium rates, bonuses or other payments negotiated locally.

wage-fund theory. Classical economists believed that the total amount of capital available for paying wages was fixed in the short run, and that the average wage was obtained by dividing this fixed fund by the number of workers. Over time the capital fund could be increased by saving.

wage-price spiral. *See* INFLATION.

wage rate. The price of labour. The wage rate is usually quoted per hour or per week.

wages councils. Government-appointed bodies which set minimum wages. At present wages councils cover three million workers over the age of twenty-one, employed mainly in retailing, catering, clothing manufacture, hairdressing and laundries. But in November 1992 the Government announced proposals to abolish the councils.

warranted rate of growth. *See* HARROD-DOMAR MODEL.

warrants. Securities giving the right to subscribe to shares or bonds at a given price from a certain date.

wasting assets. Another term for NON-RENEWABLE RESOURCES. When a firm owns such assets, e.g. a copper mine, they are included in fixed assets.

ways and means advances. Direct lending by the Bank of England to the government. It accounts for only a very small proportion of government borrowing.

wealth. Assets that yield, or could yield, income. Wealth includes both physical assets, e.g. houses and paintings, and financial assets, e.g. shares, bank deposits and pension fund rights. (If some assets do not yield income, it may be because the owners have chosen that they should not do so.)

wealth effect. An increase in real wealth which causes an upward shift in the consumption function, i.e. consumption increases as a proportion of disposable income; or, conversely, a fall in real wealth which causes a fall in consumption. It is thought that changes in real wealth due to changes in the prices of financial assets are especially likely to affect consumption, although it seems that consumption was also affected by the steep fall in house prices in the early 1990s.

Table 24   Composition of net wealth of personal sector, 1989

	Percentages
Dwellings (net of mortgage liabilities)	36.6
Other fixed assets	6.0
Non-marketable tenancy rights	7.3
Consumer durables	7.0
Building society shares and deposits	6.1
National savings, bank deposits, notes	8.3
Stocks and shares	8.1
Other	20.6
Total	100

Source: *Social Trends*

wealth tax. In the UK total wealth is not subject to tax. However taxes are levied on two forms of wealth, two types of assets, as distinct from the income derived from those assets. The first is property, which is subject to the COUNCIL TAX and the UNIFORM BUSINESS RATE. The second is gifts which are subject to the INHERITANCE TAX.

weighted average. An arithmetic mean in which each item in the series being averaged is given a weight in accordance with its importance, e.g. in calculating the average change in product prices the weights might be the share of consumer spending accounted for by each product. The average is calculated by multiplying each item by its weight, aggregating the resulting values, and dividing by the sum of the weights.

weights. *See* WEIGHTED AVERAGE.

welfare. Welfare is usually defined with reference to one or other measure of national income. However it is recognized that these measures are imperfect and other definitions, taking account of additional factors, e.g. literacy, life expectancy, have been suggested.

welfare economics. A branch of economics dealing with normative issues, and in particular with how resources should be allocated. It involves the analysis of the conditions under which ECONOMIC EFFICIENCY would be attained, and of the nature of the trade-off between efficiency and EQUITY.

welfare loss. The loss in welfare that occurs in a country as a result of an increase in prices following the imposition of a tariff on imports.

welfare state. A country which has a comprehensive SOCIAL SECURITY system.

white knight. *See* TAKEOVER.

wholesale banking. The making of loans and acceptance of deposits on a large scale, e.g. on the INTER-BANK MARKET.

wholesalers. Intermediaries between producers and retailers. The main functions of wholesalers are 'breaking bulk' (buying in large packages and selling in smaller ones), warehousing, delivery, and the provision of credit.

Williamson trade-off model. Oliver Williamson suggested that under a discretionary anti-trust policy, a merger should be allowed if the estimated cost savings to producers exceeded the estimated reduction in consumers' surplus.

willingness-to-pay test. *See* COST BENEFIT ANALYSIS.

winding up. Another term for LIQUIDATION.

window dressing. The re-arrangement of a company's financial affairs in order to present a more favourable BALANCE SHEET at the end of the financial year.

withdrawals. *See* LEAKAGES.

withholding tax. Tax deducted from payments to non-residents.

work in progress. Stocks of unfinished products; part of a firm's INVENTORIES.

workable competition. J.M. Clark suggested in an article published in 1940 that since it was unrealistic to expect markets to be perfectly competitive, anti-trust policy should be directed towards ensuring that the behaviour of oligopolists should conform to competitive standards. It is very difficult to decide precisely what this would mean in practice, and J.W. Markham proposed that each situation should be considered on its merits, a situation being declared 'workable' if no policy change would lead to an unequivocal improvement. Later writers, e.g. H. Leibenstein, have suggested that the aim of a workable competition policy should be to ensure that competitive pressures force firms to avoid X-INEFFICIENT operations.

worker participation. The involvement of workers in decisions beyond those required by their own jobs.

workforce in employment. Employees in employment, plus the self-employed, plus members of H.M. Forces, plus people on work-related government training programmes.

working capital. *See* CAPITAL.

working population. The WORKFORCE IN EMPLOYMENT plus the REGISTERED UNEMPLOYED.

workplace bargaining. *See* BARGAINING.

Workplace Industrial Relations Survey. Provides detailed information on industrial relations in some 2000 workplaces in each survey.

World Bank. *See* INTERNATIONAL BANK FOR RECONSTRUCTION AND DEVELOPMENT.

World Development Report. An annual publication of the WORLD BANK giving details of changes in various indices of development. The Report classifies countries as low income (income per head below $460 in 1986), lower middle income (below $1810), upper middle income (below $7410), high income oil exporters, and industrialized market economies.

write down. To reduce the book value of an asset.

write off. To remove an asset completely from a firm's books, e.g. a debt that becomes uncollectable.

writing-down allowance. *See* CAPITAL ALLOWANCES.

X Y Z

***x*-axis.** The horizontal axis on a graph.

x-inefficiency. A failure of management to ensure that production occurs at as low a cost as possible. When x-inefficiency occurs it means that the firm's cost curves in practice are above the curves as assumed in traditional economic theory. This failure to minimize cost is felt to indicate that the firm is not subject to sufficient competitive pressure. With greater competition the firm would have to become x-efficient in order to survive.

***y*-axis.** The vertical axis on a graph.

yardstick regulation. Where a regulated industry has a regional structure, yardstick regulation relates the allowable price in one region to cost levels not only in that region but also in other regions.

yield. The return obtained on a security. Several alternative measures of yield are available. The flat yield of a fixed-interest security is the annual interest received as a percentage of the net price. The gross redemption yield is the flat yield plus an apportionment of any capital gains or losses on dated securities held to redemption. The dividend yield on shares, which may be quoted gross or net of tax, is the current dividend as a percentage of the market price. The earnings yield of a share is the last dividend paid as a percentage of the market price. The return on capital expenditure may also be known as its yield.

yield curve. A graphical representation of the TERM STRUCTURE OF INTEREST RATES.

yield gap. The difference between the average yield on ordinary shares and on gilt-edged securities. At one time ordinary shares offered the higher yield in compensation for the higher risk. But as investors have become aware that over a long period shares have provided a better protection against inflation, they have been willing to accept a lower immediate yield on shares than on gilt-edged, a situation known as a reverse yield gap.

Youth Training Scheme. The YTS provides a two-year training programme for 16-year-old school leavers, and a one-year programme for 17-year-old leavers. The two-year programme involves at least 20 weeks off-the-job training, e.g. at a local technical college, in addition to on-the-job training and planned work experience. YTS trainees receive a tax-free allowance from the government.

zero-coupon bonds. Bonds on which no interest is payable. They are issued at a substantial discount on their face value, guaranteeing a capital gain if held to maturity.

zero-sum game. In GAME THEORY, one player's gain always balances another player's loss in a zero-sum game; it is not possible to increase the overall gain through collusion.